Praise for
The Halo Effect

One of the Best Business Books of 2007
—Financial Times and *The Wall Street Journal*

Annual Accenture Award for Best Article of the Year: "Misunderstanding the Nature of Company Performance: The Halo Effect and Other Business Delusions"
—California Management Review, summer 2007

"I was taken by this book. It destroys myths concerning the attribution of success in the management literature using potent empirical arguments. It should stand as one of the most important management books of all time, and an antidote to these bestselling books by gurus presenting false patterns and naive arguments."
—Nassim Nicholas Taleb, author of *The Black Swan*

"In *The Halo Effect,* Phil Rosenzweig has done us all a great service by speaking the unspeakable. His iconoclastic analysis is a very welcome antidote to the kind of superficial, formulaic, and dumbed-down matter that seems to be the current stock in trade of many popular business books. It's the right book at the right time."
—John R. Kimberly, Henry Bower Professor of Entrepreneurial Studies, The Wharton School, University of Pennsylvania

"Business books all too rarely combine real-world savvy with scientific rigor. Rosenzweig's book is an outstanding exception—it's a superb work and long overdue."
—Philip E. Tetlock, Lorraine Tyson Mitchell Chair II in Leadership and Communication, Haas School of Business, University of California, Berkeley

"Rosenzweig doesn't only poke fun at the mass of bad writing and bad science in the management world. He explains why it is so bad—

and how you can learn from it despite the efforts of the authors."
—John Kay, *Financial Times* columnist and author of *Everlasting Light Bulbs: How Economics Illuminates the World*

"He writes with a relaxed sense of mastery, uses simple but compelling examples, is rigorous without being pedantic, and bends over backward to be fair to the so-called experts he demolishes."
—*The Conference Board*

"A trenchant view of business and business advice."
—*The Wall Street Journal*

"This is a fascinating, tightly argued book that challenges much of what we know about business, prodding us to view the research findings with more skepticism. It is an appeal to the mind, rather than a practical handbook for managers, but it does help us evaluate the foundation for the new (and old) ideas we hear."
—*Globe and Mail* (Toronto)

"A dismantling of much business writing, which finds that the advice peddled in countless best-selling business books may be much less useful than it appears . . . A thorough, occasionally devastating, de-boning of a clutch of business books and popular business reporting."
—*The Guardian*

"Rosenzweig offers a telling indictment of the superficiality of much management literature, and a critique of the many studies that claim to illuminate the source of high performance through the experience of successful companies."
—John Kay, *Management Today*

"[A] feisty and entertaining new book [that shows how] problems of research methodology and corrupt data bedevil much management literature, turning it into reassuring parables rather than reliable guidance based on empirical evidence . . . has the temerity to name names . . . gives a seeing-to to Jim Collins and Jerry Porras's *Built to*

Last and Collins's *Good to Great,* perhaps the most influential management volumes of recent years."

—Simon Caulkin, *The Observer*

"A refreshing corrective."

—Simon Hoggart, *The Guardian*

"Makes sturdy sense."

—*The Economist*

"[Rosenzweig] deserves acclaim for this brave, provocative piece of work . . . He has thrown down a serious challenge to his business school peers and the business media as well."

—*The Financial Times*

"A masterly exposé of many myths and sloppy thinking in management. If you want to avoid the next dumb fad, and, in Kipling's famous line, 'keep your head when all about you are losing theirs,' this is an essential primer."

—Professor Andrew Campbell,
Ashridge Business School, and author of *The Growth Gamble*

"A brilliant and sobering book."

—Vuyo Jack, *Business Report* (South Africa)

THE HALO EFFECT

...and the Eight Other Business Delusions That Deceive Managers

Phil Rosenzweig

FREE PRESS

NEW YORK   LONDON   TORONTO   SYDNEY

*f*P
FREE PRESS
A Division of Simon & Schuster, Inc.
1230 Avenue of the Americas
New York, NY 10020

First Free Press trade paperback edition January 2009

FREE PRESS and colophon are trademarks
of Simon & Schuster, Inc.

For information about special discounts for bulk purchases,
please contact Simon & Schuster Special Sales:
1-800-456-6798 or business@simonandschuster.com

Designed by Davina Mock

Manufactured in the United States of America

5   7   9   10   8   6

The Library of Congress has cataloged the hardcover edition as follows:

Rosenzweig, Philip M., 1955–
The halo effect . . . and the eight other business delusions
that deceive managers / Phil Rosenzweig.
p. cm.
Includes bibliographical references (p.   ) and index.
1. Industrial management–Philosophy. 2. Business enterprises–Public opinion.
3. Fallacies (Logic) 4. Success in business. I. Title.

HD30.19.R67 2007
658–dc22
2006049010

ISBN-13: 978-0-7432-9125-5
ISBN-10:   0-7432-9125-5
ISBN-13: 978-0-7432-9126-2 (pbk)
ISBN-10:   0-7432-9126-3 (pbk)

Lyrics to "How Little We Know," words by Carolyn Leigh
and music by Philip Springer, courtesy of Alfred Publishing Co., Inc.

To my parents,

Mark and Janine Rosenzweig

Contents

tactical
J strategic

The Halo Effect and
Other Business Delusions

Delusion One: *The Halo Effect*
The tendency to look at a company's overall performance and make attributions about its culture, leadership, values, and more. In fact, many things we commonly claim drive company performance are simply attributions based on prior performance.

Delusion Two: *The Delusion of Correlation and Causality*
Two things may be correlated, but we may not know which one causes which. Does employee satisfaction lead to high performance? The evidence suggests it's mainly the other way around—company success has a stronger impact on employee satisfaction.

Delusion Three: *The Delusion of Single Explanations*
Many studies show that a particular factor—strong company culture or customer focus or great leadership—leads to improved performance. But since many of these factors are highly correlated, the effect of each one is usually less than suggested.

Delusion Four: *The Delusion of Connecting the Winning Dots*

> If we pick a number of successful companies and search for what they have in common, we'll never isolate the reasons for their success, because we have no way of comparing them with less successful companies.

Delusion Five: *The Delusion of Rigorous Research*

> If the data aren't of good quality, it doesn't matter how much we have gathered or how sophisticated our research methods appear to be.

Delusion Six: *The Delusion of Lasting Success*

> Almost all high-performing companies regress over time. The promise of a blueprint for lasting success is attractive but not realistic.

Delusion Seven: *The Delusion of Absolute Performance*

> Company performance is relative, not absolute. A company can improve and fall further behind its rivals at the same time.

Delusion Eight: *The Delusion of the Wrong End of the Stick*

> It may be true that successful companies often pursued a highly focused strategy, but that doesn't mean highly focused strategies often lead to success.

Delusion Nine: *The Delusion of Organizational Physics*

> Company performance doesn't obey immutable laws of nature and can't be predicted with the accuracy of science—despite our desire for certainty and order.

Preface

This book is about business and management, success and failure, science and storytelling. It's written to help managers think for themselves, rather than listen to the parade of management experts and consultants and celebrity CEOs, each claiming to have the next new thing. Think of it as a guide for the reflective manager, a way to separate the nuggets from the nonsense.

Of course, for those who want a book that promises to reveal the secret of success, or the formula to dominate their market, or the six steps to greatness, there are plenty to choose from. Every year, dozens of new books claim to reveal the secrets of leading companies, from General Electric and Toyota to Starbucks and Google. *Learn their secrets and apply them to your company!* Other books profile hugely successful business leaders like Michael Dell or Jack Welch or Steve Jobs or Richard Branson. *Find out what makes them great, then go do likewise!* Others tell you how to become an innovation powerhouse, or craft a failsafe strategy, or devise a boundaryless organization, or make the competition irrelevant. *Here's the way to beat your rivals!*

In fact, for all the secrets and formulas, for all the self-proclaimed thought leadership, success in business is as elusive as ever. It's probably *more* elusive than ever, with increasingly global competition and technological change moving at faster and faster rates—which might explain why we're tempted by promises of breakthroughs and secrets and quick fixes in the first place. Desperate circumstances push us to look for miracle cures.

What's going on here isn't some vast right-wing conspiracy, or left-wing conspiracy or Wall Street conspiracy or Ivy League conspiracy, for that matter. In part it's a marriage of convenience. Managers are busy people, under enormous pressure to deliver higher revenues, greater profits, and ever larger returns for shareholders. They naturally search for ready-made answers, for tidy plug-and-play solutions that might give them a leg up on their rivals. And the people who write business books—consultants and business school professors and strategy gurus—are happy to oblige. Demand stimulates supply, and supply finds a ready demand. Around and around we go.

But there's more going on than just laziness or greed. Many thoughtful people work very hard to pinpoint the reasons for company success. If they have trouble finding definitive answers, we ought to ask why. *Why* is it so hard to determine the factors that lead to high performance? *Why* is it that even clever minds that earnestly want to uncover the secrets of success don't find solid answers—even when they gather huge amounts of data about hundreds of companies over many years? Is there something about the way we ask the question, or the way we go about trying to find answers, that keeps us from getting it right?

The central idea in this book is that our thinking about business is shaped by a number of delusions. There are good precedents for investigating delusions in business and economics. Charles Mackay's 1841 classic, *Extraordinary Popular Delusions and the Madness of Crowds,* chronicled the follies of public judgment, from Dutch tulip mania to speculative bubbles and more. More recently, cognitive psychologists have identified biases that affect the way individuals make decisions under uncertainty. This book is about a different set of delusions, the ones that distort our understanding of company performance, that make it difficult to know why one company succeeds and another fails. These errors of thinking pervade much that we read about business, whether in leading magazines or scholarly journals or management bestsellers. They cloud our ability to think clearly and critically about the nature of success in business.

Is delusion too strong a word? I don't think so. A longtime friend of mine, Dick Stull, explains the difference between illusion and delusion this way. When Michael Jordan appears to hang motionless in midair for a split second while on his way to a slam-dunk, that's an *illusion*. Your eyes are playing tricks on you. But if you think *you* can lace up a pair of Nikes, grab a basketball, and be like Mike, well, that's a *delusion*. You're kidding yourself. It ain't gonna happen. The delusions I describe in this book are a bit like that—they're promises that you can achieve great success if you just do one thing or another, but they're fundamentally flawed. In fact, some of the biggest business blockbusters of recent years contain not one or two, but several delusions. For all their claims of scientific rigor, for all their lengthy descriptions of apparently solid and careful research, they operate mainly at the level of storytelling. They offer tales of inspiration that we find comforting and satisfying, but they're based on shaky thinking. They're deluded.

Mark Twain once said: "Always do right. This will gratify some people and astonish the rest." My purpose is a bit different. Rather than gratify and astonish, I hope this book will stimulate discussion and raise the level of business thinking. The point isn't to make managers smarter. The business world is full of people who are plenty smart—clever, quick of mind, and conversant in current management concepts. In short supply are managers who are wise—by which I mean discerning, reflective, and able to judge what's correct and what's wrong. I'd like this book to help managers become wiser: more discerning, more appropriately skeptical, and less vulnerable to simplistic formulas and quick-fix remedies. Why is this a worthwhile goal? I've lived in and around the business world for more than twenty-five years, first as a manager for a leading U.S. company, then as a professor at Harvard Business School, and for these past ten years as a professor at IMD in Lausanne, Switzerland. I work on a daily basis with executives from a wide variety of industries. What I've observed, over and over, is a tendency by managers and professors alike to embrace simple answers, some of them patently simpleminded and wrongheaded, and to latch on to quick solutions rather than to question and think for themselves.

But rather than tell you *what* to think, I'd rather have you think critically for yourself. You may find some parts of this book to be a bit provocative. If so, that's fine. I want you to challenge what I write rather than accept it. One of my role models here is the late Herbert Simon, father of artificial intelligence, Nobel Prize winner in economics for his work on decision making, and professor at Carnegie Mellon University from the late 1940s until his death in 2001. In his memoirs, *Models of My Life,* Simon described how his service on several foreign fact-finding missions in the 1960s, often time-consuming and very costly, led him to formulate his Travel Theorem, which goes like this:

> Anything that can be learned by a normal American adult on
> a trip to a foreign country (of less than one year's duration) can
> be learned more quickly, cheaply, and easily by visiting the San
> Diego Public Library.

The response? Simon wrote: "People react almost violently to my Travel Theorem. I try to explain that it has nothing to do with the pleasures of travel, but only with the efficiency of travel for learning. They don't seem to hear my explanation; they remain outraged. They point out that I seem to be traveling all the time. Why shouldn't other people travel too? After they simmer down enough to understand the theorem, they still attack it. It takes a long time to calm their passion with reason—and usually it isn't extinguished, but temporarily subdued. Why, they think, argue with a madman?"

Well, I think the Travel Theorem is wonderful—not because I

agree with it, but because it makes me think. It forces me to ask: *What is the real purpose of this trip?* Is it for enjoyment or for learning? If the latter, exactly what am I trying to learn, and what's the best way to learn it? Could my time and money be better spent searching available sources rather than running off to the ends of the earth? Disagree with Simon's Travel Theorem if you wish, but that's not the point. The point is to force us to ask under what circumstances it's correct and when it's false—and that sort of critical thinking is always useful.

Most management books ask the first-order question: *What leads to high performance?* This book sets out to answer a different question: *Why is it so hard to understand high performance?* My aim is to pull back the curtains and ask the questions we don't often raise, to point out some of the delusions that keep us from seeing clearly. Much of this book, chapters 2 through 8, shows why the experts—gurus, consultants, professors, and journalists—are so often wrong. It exposes delusions that are all around us—in the business press, in academic research, and in recent bestsellers. But that takes us only so far. Once we've cleared away the delusions that permeate so much popular thinking about business, what then? The second thing a wise manager must do is focus on the elements that drive company performance while recognizing the fundamental uncertainty at the heart of the business world. The remainder of the book, chapters 9 and 10, takes up these questions, suggesting how managers might replace delusions with a more discerning way of understanding company performance, one that respects probabilities. Fortunately, there are managers on the scene today who provide good role models, and the final chapter offers a few brief portraits that can serve as examples for the rest of us.

Is there a pot of gold at the end of this rainbow? Not in the usual sense of the term. You won't find any promises of guaranteed results anywhere in these pages. There's no assurance that success follows predictably if you adopt these four rules, or live by that five-point plan, or commit yourself to those six steps. Yet I'm convinced that a clear-eyed and thoughtful approach *is* a better way to think about management—better, anyway, than the kind of casual thinking that characterizes so much of what's on business bookshelves today.

Another of the wise men whose voice appears in these pages, the physicist Richard Feynman, once remarked that many fields have a tendency for pomposity, to make things seem deep and profound. It's as if the less we know, the more we try to dress things up with complicated-sounding terms. We do this in countless fields, from sociology to philosophy to history to economics—and it's definitely the case in business. I suspect that the dreariness in so much business writing often stems from wanting to sound as though we have all the answers, and from a corresponding unwillingness to recognize the limits of what we know. Regarding a particularly self-important philosopher, Feynman observed:

> It isn't the philosophy that gets me, it's the pomposity. If they'd just *laugh* at themselves! If they'd just say, "I think it's like this, but von Leipzig thought it was like that, and he had a good shot at it, too." If they'd explain that this is their best guess.

Well, this is *my* best guess. This is the way I see it.

CHAPTER ONE

How Little We Know

How little we know, how much to discover . . .
Who cares to define what chemistry this is?
Who cares, with your lips on mine, how ignorant bliss is?

"How Little We Know (How Little It Matters)"
Words by Carolyn Leigh, music by Philip Springer, 1956

In January 2004, after a particularly disastrous holiday season, Lego, the Danish toy company, fired its chief operating officer. No one doubted that Poul Plougmann had to go. Miserable Christmas sales were the last straw at the end of a terrible year—Lego's revenues were down by 25 percent, and the company lost $230 million for the year, the worst in its history. What went so badly wrong? Chief executive Kjeld Kirk Kristiansen, grandson of the founder, explained it simply: Lego had "strayed too far from its roots and relied too heavily on merchandising spin-offs, such as Harry Potter figures, which proved unpopular this season despite the continuing success of J. K. Rowling's books." The solution? Lego announced that it would "return to basics." Kristiansen vowed: "We will focus on profitability, especially the attractive potential of our core products."

There's nothing especially remarkable about a story like this. Every day we read about companies that are doing well and someone gets promoted, and other companies that fail and someone gets the ax. Today it's Lego, and tomorrow it'll be someone else. The beat goes on.

Now, I'm really not very interested in Lego. As Rick might have said in *Casablanca*, the problems of one family-owned Danish toy maker don't amount to a hill of beans in this crazy world. What *does* interest me is how we explain Lego's performance, because the way we think about what happened at Lego is typical of how we think about success or failure in countless other companies. We don't want to read just that Lego's sales were sharply down, we want an explanation of what happened. It can't just have been bad luck—there must have been some reason why a proud company, a fixture on toy store shelves all around the world, a faithful playtime companion to generations of children, suddenly did so badly. So how did the business press explain Lego's downfall? A few newspapers reported that Lego was hurt by the fall of the U.S. dollar against the Danish kroner, which meant that North American sales—about half of Lego's total—were worth less on Lego's books. Some reporters also noted that a strong new rival, Montreal-based Mega Bloks Inc., was chipping away at Lego's dominant market share. But these were side issues. The main explanation for Lego's losses? *Lego had strayed from its core. It lost sight of its roots.* That's what Lego's chief executive said, and that's what the media reported, including the *Financial Times, The Wall Street Journal,* the Associated Press, Bloomberg News, *Nordic Business Report, Danish News Digest, Plastics News,* and about a dozen others. Depending on the source, Poul Plougmann was variously *sacked, fired, axed, ousted, removed, dismissed, replaced,* or simply *relieved of his duties.* But aside from the verb used to describe his departure, not much differed among the articles. Lego's big blunder was *straying from the core.*

Consider for a moment the word *stray. The American Heritage Dictionary of the English Language* defines *to stray* as "to wander beyond established limits," "to deviate from a course that is regarded as right," and "to become lost." A guided missile can *stray off course* and hit the wrong target. A dog that runs away from home is called *a stray.* A company can *stray,* too, if it goes off on a foolish adventure, if it wanders off course, if it gets lost. Apparently that's what Lego did—it chased merchandising spin-offs when it should have been focusing on its core product line. It *strayed.*

Chris Zook at Bain & Company argued in his 2001 book, *Profit from the Core,* that companies often do best when they focus on relatively few products for a clear segment of customers. When companies get into very different products or go after very different sets of customers, the results often aren't pretty. But here's the catch: Exactly how do we define a company's core? Zook identifies no fewer than six dimensions along which a company can reasonably expand its activities—into new geographies, new channels, new customer segments, new value chain steps, new businesses, and new products. Any one of them might be a sensible step into an adjacent area, radiating out from the core and bringing success. It's also possible that any one of them might be fraught with danger and lead to disaster. So how do we know which path to take? Where does the core end and where does straying off course begin? Of course, it's easy to know in retrospect—but how can we know in advance?

Which brings us back to Lego. For years, our friends at Lego did just one thing: They manufactured and sold construction building blocks for children. That was the core. Lego made millions of blocks thanks to modern injection molding manufacturing techniques, it turned out blocks in plenty of different colors, and it made them in different shapes and sizes so they could be easily manipulated by little hands. Children could build just about anything out of Lego blocks—the only limit was their imagination. Lego was always about construction building blocks, nothing else. It built a dominant market share and had huge power over distributors and retailers. In this segment, Lego was king.

Unfortunately, nothing in the business world stands still—customer preferences change and technology marches on and new competitors appear. The market for traditional toys stagnated as kids shifted to electronic games at an earlier and earlier age. By the 1990s, simple plastic building blocks were a mature product and, in a world of video games and electronic toys, well, a bit *boring.* If Lego wanted to grow, or even if it wanted to stay the same size, it would have to try some new things—the question was what. Of all the things Lego might try, what would make the most sense? If Lego decided to expand into, say, financial services, *that* would be straying from its core. No one would be surprised if the venture flopped— *"What's a toy company doing trying to become a bank? What do they know about banking?"*—and the responsible manager would have been removed without a second thought. What if Lego launched a line of children's clothing? That one's not so clear—Lego knows a lot about kids, and it understands consumer products. It has plenty of power over retail distribution, just not in clothing, at least not yet. Maybe it could succeed, maybe not. What about *electronic* toys? Again, debatable—maybe Lego could build on its experience in toys, and with all the growth in video games, why not? And in fact, Lego had developed Bionicle CD-ROM games and Mindstorm robots made of building blocks controlled by personal computers. But Harry Potter figures? Little toys with little plastic parts that snap together? That should be smack *inside* Lego's core. If Harry Potter figures are *outside* Lego's core, we ought to ask exactly how broad Lego's core really is. Because if Lego's core is nothing but traditional blocks, we'd have to wonder how it could possibly provide sufficient growth opportunities for a company with revenues of $2 billion.

In fact, Plougmann had been brought in from Bang & Olufsen, a Danish maker of high-quality audio equipment, in part to go after new opportunities. His hiring was seen as a coup, symptomatic of Lego's commitment to new avenues of growth after the company posted its first loss ever in 1998. Under his guidance, Lego began to branch out into electronic toys and merchandising spin-offs, and the initial response was good. At the time, no one said Lego was moving outside its core. But when sales fell sharply in 2003, Kristiansen lost patience and pulled the plug on Poul Plougmann. "We have been pursuing a strategy based on growth by focusing on totally new products. This strategy did not give the expected results." So in 2004, Lego decided to "return to its core" and "focus on profitability." Strange, because profitable growth was presumably what

Lego had in mind when it went after those new opportunities in the first place.

Imagine, if we could turn the clock back to 1999, that Lego had decided to stick to plastic building blocks, nothing more. Nope, we're *not* interested in a tie-in to Harry Potter, which was only the most popular children's book of all time, whose first two movies racked up box office receipts of $1.2 billion worldwide. Next year's headline? Probably something like this: EXECUTIVE SACKED AS LEGO SALES FLAT. And the story line? Something like this: "Danish family firm stays too long with a mature product line and misses out on growth opportunities to more innovative rivals." Analysts will comment that Lego failed to go boldly forward. *It lacked vision. It was inward looking. Its managers were timid and complacent*—or maybe even *arrogant*.

Of course, some ventures outside the core are spectacularly successful. During the 1980s, General Electric, America's largest industrial company long associated with light bulbs, refrigerators, airplane engines, and plastics, sold some of its traditional businesses—home appliances and televisions—and went in a big way into financial services—commercial finance, consumer finance, and insurance. Today, these financial services bring in more than 40 percent of GE's revenues and a corresponding amount of its profits, close to $8 billion. Did GE go beyond its core? Absolutely. But nobody called for the boss's head because GE was successful. In fact, GE was ranked at the top of *Fortune* magazine's 2005 survey of *Global Most Admired Companies,* ahead of Wal-Mart, Dell, Microsoft, and Toyota, and was ranked second in the *Financial Times*'s 2005 *World's Most Respected Companies* survey, down one notch after six consecutive years at number one. So much for the perils of straying from the core.

In the weeks following Plougmann's ouster, the U.K. magazine *Brand Strategy* looked a bit more closely into Lego's prospects. Like everyone else, it reported that Lego's problems were the result of "focusing on new products such as licensed Star Wars and Harry Potter ranges, to the detriment of its core business." But *Brand Strategy* went a step further and asked several industry experts what Lego should do. Maybe these industry experts, who presumably know the toy industry and its major players very well, would be able to offer some incisive advice. They were asked: *What should Lego do now?*

Here was the view of a marketing manager at Hamley's, London's legendary toy store:

> Lego mustn't lose sight of what it's become known for–reliable, colorful construction toys. Its marketing is impressive but Lego needs to continue having the wow factor.

This was the advice from a toy and games industry analyst:

> Lego has lost its way to some extent in recent years. It has diversified into a number of sectors and this hasn't worked. Lego should focus on what it does best and it's right to focus back on toys.

And here was the view from another toy industry expert:

> Lego has to remember its heritage; listen to customers; be innovative; focus on the key issues for long-term success; and go for evolution, not revolution.

A nice set of advice! Every one of these industry experts wants Lego to have it both ways: on the one hand to remember its heritage and focus on what it's known for, and on the other hand to be innovative and achieve a wow factor. (Remember, pursuit of the wow factor was exactly what Lego had tried to do–and it got creamed for losing sight of its core. Guess that was the wrong wow factor!) Not a single expert suggested that Lego make a clear choice and follow a definitive direction–they all want Lego to have the best of everything. You can bet that if Lego returned to profitability, every one of these experts would say, *See, Lego followed my advice,* and if Lego continued to lose money, they could say, *Lego didn't do what I told them.* And these are industry experts, who presumably understand the toy industry better than you and I do.

Ted Williams, the great Red Sox outfielder, once said there was one thing he always found irritating: With runners on base and the opposing team's slugger coming to the plate, the manager walks to the mound and says to the pitcher, "Don't give the batter a good pitch, but don't walk him," then turns around and marches back to the dugout. *Pointless!* said Ted. *Of course* the pitcher doesn't want to give the batter anything good to hit, and *of course* he doesn't want to walk him. The pitcher already *knows* that! The only useful advice is, "In *this* situation, it's better to throw a strike because you really don't want to walk this hitter," or, "It's better to walk this hitter because in *this* situation you really don't want to throw him a strike." But baseball managers, like industry analysts, find it easier to ask for the best of both.

One final note about the toy business. Lost in all the sound and fury about Lego was the fact that other toy makers were struggling, too. The largest U.S. toy maker, Mattel, in the midst of a multiyear turnaround after several poor years, announced in July 2004 that sales of its best-known product, the Barbie doll, had fallen by 13 percent. Part of Barbie's woes stemmed from a rival product, MGA Entertainment's Bratz dolls, said to be an "edgier fashion doll," which had eaten into Barbie's market share. What was Mattel planning to do in order to revive Barbie sales? Focus on its core? No, it planned a new line based on the *American Idol* television show and a fashion-based line called "Fashion Fever." Months after Lego concluded that merchandising spin-offs were a bad idea, Mattel decided to take that very approach.

Drifting with WH Smith, *Expanding* with Nokia

Lego isn't the only company to be criticized for wandering off course. Consider WH Smith, the troubled newspaper and magazine retail chain. WH Smith got its start more than a hundred years ago as a London newspaper distributor, and over time moved into bookstalls and stores. Nothing odd about that. *The*

New York Times reported: "It was in the 1980s that WH Smith began to diversify well beyond books and periodicals, adding music, office supplies, stationery, and gifts to its store shelves. But in drifting away from its core products, analysts said, the company also made itself vulnerable to competition." WH Smith now found itself competing with supermarkets and other large surface stores—a dangerous game.

Note the word: *drifting*. According to the *Times*, WH Smith didn't *expand* or *diversify*, it *drifted*. *The American Heritage Dictionary* defines *to drift* as "to move from place to place with no particular goal," "to be carried along by currents of air or water," "to wander from a set course or point of attention; to stray." A raft can be *cast adrift*, left to move with the currents. Wood that flows in and out with the tides is *driftwood*. A person with no direction or aims is a *drifter*. (At the start of *The Magnificent Seven*, the rootlessness—and availability for hire—of the gunfighters is conveyed in this exchange between Steve McQueen and Yul Brynner. "Where are you heading?" asks McQueen. Brynner answers: "I'm drifting south, more or less. And you?" McQueen shrugs. "Just drifting.")

Well, who says that WH Smith *drifted*? Who says that selling music and office supplies is an example of wandering off course? Why should we think that WH Smith had no particular goal when it added stationery and gifts? It didn't get into book publishing. It didn't try to sell fresh food or alcoholic beverages. WH Smith didn't add products that call for explanations by salespeople, like electronic equipment, or products that might involve returns. All it did was add a few other fast-moving consumables. It expanded the range of products on its shelves, nothing more. Isn't that exactly what WH Smith should be doing—identify adjacent areas that draw on its existing capabilities and that appeal to its core customers? In fact, WH Smith's dilemma sounds like a classic problem of format expansion: As large stores and supermarkets expanded their formats to include some of WH Smith's products, WH Smith had to decide whether to sit still and suffer the consequences, or respond by expanding its format. It could well be that given the circumstances, adding music and office supplies was the best move it could have made. Maybe WH Smith was unable to execute its new format for some reason—bad inventory management or poor logistics—or maybe it simply couldn't match the buying power of Wal-Mart and Safeway. But that's very different from saying WH Smith *drifted*.

Let's fast-forward and see if we can spot a good strategy while it's happening. Nokia had been the leader in mobile phone handsets since the mid-1990s, combining technological excellence, sleek designs, and shrewd branding to build the world's largest market share. But by 2004, the Finnish-based company had begun to feel the heat from tougher competition, much of it coming from low-cost Asian rivals. Mobile phones, those clever compact items, that now included cameras and calendars and calculators and radios, were in danger of becoming a commodity—and Nokia's margins were under pressure. So what was Nokia going to do? Would it redouble its focus on the core and ramp up its investment in handsets? Not at all. According to *Business Week*, Nokia was intent on "expanding into mobile gaming, imaging, music, and even complex wireless systems for corporations." These new areas were appealing for their growth and promise of higher margins, but they were far from Nokia's core of handset design and manufacturing. They were further from Nokia's core than stationery was from WH Smith's core or Harry Potter toys were from Lego's core. So why didn't *Business Week* say that Nokia was *straying* or *drifting*? Why was Nokia merely *expanding*? Because, at the time, no one knew if Nokia would succeed or fail, so *Business Week* chose a nice neutral verb, *expand*. Plus, in plenty of ways, Nokia's strategy made sense—it was shifting from a tough low-margin business into new areas that promised higher margins. If Nokia could make this change work, it would be celebrated for its nimble strategy and clever management. Of course, if Nokia failed, reporters would say it had erred by moving into areas it didn't understand; it *strayed* or *drifted*. The chief executive (or his replacement, if he met the same fate as Poul Plougmann) might then decide Nokia should go back to basics and try even harder with the girl it brought to the dance in the first place, handsets. Yet if

Nokia had decided to stick to handsets while its market share was collapsing and margins were imploding, we'd have probably read that Nokia was complacent, inward looking, and conservative. *No wonder Nokia failed,* we'd be told. *It didn't react to a shift in the market. It didn't change with the times.*

The Mother of All Business Questions

These accounts about Lego, WH Smith, and Nokia are all variants of the most basic question in the business world: *What leads to high performance?* It's the mother of all business questions, a Wall Street equivalent of the Holy Grail. Why does one company achieve great success, turning its shareholders into millionaires, while another company just muddles through, earning a modest profit but never catching fire or, even worse, failing altogether? The fact is, it's often hard to know exactly why one company succeeds and another fails. Did Lego make a mistake when it added merchandising tie-ins? At the time, the decision seemed to make sense. It was only later, after the results were in, that Lego's initiatives were described as misguided and ill considered. But that's in retrospect. Lego's venture turned out badly, yes, but that does not necessarily make it a mistake. Plenty of other things, from currency shifts to competitors' actions to sudden shifts in consumer taste, could have helped bury Lego. Plus it's not clear that any of the alternatives would have been more successful. Yet when we read a word like *stray,* it's hard to escape the conclusion that Lego erred—the very word implies a damning judgment. If we had a better idea of what Nokia's new directions would lead to, we would use a more precise term than *expand*—we might more confidently describe it either as *ill-advised* or as *brilliant.* But we don't.

Or consider a little discount retailer, founded in a small Arkansas town in 1962. How did Wal-Mart grow up to be the biggest company in the world, spinning its cash registers to the tune of \$1 billion per day, so big that it accounts for 30 percent of the sales of Procter & Gamble, that it sells 25 percent of all disposable diapers and 20 percent of all magazines sold in the United States, so powerful that it can censor magazines and CDs by threatening not to carry them? How did Wal-Mart become such a success? There's no shortage of theories: Perhaps it was a strategy of "everyday low prices," or a relentless obsession with detail, or a culture that gets ordinary people to do their best, or a sophisticated use of information technology in supply chain management, or maybe a bare-knuckled approach to squeezing its suppliers. Are *some* of these explanations right? Are *all* of them right? Which are most important? Do some work only in combination with others? Some explanations, like Wal-Mart's use of its sheer scale to get the lowest input costs, help explain high performance today but don't tell us how the company got so big in the first place. These questions are important because if we want to learn from Wal-Mart, if we want some of Wal-Mart's success to rub off on our companies, which lessons should we learn? The fact is, it's hard to be sure. As Frank Sinatra, the Chairman of the Board, used to sing: *"How little we know, how much to discover."*

Of course, we don't like to admit how little we know. The social psychologist Eliot Aronson observed that people are not rational beings so much as *rationalizing* beings. We want explanations. We want the world around us to make sense. We may not know exactly why Lego ran into a brick wall, or why WH Smith fell on hard times, or why Wal-Mart has done so well, but we want to feel that we know what happened. We want the comfort of a plausible explanation, so we say that a company *strayed* or *drifted*. Or take the stock market, whose daily fluctuations, edging higher one day and a bit lower the next, resemble Brownian motion, the jittery movement of pollen particles in water or of gas molecules bouncing off one another. It's not very satisfying to say that today's stock market movement is explained by random forces. Tune in to CNBC and listen to the pundits as they watch the ticker, and you'll hear them explain, "The Dow is up slightly as investors gain confidence from rising factory orders," or, "The Dow is off by a percentage point as investors take profits," or, "The Dow is a bit higher as investors shrug off worries about the Fed's next move on interest rates." They have to say *something*. Maria Bartiromo can't exactly look into the camera and say that the Dow is down half a percent today because of random Brownian motion.

Science and the Study of Business

But all of this begs a larger question. If we have difficulty pinpointing what drives company performance, why is that? It's certainly not for lack of trying. Thousands of very smart and hardworking people in business schools and research centers and consulting firms spend a great deal of time and effort looking for answers. There's a huge amount at stake. So why are explanations about company performance so often riddled with clichés and simplistic phrases?

In other fields, from medicine to chemistry to aeronautical engineering, knowledge seems to march ahead relentlessly. What do these fields have in common? In a word, these fields move forward thanks to a form of inquiry we call *science*. Richard Feynman once defined science as "a method for trying to answer questions which can be put into the form: *If I do this, what will happen?*" Science isn't about beauty or truth or justice or wisdom or ethics. It's eminently practical. It asks, If I do something over here, what will happen over there? If I apply this much force, or that much heat, or if I mix these chemicals, what will happen? By this definition, *What leads to sustained profitable growth?* is a scientific question. It asks, If a company does this or that, what will happen to its revenues or profits or share price?

How should we answer a scientific question? Feynman explained: "The technique of it, fundamentally, is: Try it and see. Then you put together a large amount of information from such experiences." In other words, you conduct experiments and put together information in systematic ways to deduce rules that govern the phenomena and that can lead to accurate predictions. The great thing about sciences like physics and chemistry is that we can run experiments—*try it and see*—in carefully constructed laboratory settings that let us control the settings, adjust the inputs, and observe the results. Then we can tinker with a few variables, alter some settings, and try again. Scientific progress owes a great deal to the careful and incremental refinement of experiments.

But what about the business world, which takes place not in a laboratory, but in the messy and complex world around us? Do business questions lend themselves to scientific investigation? Can we devise alternative hypotheses and test them with carefully designed experiments, so that we can support some explanations and reject others? In many instances, the answer is *yes*. Plenty of business questions lend themselves to scientific experimentation. Imagine you want to know where to place an item in a supermarket, or what effect a price change will have on the quantity of a product sold, or what effect a special promotion will have. What can you do? Simple, you can run trials in different stores and compare the answers. You can find out what works in a given setting. *If I do this, what will happen?* In fact, just about any situation with an abundance of similar transactions affords a natural setting for experiments. One explanation of Wal-Mart's success is that it was among the first retailers to apply scientific rigor to merchandising, studying the patterns of consumption and understanding the behavioral traits of its customers, then applying its findings to everything from logistics management to store layout. Likewise, some of the best Internet companies, such as Amazon.com and eBay, use highly sophisticated techniques to track customer clicks and understand their choices. Another example is Harrah's Entertainment, one of America's leading gambling companies—the polite word is *gaming*—with hundreds of thousands of customers visiting its casinos every day. When Gary Loveman came on board as chief operating officer in 1998, he didn't just see rows of slot machines and card tables and roulette wheels—he saw a fabulous laboratory for running experiments. He saw that Harrah's loyalty card, *Total Gold*, gathered huge amounts of data about thousands of customers and their preferences. Using these data, Harrah's could run experiments and analyze the outcomes, then make adjustments to improve customer satisfaction and retention. For example, Harrah's could configure casino floors with just the right mix of slot machines to benefit both customers and the company. Did Loveman's experiments meet the standard of science? You bet. And the results were dramatic: Revenues and profits were way up, both in absolute terms and relative to Harrah's competitors. Scientific thinking—*try it and see*—helped Harrah's improve its performance.

But other questions in business don't easily lend themselves to this sort of experimentation. Take a major strategic initiative, like the launch of a new product. Coca-Cola didn't get two chances to launch New Coke in 1985—it got one bite at the apple and famously got it completely wrong. Daimler had just one shot at acquiring Chrysler, and mistakes were hard, if not impossible, to undo. Ditto AOL and Time Warner—a complex merger between two entirely different corporate cultures in a rapidly changing industry. Steve Case and Gerald Levin had no way to conduct experiments. There's simply no way to bring the rigor of experimentation to questions like these. Want to know the best way to manage an acquisition? We can't buy 100 companies, manage half of them in one way and half in another way, and compare the results. We can't run that sort of experiment.

Science, Pseudoscience, and Coconut Headsets

Our inability to capture the full complexity of the business world through scientific experiments has provided fodder for some critics of business schools. Management gurus Warren Bennis and James O'Toole, in a 2005 *Harvard Business Review* article, criticized business schools for their reliance on the scientific method. They wrote: "This scientific model is predicated on the faulty assumption that business is an academic discipline like chemistry or geology when, in fact, business is a profession and business schools are professional schools—or should be." The notion seems to be that since business will never be understood with the precision of the natural sciences, it's best understood as a sort of humanity, a realm where the logic of scientific inquiry doesn't apply. Well, yes and no. It may be true that business cannot be studied with the rigor of chemistry or geology, but that doesn't mean that all we have is intuition and gut feel. There's no need to veer from one extreme to the other. There's plenty of room between the natural sciences and the humanities, after all. We might not be able to buy 100 companies and run an experiment, but we *can* study acquisitions that have already taken place and look for patterns. We *can* examine some key variables like company size, industry, and the integration process, and then see what leads to better or worse results. That approach—called *quasi-experimentation*—is a staple of social science. It may never reach the ideal of the natural sciences, but it comes about as close as we can get to applying the spirit of scientific inquiry to some key business decisions.

In fact, there's a great deal of very good social science research about company performance, and I'll review some of it in future chapters. But much of it, precisely because it's done carefully and is circumspect in its findings, tends not to provide clear and definitive guidelines for action. It's just not very appealing to read that a given action has a measurable but small impact on company success. Managers don't usually care to wade through discussions about data validity and methodology and statistical models and probabilities. We prefer explanations that are definitive and offer clear implications for action. We want to explain Lego's fortunes quickly, simply, and with an appealing logic. We like stories.

It's useful to make the distinction between reports and stories. A *report* is above all responsible for providing the facts, without manipulation or interpretation. If the accounts about Lego and WH Smith are meant to be reports—which presumably they are, since they're written by *reporters*—then words like *stray* and *drift* are problematic. Stories, on the other hand, are a way that people try to make sense of their lives and their experiences in the world. The test of a good story isn't its responsibility to the facts as much as its ability to provide a satisfying explanation of events. As *stories*, the news accounts about Lego and WH Smith work just fine. In a few paragraphs, the reader learns of the problem (sales and profits are down), gets a plausible explanation (the company lost its direction), and learns a lesson (don't stray, focus on the core). There's a neat end with a clean resolution. No threads are left hanging. Readers go away satisfied.

Now, there's nothing wrong with stories, provided we understand that's what we have before us. More insidious, however, are stories that are dressed up to look like science. They take the form of science and claim to have the authority of science, but they miss the real rigor and logic of science. They're better described as *pseudoscience*. Richard Feynman had an even more memorable phrase: Cargo Cult Science. Here's the way Feynman described it:

> In the South Seas there is a cult of people. During the war they saw airplanes land with lots of materials, and they want the same thing to happen now. So they've arranged to make things like runways, to put fires along the sides of the runways, to make a wooden hut for a man to sit in, with two wooden pieces on his head like headphones and bars of bamboo sticking out like antennas—he's the controller—and they wait for the airplanes to land. They're doing everything right. The form is perfect. But it doesn't work. No airplanes land. So I call these things Cargo Cult Science, because they follow all the apparent precepts and forms of scientific investigation, but they're missing something essential, because the planes don't land.

That's not to say that Cargo Cult Science doesn't have some benefits. The folks who wait patiently by the landing strips on their tropical island, dressed up like flight controllers and wearing a pair of coconut headsets, may derive some contentment from the whole process—they may live in hope of a better future, they may enjoy having something to believe in, and they may feel closer to supernatural powers. But it's just that—it's a story. It's not a good predictor of what will happen next.

The business world is full of Cargo Cult Science, books and articles that claim to be rigorous scientific research but operate mainly at the level of storytelling. In later chapters, we'll look at some of this research—some that meet the standards of science but aren't satisfying as stories, and some that offer wonderful stories but are doubtful as science. As we'll see, some of the most successful business books of recent years, perched atop the bestseller lists for months on end, cloak themselves in the mantle of science, but have little more predictive power than a pair of coconut headsets on a tropical island.

CHAPTER TWO

The Story of Cisco

Those who rewrite history probably do believe with parts of their minds that they are actually thrusting facts into the past. . . . They feel that their own version was what happened in the sight of God, and that one is justified in rearranging the records accordingly.

George Orwell
Notes on Nationalism, 1945

The examples we've seen so far, about Lego, WH Smith, and Nokia, were drawn from articles in the business press, by reporters writing under a tight deadline, perhaps based on little more than a company press release. It's no wonder so many of them relied on clichés and stock phrases. But what about studies of a single company over several years? Perhaps examining a company over time can offer a better understanding of its performance.

One of the most basic measures of company performance is shareholder value, and by that measure, Cisco Systems ranks as one of the highest performers of all time. It reached a market value of $100 billion faster than any other company in history, and then, for one brief, shining moment—two weeks, actually, in March 2000— Cisco was the tops, surpassing Microsoft as the most valuable company in the world, worth a staggering $555 billion. In the five years after he became Cisco's chief executive, John Chambers presided over an increase of $450 billion in shareholder value, a clip of more than $90 billion per year—which works out to $1 billion every four days, or $250 million every single day of the year, including Sundays and holidays, for five straight years. High performance indeed.

Was it all just a bubble? True, Cisco's share price slumped badly at the end of 2000 and fell further in 2001, then languished far below its peak levels for the next two years. But as the economy began to revive, Cisco's market capitalization picked up, and by 2005 it stood at $116 billion, making Cisco the seventeenth most valuable company in the United States. It ranked ahead of durable legends like Coca-Cola, ChevronTexaco, and Disney. It was worth more than 3M and American Express put together. Not exactly what you'd expect if the company was nothing but smoke and mirrors.

Another way to measure firm performance is to leave Wall Street aside and look at a company's ability to generate profits on a sustained basis. If we take that approach, Cisco *still* deserves very strong marks thanks to its ever growing sales, topping $24 billion in 2005, while also generating very high profit margins. Any way we look at it, Cisco Systems has been a stellar performer. If we want to explain firm performance, the obvious place to look is at a company with one of the best performances of all—because if we can't explain Cisco's success, how can we hope to explain a lesser case? Fortunately, Cisco has been the subject of dozens of magazine articles, case studies, and at least a couple of books. So let's take a look at how reporters and managers and professors explained one company's success.

Once upon a Time in the Valley

Right from the start, the story of Cisco had a fairy-tale quality. In *John Chambers and the Cisco Way,* John K. Waters began the tale this way:

> The legend of the founding of Cisco Systems is a Silicon Valley classic. Sandra K. Lerner and Leonard Bosack met in graduate school, fell in love, and married. After graduating, they took jobs managing computer networks located at different

corners of the sixteen-square-mile Stanford campus. They
longed to exchange romantic e-mail, but their networks were
incompatible. Sandy supervised the computers at Stanford's
graduate school of business, while Bosack worked five hundred
yards away at the computer science lab.

The solution to incompatible networks was something called a
multiprotocol router, which allowed computers to exchange data.
Lerner and Bosack devised the router, founded the company, and
the rest was history. Well, that's the legend—the story we read over
and over. And it's about right, at least as far as I can tell, twenty
years later and more than a few hundred miles away.

Like many start-ups, Cisco began by operating out of a basement
and at first sold its wares to friends and professional acquaintances.
Once revenues approached $1 million, Lerner and Bosack went in
search of venture capital. The man who finally said *yes* was Donald
Valentine at Sequoia Capital, the seventy-seventh moneyman they approached, who invested $2.5 million in exchange for a third of the
stock and management control. Valentine began to professionalize
Cisco's management, bringing in as CEO an industry veteran, John
Morgridge. Sales grew rapidly, from $1.5 million in 1987 to $28 million in 1989, and in February 1990, Cisco went public. At the end of
the first day of trading, its market capitalization stood at $222 million.
Over the next years, Morgridge and Valentine continued to guide the
company upward, and in a pattern repeated often in Silicon Valley,
the founders soon left, squeezed out, their time done.

In 1991, when Cisco was still a relatively small and rather speculative venture, one of dozens like it in the Valley, Valentine and
Morgridge brought on board a sales executive named John Chambers. Most profiles of Chambers describe him in the same way:
humble but also driven, charismatic but self-effacing, a low-key supersalesman. He had grown up in the white-shirt culture of IBM
and then moved to Wang Labs, two big computer companies that
had suffered sharp downturns. Now Chambers was ready to hitch
his star to a smaller company, one he could help shape.

A turning point for Cisco came in 1993. Although sales of the core product, routers, remained strong, Chambers devised a new strategic plan. Along with CEO Morgridge and Chief Technology Officer Ed Kozel, Chambers decided that Cisco would put together a broad product line and become a one-stop shop for the wired world, dominating the market for Internet infrastructure. There was only one hitch. The market was growing so fast, and new technologies were so unpredictable, that Cisco couldn't hope to grow on its own. Drawing up a grid that showed the full range of products, Chambers suggested that Cisco fill in the blanks by acquiring small companies. Over the next weeks, Cisco scouted for start-ups, identifying hot new technologies and clever engineers. Soon it made a first acquisition, buying Crescendo Communications, a LAN-switching company, for $97 million. That was just an appetizer—over the next three years, Cisco would acquire two dozen companies.

In 1995, John Morgridge retired and John Chambers became Cisco's CEO. Under his guidance, Cisco soon morphed into a New Economy juggernaut. It bought thirteen more companies in 1996, almost all of them small, but one "really big fish," StrataCom, a maker of frame relay devices and switches with 1,200 employees and revenues of $400 million. With the Internet economy exploding all around, and bolstered by its several acquisitions, Cisco's revenues reached $4 billion in 1997. Now it began to attract notice in the press. A March 1997 article in *Wired* described Cisco in cultlike terms, filled with "shiny, happy people" working long hours but "loving every minute of it." It elaborated: "These folks do work that is difficult, that takes long hours, that can be exquisitely frustrating and twisted. They are basically very, very good mechanics of a type that is peculiar to our age: they build the plumbing of the Internet." Yet there was something unusual about this company: "*Nobody* has this much fun going to work," *Wired* commented. "And all they do is smile, smile, smile." One month later, *Business Week* ran a feature story about Cisco, calling it a "high tech whiz." It was "the undisputed king of networking equipment and one of the troika that sets the industry's agenda: Cisco is to the information highway what Microsoft Corp is to software and Intel is to computer chips." And the reasons for this success? *Business Week* explained it was due to more than happy, shiny people: "Thanks to Chambers' seemingly flawless management, slick salesmanship, and a scorching series of acquisitions . . . Cisco has gone from relative obscurity to computer industry superstardom." Two weeks later, in May 1997, *Fortune* ran its own feature article on Cisco, anointing it as "Computing's New Superpower." In *Fortune*'s words, Cisco had "surfed the internet tsunami with more aplomb than perhaps any other company, deftly maneuvering into new areas of networking technology with lightning quick acquisitions." Note the words: Cisco wasn't *straying from its core* or *drifting*, but *deftly maneuvering into new areas*.

Cisco rode the crest of the Internet wave in 1998. Revenues reached $8.5 billion, six times the 1995 level. Cisco had a 40 percent share of the $20 billion data-networking equipment industry—routers, hubs, and devices that made up the so-called plumbing of the Internet—and a massive 80 percent share of the high-end router market. But Cisco wasn't just growing revenues. It was profitable, too. At a time when even the most admired Internet start-ups, like Amazon.com, were losing money, Cisco posted operating margins of 60 percent. This wasn't some dot-com with a business plan, way out there in the blue, riding on a smile and a shoeshine. It wasn't panning for Internet gold, it was selling picks and shovels to miners who were lining up around the corner to buy them. And Wall Street loved it. Cisco was "Big C," an unstoppable force that slightly surpassed Wall Street expectations quarter after quarter. In July 1998, *The Wall Street Journal* reported: "Of all the recent bull market milestones, fewer were as impressive as the one reached last Friday by Cisco Systems. The maker of computer-networking gear saw its market capitalization roll past $100 billion." Cisco had reached the magic mark in record time, after just twelve years. Microsoft, the former champ, had taken twenty years to reach that size. In September 1998, *Fortune* crowned Cisco as "The Real King of the Internet." It wrote that Chambers "has spun nothing but sweetness for investors, turning Cisco's stock into the closest thing to a sure bet in the technology business." By now, Cisco had bought twenty-nine companies. Chambers's willingness to buy, rather than invent, the technology he needed was unusual for Silicon Valley. While many high-tech companies looked at acquiring new technology as a sign of weakness, Chambers took the opposite view—in fact, he thought that a refusal to look outside was an example of the insular thinking that had hurt IBM.

It was onward and upward for Cisco in 1999. The larger it got, the faster it grew—and vice versa. And where was Cisco going next? Beyond routers and switches, into a much bigger league—the $250 billion–a–year market for telecom equipment, where Cisco so' far had only a tiny share. The room for growth was immense! Of course, expanding into this segment would put Cisco in direct competition with some heavy hitters—Lucent, Nortel, and Alcatel. Were analysts worried that Cisco was straying from the core? Not at all. As long as Cisco delivered good results, analysts wrote that diversification made sense. JP Morgan commented: "Chambers has diversified the product line and motivated his managers to stay completely focused on customers. Cisco is off to a very fast start, and if you give them a lead they're nearly impossible to catch." SG Cowen Securities added: "They're just getting started" with telephone companies. MCI WorldCom, Sprint, Swisscom, and other major telecoms were all planning to buy Cisco products.

Explaining Cisco's Success

From 1997 through 2000, Cisco was featured in numerous lengthy articles in the leading American business magazines. The question implicit in these stories? Why was this company—this one rather than some other one—doing so well? A few themes emerged. In just about every account, credit was given to John Chambers, Cisco's chief executive. Many profiles touched on the same points. How Chambers was the son of two doctors in Charleston,

West Virginia. How he had overcome dyslexia to go to law school, then taken a job with IBM. How he had seen IBM and Wang stumble by failing to react to important shifts in technology. Chambers reflected: "I learned at both companies that if you don't stay ahead of trends, they'll destroy everything you work for and tragically disrupt the lives of your employees. I don't ever want to go through that again." It was an inspiring story. And with Chambers at the helm, Cisco would never repeat those mistakes—it would remain lean and humble and nimble. It would take the best points from IBM and combine them with the drive and passion and vision of the New Economy.

A second element often mentioned was Cisco's remarkable skill at acquiring companies. *Fortune* wrote: "Think of Cisco as an acquisition engine, as cleverly designed and highly tuned as the giant routers it builds to handle vast surges of Internet traffic." What made Cisco so good at acquisitions? Part of the explanation was Cisco's ability to select the best companies to buy. There was no shortage of possible candidates, from small start-ups to large established companies. Identifying the right companies was the job of thirty-three-year-old wunderkind Michelangelo (Mike) Volpi, said to have a knack for identifying start-up companies at just the right moment. A Harvard Business School case study focused on Cisco's strategy of growth through acquisitions. It agreed that Cisco was highly disciplined, going after small companies with products that could immediately take their place in Cisco's offerings, but avoiding speculative and unrelated acquisitions. It would buy no large companies, or any far away from its California base, or any with a very different corporate culture. Why? Because Cisco wanted to pick off small and similar companies that could be easily absorbed. Prior to every acquisition, Cisco performed a thorough due diligence using a cross-functional team with representatives from marketing, engineering, and manufacturing. It was said to care as much about cultural fit as technology fit.

Finding the right companies to acquire was only part of the story. Cisco wasn't just doing deals, it was integrating new companies with great results. *Fortune* observed that Cisco excelled at digesting acquisitions smoothly. What were the keys to its success? First, Cisco had a dedicated team whose sole job was to "repot" start-ups into the larger company. The Harvard case study reported that after a deal closed, Cisco followed a systematic postacquisition integration process with clear expectations for specific milestones at 90 days and 180 days. It commented: "Integration success was due in large part to the very organized, methodical approach that Cisco took toward managing the experience of acquired employees." But Cisco was also said to address the human dimension of integrations. After all, small high-tech companies didn't just bring assets or customers—they were attractive mainly for their people. Smooth integration was critical to keep talent on board, and on this score Cisco was said to do a terrific job. It cared about the soft side of merger integration, helping to bring new employees on board, making them feel part of the team—by handing out Cisco baseball caps, for example, to help build company identity. *Fortune* wrote: "When Cisco absorbs a company, it makes a no-layoffs pledge; its turnover rate for employees acquired through mergers is a scant 2.1% vs. an industry average of 20%." Finally, Cisco's approach struck the right balance between flexibility and discipline. While each acquisition was unique and required some customization, there were numerous mandatory steps, including the merger of information systems and adoption of manufacturing methods. Whereas other companies made infrequent acquisitions and had to learn tough lessons each time, Cisco was making a science of acquisitions. In 1999, it was ranked number one by the Chapel Hill, N.C., consulting company Best Practices, following a client survey about successful merger-and-acquisition policies.

As Cisco's fortunes soared in the late 1990s, two professors at Stanford Business School, Charles O'Reilly III and Jeffrey Pfeffer, were at work on a book, *Hidden Value: How Great Companies Achieve Extraordinary Results with Ordinary People*. They included a chapter about Cisco, in their view an exemplar when it came to managing people. The authors spent a few pages recounting Cisco's history and discussing its strategy, and offered a standard profile of John Chambers, the humble supersalesman with the West Virginia drawl. They referred to Cisco's management of acquisitions and noted its ability to retain talent. Yet none of these seemed adequate to explain Cisco's phenomenal success. "So the question remains," wrote O'Reilly and Pfeffer, "What accounts for Cisco's competitive advantage?" And the answer? "Think about it deductively," they urged. If Cisco was more successful than other companies, that must mean it "has been more adept than its competitors at providing customers with the technology and equipment they want." And that meant two things: Cisco had "the strong belief in having no technology religion, and listening carefully to the customer." According to O'Reilly and Pfeffer, that's what Cisco really did well—it had no technology of its own but listened intently to customers. It observed where the market was going, then acquired the necessary technology and retained the people who developed it. In the last analysis, the key to Cisco's success had everything to do with its ability to tap the talent and energy of its workforce.

Cisco at Flood Tide

The NASDAQ surged in the last month of 1999, and after a short pause following the New Year, it zoomed past 4000 and then touched 5000. On March 27, 2000, Cisco reached a market cap of $555 billion and eclipsed Microsoft as the most valuable company in the world. In April the NASDAQ began to waver, and by May Cisco's shares had slid by 20 percent from its high of $80. Today we see that as the first shudder before the house of cards collapsed, but at the time many observers saw a softening in tech stocks only as a much-needed correction, a pause before going still higher. In fact, some believed that Cisco's stock looked more attractive than ever. In May 2000, *Fortune* ran a cover story on Cisco and its chief executive. The cover headline asked: "Is John Chambers the world's best CEO? Is it too late to buy his stock?" Inside was a six-page article with photos and graphs, based on extensive interviews and visits on-site (including a fawning visit to the home vineyard of a couple of top executives). *Fortune* wrote that "Cisco, with CEO John Chambers at the helm, must be considered one of America's truly outstanding companies, in the same league as Intel, Wal-Mart, and yes, GE." It was as positive a story as one can imagine, a high-water mark of hype.

The reasons that *Fortune* gave for Cisco's amazing success? The same basic themes were stressed yet again. Cisco was credited with "extreme customer focus." "Put simply," wrote *Fortune*, "no networker has ever had the laser focus on customers that Cisco has had from day one." It quoted a venture capitalist, John Doerr, who agreed: "That's the focus—customers. John Chambers is the most customer-focused human being you will ever meet." Chambers himself commented: "When it comes to our customers, we will do whatever it takes to win them." A second theme was acquisition integration. *Fortune* wrote that Cisco was "making a science of acquisitions," noting its "ability to integrate acquired companies is legendary." Third was Cisco's special corporate culture, which blended personal empowerment with discipline. "You have to understand," said a rival Silicon Valley executive, "managers are empowered there in a way they just aren't at Oracle or Sun or HP or Intel." Yet Cisco was also credited with a culture of discipline and an obsession about costs: "John and [CFO] Larry Carter run such a tight ship, it's almost unbelievable," said one manager. Cisco's offices were simple and frugal. Everyone flew coach. No one, least of all top managers, enjoyed ostentatious perks. Fourth, but by no means last, was John Chambers. Much of the credit for Cisco's success went to Cisco's chief executive. Jeff Bezos of Amazon.com might have been *Time* magazine's 1999 *Person of the Year*, but according to *Fortune*, the best CEO in the information age was John Chambers.

As for holding Cisco's stock, *Fortune* pointed out that Cisco's growth was twice that of GE's annual rate of 15 percent. If you owned stock in just one company, wrote *Fortune* in May 2000, then

Cisco was the one to have. And for a time, that advice seemed justified. The NASDAQ stabilized during the summer of 2000, and by October, when *Fortune* announced its annual poll of most admired companies, Cisco was ranked at number two, right behind General Electric—the most successful diversified company in the world, led by the legendary Jack Welch. So there it was. Cisco was at the summit, immensely successful, wonderfully customer oriented, with a terrific culture and an unsurpassed mastery of acquisitions. The only question, as *Fortune* had phrased it in May 2000, was whether it was too late to buy Cisco's stock.

The answer turned out to be *yes*.

Reversal at *Fortune*

Tech stocks started to slide in September, then fell faster in October. By November, Cisco's shares were trading at just $50 amid a full rout. The implications for Cisco weren't lost on the more astute reporters. Scott Thurm of *The Wall Street Journal* noted: "At stake are tens of billions of dollars of Cisco's stock market value, now $393 billion. And because Cisco relies on its stock to hire and retain employees, as well as to acquire promising technology, a weaker stock could further hamper Cisco's business. As the stock stagnated in recent months, Cisco's attrition rate inched higher, as some employees sought more lucrative opportunities." By the end of 2000, Cisco's share price had dropped all the way to $38, less than half of its record high. Yet John Chambers remained bullish, announcing that the slump was an opportunity to expand market share, and he continued to order more inventory. But this time things were different. Orders fell, backlog dropped, and in April 2001, Cisco wrote off a staggering $2. 2 billion of inventory, finally recognizing that it had utterly misread customer demand. Then Chambers was forced to do what he had most dreaded, a layoff of thousands of employees. By April 2001, exactly one year after peaking at $80, Cisco's stock bottomed out at $14. More than $400 billion in market capitalization had vanished in twelve months. Acquisitions weren't just out of the question, they were pointless.

In May 2001, exactly one year after its last and greatest puff piece, *Fortune* ran a very different story about Cisco. The title: "Cisco Fractures Its Own Fairy Tale." Now it wrote:

> On the way up to a stock market value of half a trillion dollars, everything about Cisco seemed perfect. It had a perfect CEO. It could close its books in a day and make perfect financial forecasts. It was an acquisition machine, ingesting companies and their technologies with great aplomb. It was the leader of the new economy, selling gear to new-world telecom companies that would use it to supplant old-world carriers and make their old-world suppliers irrelevant.
>
> Over the past year, every one of those characterizations has proved to be false.

According to *Fortune,* Cisco's prowess hadn't just been exaggerated, it had been false. And its problems weren't just external—a bubble bursting and orders slowing down faster than anyone could have forecast. Rather, *Fortune* concluded, based on "dozens of conversations with customers, past and present Cisco executives, competitors, and suppliers reveal, Cisco made its own mess."

What about its extreme customer focus? Now *Fortune* reported that Cisco "had exhibited a cavalier attitude toward potential customers." Cisco's sales techniques had been "irksome" and had "alienated" competitors. Its legendary forecasting ability? Sorry. Cisco "had signed long-term contracts with suppliers at just the wrong time." Its skills at innovation? Now it turned out that "a few of its products weren't very good." Nothing was spared: "Acquisitions, forecasting, technology, and, yes, senior management—all have failed Cisco in the past year." And what had led to such mistakes? At the heart of these problems was an arrogance brought on by success. *Fortune* remarked that Cisco had been "basking in a culture of confidence," that its venture into telecom products was evidence of Cisco's "swagger," that it "strode cocksure," and that its "assuredness bordered on the naïve." Pride before the fall, a theme as old as the Greeks. Other companies had stumbled, sure, but "Cisco's stumbles are fascinating because Chambers promoted the company as a new breed of behemoth—one that was faster, smarter, and just plain better than the competition." Of course, all of this was even more intriguing because it wasn't Chambers who had made these claims, but the journalist's colleagues at *Fortune*.

Business Week wasn't far behind in shifting its story. In August 2001, in an article titled "Management Lessons from the Bust," it wrote:

> Only a year ago, Cisco Systems Inc. was widely hailed as the shining exemplar of the New Economy. Management gurus viewed Cisco as the prototype of the 21st century organization where information technology linked suppliers and customers in ways that allowed the company to nimbly respond to every market nuance.
>
> Cisco had flattened the corporate pyramid, outsourced capital-intensive manufacturing, and forged strategic alliances with suppliers that were supposed to eliminate inventory almost entirely. Sophisticated information systems gave its managers real-time data, allowing them to detect the slightest change in current market conditions and to forecast with precision. If anyone had "the vision thing" nailed for the new digital era, it was supposed to be Cisco CEO John T. Chambers.
>
> Oops! The surprising abruptness and severity of Cisco's downturn—marked by a shocking $2.2 billion write-off of inventory in April—showed that it was just as vulnerable as any other company to an economic slowdown.

The same magazines that had rushed to applaud Cisco just a year before—*King of the Internet, World's Best CEO, on par with General*

Electric and Microsoft–now elbowed one another aside to heap criticism. In January 2002, *Business Week* published another exposé, this one called "Cisco Behind the Hype." It wrote:

> There has always been a good deal of myth-making where Cisco is concerned. At the height of the Internet frenzy, it was the very embodiment of the age. When it came to Cisco, everything seemed faster, bigger, and better. Its sales and earnings were second to none. It sold more sophisticated gear over the Internet than any other company as it raced to fill demand that seemed unquenchable. It could close its books in a day, thanks to its powerful information systems. For 43 quarters in a row, Cisco met or beat Wall Street's hungry expectations for higher earnings. For one brief, heady moment, it became the most valuable corporation on the planet.

All the major themes were addressed: Cisco's customer focus, its culture, its ability to manage acquisitions, and its leadership. But now the company was found lacking in every department. Of course, it's possible that Cisco had changed. Success *can* engender complacency. Rapid growth *can* lead to difficulties in maintaining control. Some companies *do* take their customers for granted. And so on. But that's *not* what was being said. No one was saying that Cisco had changed between 2000 and 2001. It was just that now, in retrospect, Cisco was described through a different lens–one of falling performance.

Springtime for Cisco

But the story of Cisco doesn't end there. First a thesis, then antithesis, and next synthesis. After summer, a hard winter; and after winter, signs of spring.

For the next two years, 2001 through 2003, while the tech sector remained in the dumps, John Chambers and his colleagues persevered, insisting that Cisco would emerge from the slump stronger than ever. Recovery came slowly, but by 2003 there were distinct signs of an upturn in the high-tech industry and Cisco began to rack up stronger figures. In November 2003, with sales now on the mend, *Business Week* again put Chambers on its cover, this time with the caption "Cisco's Comeback." The story line was fascinating, not so much for what it said Cisco was doing right in 2003, but for its account of all the things Cisco was said to have done *wrong* in 2000.

Once Cisco had been lauded for organizational excellence, for its *discipline* and *coordination*. Now *Business Week* reported that, in fact, Cisco had been out of control. It had a "Wild West culture" that used to "operate like a band of independent tech tribes. Each unit could choose its own suppliers and manufacturers." Cisco had been "known for its carpe diem culture—with little coordinated planning." Instead, "engineers followed their geek muses wherever they led." The company was characterized by "chaos that comes with growth at any cost" and "staffers were too busy taking orders and cashing stock options to bother with efficiency, cost-cutting, or teamwork." Its many engineering efforts "were a jumble of overlapping development projects." This portrait of a chaotic and disorganized company was nothing like the ones we had read in 2000, but never mind, because all of those problems were in the past and now, in 2003, Cisco was "more disciplined and cohesive." We ought to be relieved at Cisco's improvements—at least until we remember that discipline and cohesion were the very sorts of words used to describe Cisco from 1997 through 2000!

What about *customers*? Stanford professors O'Reilly and Pfeffer had observed that listening closely to customers was a chief reason for Cisco's success, and *Fortune* had described customer focus as first among Cisco's strengths. Now *Business Week* wrote that even at the peak of its success, in 2000, Cisco had overlooked its customers. Chambers himself said that maybe Cisco had forgotten one of its cardinal rules: Listen to your customer. Well, then, what about *acquisitions*, cited time and again as a key reason for Cisco's success? Sorry, said *Business Week*, Cisco really hadn't been good at acquisitions after all: "Cisco had long been a binge buyer—of even un-proven start-ups with no profits." Rather than following a clear strat-egy, Cisco was said to have embarked on a "73-company buying binge from 1993 to 2000 by scooping up any networking outfit with a shot at success." It had been on an "acquisition free-for-all" charac-terized by "haphazard" and "freewheeling investment practices." These accounts spared nothing. Where Cisco had once been de-scribed as a focused, disciplined company, making a science out of merger integration, it was now remembered as a binge buyer. As for buying "unproven start-ups with no profits"—well, at the time that had been the whole point, finding young companies with smart people and great ideas. But in retrospect, it was fodder for blame.

Read in the context of their times, each of these articles seems plausible. They offer a reasonable explanation of events. But look at them over the course of a few years, and we have to question whether the reporters got the story right—or if their descriptions were colored by the story they wanted to tell. Facts were assembled and shaped to tell the story of the moment, whether it was about great performance or collapsing performance or about rebirth and recovery. Placing these accounts together, the impression is nothing short of Orwellian—a rewriting of history that thrusts facts into the past, rearranging the record to tell a more coherent story. It's an ex-ample of reinterpreting the past to suit present needs.

Intrigued at these sharply different accounts, I contacted the au-thor of one of the most effusive articles, *Fortune*'s laudatory May 2000 piece. What, I asked Andy Serwer, *Fortune*'s editor-at-large, could explain the adulation in 2000 and the extreme criticism later? Serwer candidly replied: "I think there is a pendulum effect, and that we all may get too caught up and perhaps overaccentuate what's going on." I also contacted Peter Burrows of *Business Week*, author of the November 2003 article "Cisco's Comeback," which had portrayed Cisco, three years prior, in 2000, as full of problems. Burrows is a smart and experienced Silicon Valley journalist who has written extensively about Cisco, Hewlett-Packard, and other compa-nies in the region. What was going on? I asked. Burrows explained that in his view, Cisco had never really been a cost-conscious company, but that it *had* been customer focused. He then added: "Generally speaking, I think there's a tendency to exaggerate a company's strengths during boom times—never more than during the biggest boom of them all, in the late 1990s."

No doubt Serwer and Burrows are correct. There's a natural tendency, even at leading publications like *Fortune* and *Business Week,* to exaggerate the highs and lows, and to rely on simple phrases to explain a company's performance. It makes for a better story, yet it leads us down a dangerous path. It's often said that journalism is the first draft of history, and these journalistic accounts become the primary sources for later studies. The Harvard case study mentioned previously, for example, was based on these same newspaper and magazine articles, and the chapter about Cisco in O'Reilly and Pfeffer's *Hidden Value* also cited these same *Fortune* articles reviewed earlier. These case studies and book chapters are only as good as the sources on which they're based.

But there's an even deeper problem. The story of Cisco is perhaps less an example of intentional journalistic hyperbole than it is of something more basic: the difficulty we have in understanding company performance, even as it unfolds before us. For all the attention that Cisco received, for all its prominence in the press over several years, even experienced journalists and respected academics had trouble identifying with any precision the reasons for Cisco's outstanding success or its stunning decline. There was talk, over and over, about customer orientation and leadership and organizational efficiency, but these things are hard to measure objectively, so we tend to make attributions about them based on things we *do* feel certain about—revenues and profits and share price. We may not *really* know what leads to high performance, so we reach for simple phrases to make sense of what happened.

CHAPTER THREE

Up and Down with ABB

Milo went pale again. "He did *what*?"

"He mashed hundreds of cakes of GI soap into the sweet potatoes just to show that people have the taste of Philistines and don't know the difference between good and bad. Every man in the squadron was sick. Missions were canceled."

"Well!" Milo exclaimed with thin-lipped disapproval. "He certainly found out how wrong *he* was, didn't he?"

"On the contrary," Yossarian corrected. "He found out how right he was. We packed it away by the plateful and clamored for more. We all knew we were sick, but had no idea we'd been poisoned."

Joseph Heller
Catch-22, 1961

It might not be surprising to find a strong bandwagon effect in the story of Cisco. The business world seemed to lose touch with reality during the high-tech bubble of the late 1990s. Maybe we can forgive a few journalists for losing their sense of perspective. But the same thing can be seen at other companies, including some that are neither new, high-tech, nor American.

Consider ABB, the Swedish-Swiss industrial company. ABB was created in 1988 by the merger of two leading engineering companies, Sweden's ASEA and Switzerland's Brown Boveri. The fusion was the brainchild of ASEA's chief executive, Percy Barnevik, who saw that national power markets were giving way and reasoned that a company that operated across borders could have a big competitive advantage. The newly combined company was a leader in power generation, transmission, and distribution, as well as a few other businesses including process automation, robotics, and plastics.

Barnevik quickly set about blending the two companies into one. The speed of integration was breathtaking, the cost savings unprecedented. A number of plants were closed across Europe, jobs were cut, and overhead was slashed. At the same time, ABB expanded its global position through a series of acquisitions. In 1989, it made headlines by paying $700 million for Westinghouse Electric's North American power transmission and distribution business, and then bought U.S.-based Combustion Engineering for $1.6 billion. Next, ABB expanded into Central and Eastern Europe, taking advantage of liberalization and privatization after the fall of Communism. It also moved into Asian markets, where demand for power and engineering was growing rapidly. By 1994, ABB's profile had been completely transformed, with reduced head count in Western Europe, consolidation in North America, and expansion into emerging markets. All the while, sales and profits were up. Between 1988 and 1996, ABB's revenues almost doubled to $34.7 billion, and profit tripled to $1.2 billion. Its share price grew rapidly, and ABB's market capitalization surpassed $40 billion.

Explaining ABB's Success

For roughly a decade, from the late 1980s through the late 1990s, the business press was full of stories about ABB. What could account for ABB's breathtaking success? Most explanations started at the top, with ABB's chief executive. Tall, lean, with sharp eyes and a neatly trimmed goatee, Percy Barnevik cut a striking figure. He was unprecedented for a European business leader—a Scandinavian who combined old world manners and language skills with American pragmatism and an orientation for action. It was a memorable combination. The American press was impressed with Barnevik's Stanford MBA and his command of American slang. Soon, feature articles began to appear in leading magazines. A 1991 profile in *Harvard Business Review* described Barnevik as a "corporate pioneer" who was building "the new model of competitive enterprise." He was said to believe in rapid decision making and relentless communication, and was committed to building a set of values that would hold together his vast company. In 1992, *Long Range Planning* described ABB as a "model merger for a new Europe" and was forthright in its praise for the leader: "By any standards, Barnevik is one of Europe's world-class CEOs. To meet him . . . is to become immediately aware of an incisive, original approach to management in which the ability to make swift, confident decisions is paramount." *Fortune* gushed: "If lean and mean could be personified, Percy Barnevik would walk through the door. . . . Barnevik is Europe's leading hatchet man. He is also the creator of what is fast becoming the most successful cross-border merger since Royal Dutch linked up with Shell in 1907."

More flattering stories followed. In 1993, *Business Week* ran a feature story titled "Percy Barnevik's Global Crusade." It began: "Call it Planet Barnevik. The hard charging executive of ABB has seen the future and it contains no national boundaries." Over the next pages, *Business Week* painted a vivid portrait. "Despite a manic drive and a fast-track career, Barnevik is—for a European business chief—surprisingly unpretentious and accessible." Barnevik "meets frequently with all levels of ABB management, from button-down directors at Zurich headquarters to shirtsleeved supervisors on the floor of a turbine factory in Poland—most of whom call him by his first name." He was a workaholic who was known to do "paperwork in the sauna." Barnevik was also "renowned for his speed-reading ability and sharp analytical skills" and "never bothers to prepare speeches in advance, preferring to speak extemporaneously on even such dense topics as international economic adjustments." To complete the picture, away from work Barnevik was said to climb mountains and "enjoys up to 10-hour marathon jogging sessions, pausing only for short breaks." A year later, *Forbes* wrote that "Barnevik relishes taking a scythe to bureaucratic bloat." He was "a commanding figure who speaks in a slow, rich baritone. But by no means is he the European-style imperial CEO. He is unpretentious and candid, punching the air with his fist, coloring our chat with the occasional American profanity." *Industry Week* wrote that Barnevik had "a prodigious store of personal energy, a boundless grasp of business operations, and the clear deter-

mination to enhance his company's competitive mark in industry."
He was "remarkably fresh, dynamic, and engaging."

Academics joined the chorus of praise. One of Europe's best-
known professors of management, Manfred Kets de Vries of IN-
SEAD, confirmed that Barnevik was, as widely reported, a man in a
hurry, "but what was also noticeable was his humility. He continually
played down his own contribution to the success of ABB." Over the
next years, Barnevik's reputation continued to grow. In 1996, *Director*
repeated stories about Barnevik's prodigious personal qualities: "Famously workaholic and incessantly on the move, he sometimes jokes
he spends two days a week in the office—Saturday and Sunday. . . .
Colleagues speak in awe of his ability to go deeply into the details of
a business without getting bogged down, of being able to work 20-
hour days across time zones, catnapping at will, and of keeping in
touch by phone and fax on his midsummer's sailing holiday. He has
even been seen doing paperwork in the sauna." Whether Barnevik's
sauna habits were observed directly, or whether the observation of
one reporter in 1993 was recycled by another three years later wasn't
clear—but it really didn't matter. By now, Barnevik had assumed legendary status. For four consecutive years in the mid-1990s, he was
voted "CEO/chairman of Europe's most respected company." He
was called Europe's Jack Welch. Barnevik's reputation had gained a
momentum of its own: In 1996, the Korean Management Association named him "the world's best honored top manager." Barnevik
was now getting awards for receiving the most awards!

ABB's chief executive wasn't the only explanation for its success.
Linked to Barnevik was a second theme: a dynamic corporate culture. ABB had neither a staid Swedish culture, emphasizing consen-
sus and participation, nor a conservative Swiss culture, but was
depicted as a confident blur of speed and action. Its very creation
had been a bold move, aimed at creating a world-class company
from two venerable European firms. Shortly after the merger, in a
speech to top managers in Cannes, Barnevik described ABB's modus
operandi in three principles: "1. To take action (and stick one's neck
out) and do the right things is obviously the best behavior; 2. To take

action and do the wrong things is next best (within reason and a limited number of times); 3. Not to take action (and lose opportunities) is the only unacceptable behavior." In a separate interview with the *Financial Times*, he elaborated: "If you do 50 things, it is enough if 35 go in the right direction. A basic rule is: 'Take the initiative and do the right things.' The next message is: 'Take the initiative—even if it subsequently leads to the wrong things.' The only thing we cannot accept is people who do nothing." This ethos—action, initiative, risk taking—was said to characterize the ABB culture and was frequently mentioned as a prime reason for the company's growth and success.

A third theme in stories about ABB was its complex organization design. All multinational companies have to take advantage of their global scale while also competing in local markets. For ABB, the challenge was to capture benefits of global efficiency in an industry where many customers were state-owned power companies, not global firms. Barnevik described the paradox: ABB had a simultaneous need to be "global and local, big and small, and radically decentralized with central reporting and control." All of this called for a new way to organize and manage. Barnevik never referred to ABB as a "global" company, preferring to describe it as a "federation of national companies." The goal was to find the best solutions to customers' problems and then spread them throughout the world. It was to unleash the energy of local entrepreneurs by "ripping down bureaucracy so executives in Atlanta can launch new products without meddling from headquarters, so power technicians in Sweden can make design changes, and so factories in India can alter production methods on their own."

To meet both global and local objectives, ABB devised a matrix structure with seven major sectors divided into business areas on one axis and dozens of countries on the other axis. While other multinationals were moving away from the complexity of matrix management, ABB embraced it explicitly. ABB's matrix had fifty-one business areas and forty-one country managers, which intersected in 1,300 separate companies. These companies were divided into 5,000 profit centers, each one accountable to deliver profits and empowered to achieve high performance. Such a complex organization—5,000 *sep-*

arate profit centers!—naturally invited questions. *Industry Week* speculated that "just trying to figure out who has responsibility for what would seem to impede interpersonal communications and make more difficult the maintenance of a sharp customer focus." But when reporters spoke with ABB's managers, their concerns fell away. Managers seemed satisfied, and of course the company's results spoke for themselves—so the organization *must* have been good. *Business Week* told the story of a Swiss factory manager who remembered his days at Brown Boveri, when he had no autonomy and little accountability. ABB's new organization put him in charge of a profit center, a wonderfully motivating change that led to substantial improvements as he borrowed ideas from a similar ABB plant in Sweden. Improvements weren't long in coming, and profits soon took off.

ABB's sophisticated organization was applauded by journalists, academics, and management gurus. Tom Peters, perhaps the world's best-known guru in the early 1990s, called ABB a "buckyball organization," referring to the elegant geodesic structures designed by Buckminster Fuller. According to Peters, Percy Barnevik was the most insistent enemy of bureaucracy that he had ever met. He wrote that Barnevik's "abiding hatred of bureaucracy is critical to making the ABB structure work." Christopher Bartlett at Harvard Business School wrote a case study that described not just ABB's organization structure, but also explained the sophisticated processes and management philosophy that made it work so well. Manfred Kets de Vries held up ABB's organization as a model for others to emulate. Despite its giant size and scope, ABB was said to have the agility and flexibility of a small company. According to Kets de Vries, ABB had invented a new organizational form; it exemplified the "prototypical postindustrial organization."

ABB on Mount Olympus

By the mid-1990s, ABB was atop the world, consistently named among the world's most-admired and best-managed companies. In

1996, ABB was named Europe's *Most Respected Company* for the third year in a row by the *Financial Times*. The accompanying article explained:

> As well as being the overall winner, [ABB] is rated exceptionally highly for business performance, corporate strategy and maximizing employee potential. It is also cited most frequently as the benchmark against which other companies measure their performance.
>
> Indeed, admiration for ABB's achievements is overshadowed only by esteem for Mr. Percy Barnevik, its president. Named Europe's most respected business leader, he attracted more votes than were cast for his company in the overall rankings: he was particularly praised for strategic vision and focus.

Even normally skeptical observers applauded ABB and its leader. In 1996, John Micklethwait and Adrian Wooldridge of *The Economist* wrote a stinging book, *The Witch Doctors,* which took aim at management gurus. Yet they set aside their skepticism when it came to ABB. Micklethwait and Wooldridge commented:

> Europe has produced worryingly few management superstars. But one man who unquestioningly fits the bill is Percy Barnevik. . . . A tall, fast-talking Swede, with the restless manner of a man overendowed with energy, Barnevik has won almost every honour which his profession can bestow, from "emerging markets CEO of the year" to (twice) boss of Europe's most respected company.

Was the admiration of Barnevik excessive? Not at all, said Micklethwait and Wooldridge. "For once," they continued, "the hyperbole is largely warranted." They went on to praise Barnevik for his commanding presence, his bold strategic vision, his no-nonsense style, and ABB's nimble organization, repeating the broad themes of the previous several years.

In January 1997, after more than a dozen years at the helm of ASEA and then ABB, Percy Barnevik turned over responsibilities as chief executive to Goran Lindahl, executive vice president of power transmission, but he remained non-executive chairman. The transition was smooth, and ABB's performance remained strong. The company was featured in a *Financial Times* series called *Mastering Management*, written by two researchers at the Ashridge Management Centre in England, Kevin Barham and Claudia Heimer. Noting that ABB had enjoyed spectacular financial success, the authors praised it as a "new form of global organization." They attributed ABB's success to "five guiding lights": customer focus, connectivity, communication, collegiality, and convergence. The following year, 1998, Barham and Heimer published a full-length book, *ABB: The Dancing Giant*. Based on dozens of articles and case studies as well as original interviews with ABB managers, their 382-page book was the culmination of a decade of praise. Barham and Heimer called Barnevik "the most influential manager in the world." They described ABB's organization structure and admired its high levels of employee empowerment. They likened ABB managers to "a new breed of superhumans." They concluded that ABB occupied a position on the "Corporate Mount Olympus" with General Electric and Microsoft. There wasn't a trace of irony in their words—and why should there have been? By this time, ABB had racked up a solid decade of strong financial results. Its success seemed clear to all.

Running Off the Rails: ABB After 1997

Yet even as Barham and Heimer's book arrived in stores, ABB's fortunes were beginning to shift. Lindahl and Barnevik had begun to steer ABB away from its reliance on heavy manufacturing and engineering, and toward a new mix of activities including services. At a time when management thinking was shaped by concepts such as "intellectual capital" and "intangible assets," ABB's leaders said they wanted it to become a "knowledge-based" company. Barnevik explained that "ABB is transforming its business portfolio, expanding into higher value businesses based on intellectual capital, focused on software, intelligent products, and complete service solutions. It's a strategy with significant advantages." He described "ABB's transformation to a knowledge company," which involved "moving up the value chain, delivering in effect greater competitiveness rather than products and services. ABB will also reduce its exposure to some of the cyclic swings to which it has been vulnerable in the past."

Accordingly, ABB resumed making acquisitions, but this time entering into new areas, including financial services. It also began to divest itself of some formerly core activities. ABB sold its 50 percent share of the Adtranz joint venture with Daimler Chrysler for $472 million, exiting the trains and trams business altogether. ABB sold its nuclear fuels business and combined its power generation business with Alsthom of France to create a fifty-fifty joint venture, ABB Alsthom Power. How did the public react to this fundamental shift? Did anyone worry that ABB was *straying from its core*? Not at all. ABB's new direction was met with approval. For starters, ABB's reputation was so strong that few observers doubted openly what the company could achieve. Furthermore, its strategy resembled the earlier migration of General Electric, which had shifted successfully from manufacturing to financial services. Meanwhile, ABB's share price continued to rise—nothing like Cisco, of course, but at a healthy rate, along with many other companies in those bull market years. But ABB's reputation wasn't based only on its share price—it was known as a bold company that had transformed a pair of stodgy industrial companies into a New Age dynamo. Admiration from peers continued, and ABB's glow now reflected on its new chief executive. In November 1999, Goran Lindahl was named *CEO of the Year* by the American publication *Industry Week*, becoming the first European to receive the award, joining previous winners including Jack Welch, Lou Gerstner, Michael Dell, and Bill Gates. *Industry*

Week cited Lindahl for his strategic leadership, noting with approval ABB's acquisitions into new markets and its divestiture of mature businesses.

The early evidence seemed to confirm the wisdom of ABB's strategy. Revenues continued to rise, and the mid-2000 share price reached an all-time high of $31. A business school case study talked about ABB's transformation as if it were already a success: "The results of these initiatives were clearly visible as ABB entered the new millennium. In early 2000, the company reported a 24% increase in net income to $1.6 billion, and a 4% increase in revenues to $24.7 billion in 1999. Company analysts unanimously regarded the company's prospects as outstanding. 'ABB is no longer a cost story. It is a growth story,' one such analyst observed."

In *ABB: The Dancing Giant,* Barham and Heimer predicted that the years after 1996 would be ones of "reaping the harvest." ABB had planted its garden, now it would enjoy the fruits. Brimming with optimism about the company's future success, the book ended by declaring: "We look forward to finding out about the next big surprise coming out of Zurich!"

The next years were indeed full of surprises, but not the ones anyone expected. Signs of trouble began to build in 2000, as revenue growth slowed. In November 2000, Goran Lindahl abruptly announced his resignation, taking almost everyone by surprise. The reason he gave: To turn the reins over to someone with stronger IT capabilities, critical given ABB's shift into knowledge-intensive businesses. Lindahl was replaced in January 2001 by Jürgen Centerman, who soon announced a shift in ABB's famous organization structure. From now on, ABB would be designed around industries and customer groups, not products. Explained Centerman, the old structure had up to ten entities dealing with the same customer, causing overlap and confusion. The new design would be simpler and would help deepen relationships with key clients.

New design or not, ABB's performance continued to slide. In April 2001, it reported a 6 percent decline in annual revenues as market demand softened. Reporters now speculated that worsening results had been the real reason for Lindahl's sudden departure. Then unpleasant surprises began to pop up from past acquisitions. In response to Securities & Exchange Commission filing requirements, ABB disclosed some troubling news: Combustion Engineering, the U.S. firm it had acquired in 1989, was the target of messy asbestos litigation, forcing ABB to set aside $470 million as provisions for damage claims. These provisions hurt ABB's credit rating and compounded its debt worries. Performance continued to dive through the summer, and by autumn 2001, ABB's share price had fallen by 70 percent from its peak of the previous year. *The Wall Street Journal* now reported that ABB's "vision to move away from heavy industry toward knowledge driven, high technology fields appeared to go awry as profits fell."

Under growing pressure from the board, Barnevik resigned as ABB's non-executive chairman in November 2001 and was replaced by Jürgen Dormann, a board member and former chief executive of the German chemicals group Hoechst. But ABB's performance fell still faster over the next year, and Centerman was replaced as CEO in September 2002. Jürgen Dormann now took over as chief executive as well as chairman, and began to review ABB's broad range of businesses. Sensing the extent of ABB's troubles, Dormann quickly reversed the company's course. He divested ABB's petrochemicals division, sold ABB's structured finance division to GE, and secured a $1.5 billion loan so ABB could avoid a liquidity crisis. With the sale of these "non-core" assets, ABB had narrowed its focus and now defined itself in terms of automation technologies and power technologies.

Amid ABB's steep decline came another shock. In early 2002, the news broke that Barnevik and Lindahl had secured a secret pension deal worth $150 million. The package had been agreed in 1992 with Peter Wallenberg, ABB's co-chairman and a member of Sweden's most powerful family, but hadn't been disclosed to other members of the board, much less to managers throughout the company. The size of the pension deal was huge since it had been linked to ABB's results, which had been excellent throughout the 1990s.

Yet by the time Barnevik and Lindahl stepped down, ABB was no longer a high performer, and the large payout—unheard of by European standards—set off a huge outcry. Inside and outside the company, in Sweden and throughout Europe, people were shocked by what they perceived as an example of executive greed. Under intense pressure, Barnevik agreed to return 90 million out of 148 million Swiss francs, and Lindahl returned 47 million of 85 million Swiss francs, but their reputations were damaged.

In 2002, ABB lost $600 million on flat revenues. Debt had ballooned, and some analysts speculated the company was close to bankruptcy. Market capitalization now was less than $4 billion, barely one-tenth of its peak of $40 billion. As 2003 began, ABB once again sought to restructure its activities, to cut jobs and sell assets, and it still faced huge liabilities in asbestos lawsuits. Over the next year, led by Dormann and a new executive team, ABB worked steadily to restore profitability. By summer 2004, revenues were beginning to rise again, and profitability was restored for the first time after a net loss the previous year. A new CEO, Fred Kindle, took over, and by autumn 2005, ABB was nearing a final settlement regarding asbestos claims and had driven its debt to a manageable level. Operating profits were modest, and industry demand remained uncertain, but ABB was back in the black.

ABB Through the Looking Glass

There was no absence of stories while ABB was on the way up, and the ink didn't run dry when it was in free fall, either. When times were good, ABB's culture had been celebrated as bold and daring. Action had been preferred to lengthy analysis—the willingness to act was a reason for ABB's success. But once growth stalled and U.S. asbestos claims mounted, ABB's ambitious growth strategy was perceived differently. Now ABB was described as having been impulsive and foolish. In 2003, ABB's chairman, Jürgen Dormann, remembered: "We had a lack of focus as Percy went on an acquisition spree. The company wasn't disciplined enough."

As for ABB's New Age organization? As long as times were good, the complex matrix organization had been described as a key to its success, a hypermodern mix of global and local, a flexible buckyball. Now a different picture emerged. As ABB's performance unraveled, one reporter wrote: "The decentralized management structure Mr. Barnevik created for the company's far-flung units ended up causing conflicts and communication problems between departments." ABB managers, once full of praise for the company's nimble design, now recalled an organization beset with chaos and conflict. So many divisions, so many countries, and so many profit centers had resulted in a "vast duplication of effort." Allowing local decisions had produced a fragmented back office with 576 enterprise resource planning systems, 60 different payroll systems, and more than 600 spreadsheet software programs used in the company. Sharing data had become a nightmare. Managers also recalled poor coordination among countries and dysfunctional competition—such as the lack of sharing plans for fear that managers in other countries would poach them. Not exactly the paragon of postindustrial management we had read about just a few years before! And interestingly, none of these recent articles suggested that ABB's organization had *changed* in any way—it was the same organization, but now the emphasis was on its flaws.

Perhaps the most stinging revision was saved for Percy Barnevik. When ABB was posting record performance, Barnevik had been the focus of a virtual personality cult, portrayed with powers of a superman. He had been described as charismatic, bold, and visionary. But once performance fell, Barnevik was remembered as arrogant, imperial, and resistant to criticism. He was said to have "built walls around himself." He had been "high-handed in his treatment of the board." He had "monopolized the flow of information," quite the opposite of the spirit of openness he claimed to espouse. Barnevik was now accused of having been "addicted to acquisitions" and was nicknamed "Percyfal" after the knight who searched in vain for the

Holy Grail. Others said that Barnevik suffered from an unhealthy fixation with Jack Welch and had been obsessed with matching the size and success of General Electric.

Had Barnevik changed? Perhaps. Manfred Kets de Vries at IN-SEAD explained that some successful executives "start to believe their own presses and it becomes a vicious circle of narcissism." Yet no one offered any evidence of alleged "narcissism." No one said that Barnevik now gazed at himself admiringly in the reflection of his hot tub, or devoted too much time to personal grooming, or decorated the walls of his office with his many awards, or otherwise neglected the business of ABB. No one showed how "narcissism" had led to any specific errors, whether strategic or organizational. (Nor did anyone point out that some of the most favorable press coverage that had supposedly led to narcissism came from Professor Kets de Vries himself.) In fact, looking across fifteen years of articles, Barnevik was portrayed as very much the same man throughout— bold, direct, and very sure of himself. No one offered any evidence that he had changed—it was all inferred based on the company's performance. Winners are confident, losers are arrogant. *Fortune* observed: "His reputation in tatters, the former ABB chairman faces another unkind cut: His successors are questioning his business legacy."

Naturally, Percy Barnevik wasn't terribly pleased with the revisionist view of his years at ABB. *The Wall Street Journal* wrote that Barnevik "bristles at the charges that he helped destroy the company," quoting him as saying: "I refuse to accept we were trigger happy." Being made a scapegoat "has not been much fun." Regarding asbestos claims at Combustion Engineering, Barnevik maintained it had been an acceptable risk at the time. "It is a hell of a thing to say you should have seen 13 years ago risks nobody else saw." Yet the tendency to attribute company success to a specific individual is hard to resist. In fact, one of the main reasons we love stories is that they don't simply report disconnected facts but make connections about cause and effect, often ascribing credit or blame to individuals. Our most compelling stories often place people at the center of events. When times are good, we lavish praise and create heroes. When things go bad, we lay blame and create villains. These stories offer a means of establishing right and wrong, a way of attributing moral responsibility. Of the dozens of articles about ABB, only a few tried to resist this tendency and retain a sense of perspective. In their 2002 *Fortune* article, Richard Tomlinson and Paola Hjelt wrote: "Barnevik was never as good as the rave reviews he received in the 1990s, nor was he half as bad as the recent damning press coverage might suggest. What's been missing since open season was declared on Barnevik is a sense of proportion about how much of the blame he should shoulder." A wise view, but all too rare among the scores of articles and case studies about ABB. Most writers went with the simpler story. Once widely revered, Percy Barnevik was now an exemplar of arrogance, of greed, of bad leadership. A final postscript to the saga of ABB came in late 2005, when the Office of the Prosecutor in Zurich dropped its case against Barnevik and Goran Lindahl in connection with their pension deal. Finding no fault with either manager, the prosecutor noted that the deal had been agreed in 1998, when ABB had been a very profitable company, and had been entirely proper given rules of disclosure. Yet by then the damage had been done, the perception of villainy set in stone. It was, as Barnevik said, a hell of a thing.

CHAPTER FOUR

Halos All Around Us

The difference between a lady and a flower girl is not how she behaves, but how she's treated.

George Bernard Shaw
Pygmalion, 1916

During World War I, an American psychologist named Edward Thorndike was conducting research into the ways that superiors rate their subordinates. In one study, he asked army officers to rate their soldiers on a variety of features: intelligence, physique, leadership, character, and so on. He was struck by the results. Some men were thought to be "superior soldiers" and were rated highly at just about everything, while others were thought to be subpar across the board. It was as if officers figured that a soldier who was handsome and had good posture should also be able to shoot straight, polish his shoes well, and play the harmonica, too. Thorndike called it the Halo Effect.

There are a few kinds of Halo Effect. One refers to what Thorndike observed, a tendency to make inferences about specific traits on the basis of a general impression. It's difficult for most people to independently measure separate features; there's a common tendency to blend them together. The Halo Effect is a way for the mind to create and maintain a coherent and consistent picture, to reduce cognitive dissonance. Here's a recent example: In the autumn of 2001, after the September 11 attacks, George W. Bush's overall approval rating rose sharply. No surprise there, as the American public closed ranks behind its president. But the number of Americans who approved of President Bush's *handling of the economy* also rose—from 47 percent to 60 percent. Now, whether or not you like Bush's economic policies, there's no reason to believe that his handling of the economy was suddenly better in the weeks after September 11. But it's hard to keep these things separate: General approval of the president carried over to approval of a specific policy. The American public conferred a Halo on its president and made favorable attributions across the board. After all, it's uncomfortable for many people to believe that their president might be good on issues of national security but ineffective on the economy—it's far easier to think he's about the same for both. And what goes up can also come down. By October 2005, with public support for the Iraq War fading and in the wake of Hurricane Katrina's devastation, President Bush's overall approval rating sank to 37 percent, down from 41 percent in August 2005. Interestingly, Americans also gave the president lower marks on every specific question in the poll: For his economic policies, Bush had a 32 percent approval rating in October compared with 37 percent in August; regarding Iraq, 32 percent down from 38 percent; and fighting terrorism, 46 percent versus 54 percent. Asked whether President Bush had strong qualities of leadership, 45 percent of Americans said yes, compared with 54 percent in August. Each of these individual indicators moved in parallel, suggesting they were not independent but rather based on a single, overall assessment—a Halo.

This sort of Halo Effect shows up in many places. One of the companies I work with gets thousands of calls every day to its customer support center. Sometimes the problems can be solved right away, but often the service representative has to look into the matter and call back later. When the company subsequently surveyed its customers to see how satisfied they had been with the support center, customers whose problem had been solved right away rated the service representative as more knowledgeable than did customers whose problem had not been solved. That's not surprising, since it's reasonable to infer that a quick solution came from a well-informed rep. But here's what's more intriguing: 58 percent of customers whose problem had been solved right away remembered that their call had been answered "immediately" or "very quickly," while only 4 percent remembered having been kept waiting "too long." Meanwhile, of those customers whose problem had *not* been solved right away, only 36 percent remembered their call had been answered "immediately" or "very quickly," while 18 percent recalled they had waited "too long." In fact, the company had an automated answering system and there was no difference in waiting time between the two groups. Rather, an overall impression about customer service created a powerful Halo Effect that shaped perceptions about waiting time.

But the Halo Effect is not just a way to reduce cognitive dissonance. It's also a heuristic, a sort of rule of thumb that people use to make guesses about things that are hard to assess directly. We tend to grasp information that is relevant, tangible, and appears to be objective, and then make attributions about other features that are more vague or ambiguous. For example, we may not know if a new product is good, but if it comes from a well-known company with an excellent reputation, we might reasonably infer it should be of good quality. That's what brand building is about: creating Halos so that consumers are more likely to think favorably of a product or service. Or take a well-documented setting for the Halo Effect—the job interview. What's the most relevant and tangible information we first have about job candidates? Probably the school where they earned their degree, their grade-point average, and what honors they received. With this information clearly in mind—relevant, tangible, and seemingly objective—interviewers tend to shade their evaluations about other things that are less tangible, such as a candidate's personal manner or the quality of answers to general questions. A strong record from an excellent school? The job candidate often appears to be a little brighter, with smarter answers and greater potential for success. A modest record from an unheralded local school? The very same answers may sound a little less intelligent, the same appearance a bit less impressive. Which is exactly what Thorndike found in his study about army officers and their soldiers all those years ago.

Now consider companies. What's the most relevant and tangible information we often have about a company? Financial performance, of course. Whether the company is profitable. Whether sales are growing. Whether the price of its stock is on the rise. Financial performance looks to be accurate and objective. Numbers don't lie, we like to say—which is why Enron, Tyco, and a handful of other recent scandals shake our confidence so deeply. We routinely trust financial performance figures. And it's natural that on the basis of this performance data, people make attributions about other things that are less tangible and objective. All of which helps explain what we saw at Cisco and ABB. As long as Cisco was growing and profitable and setting records for its share price, managers and journalists and professors inferred that it had a wonderful ability to listen to its customers, a cohesive corporate culture, and a brilliant strategy. And when the bubble burst, observers were quick to make the opposite attribution. It all made sense. It told a coherent story. Same for ABB, where rising sales and profits led to favorable evaluations of its organization structure, its risk-taking culture, and most clearly the man at the top—and then to unfavorable evaluations when performance fell. Journalistic hyperbole? To some extent, sure. But more importantly, a natural human tendency to make attributions based on cues that we think are reliable.

Halos in the Business World

Financial information is far from the only data on which people make attributions. Barry Staw, then at the University of Illinois and later at the University of California, conducted an experiment in which groups of participants were asked to estimate a company's future sales and earnings per share based on a set of financial data. Afterward, he told some of the groups they had performed well, making accurate estimates of sales and earnings per share, and told other groups they had performed poorly—but Staw did so completely *at random*. In fact, the "high-performing groups" and the "low-performing groups" had done equally well in their financial calculations; the only difference was what Staw *told* them about their performance. Then he asked the participants to rate how well their groups had done on a range of issues. The results? When told they had performed well, people described their groups as having been highly cohesive, with better communication, more openness to change, and superior motivation. When told they had performed poorly, they recalled a lack of cohesion, poor communication, and low motivation. Staw concluded that people attribute one set of characteristics to groups they believe are effective, and a very different set of characteristics to groups they believe are ineffective. That's the Halo Effect in action.

Of course, these findings do not mean that group cohesiveness and effective communication are unimportant in group performance. It only means that you can't hope to measure cohesiveness or communication or motivation by asking people to rate themselves when they already know something about the outcome. Once people—whether outside observers or participants—believe the outcome is good, they tend to make positive attributions about the decision process; and when they believe the outcome is poor, they tend to make negative attributions. Why? Because it's hard to know in objective terms exactly what constitutes good communication or optimal cohesion or appropriate role clarity, so people tend to make attributions based on other data that they believe are reliable. Performance is a cue by which people attribute characteristics to groups and to organizations.

Some people questioned Staw's findings. They doubted whether an experiment that put strangers together for just thirty minutes could accurately capture the perceptions of work groups. A team led by H. Kirk Downey at the University of Oklahoma therefore replicated Staw's study, using the exact same set of financial problems, but with groups of people who had a prior history of working together, and giving them considerably more time to make their calculations. Again, groups were told—*at random*—that they had performed well or poorly. The results were virtually the same as in Staw's experiment. Once again, "high-performing teams" reported that their groups had been more cohesive, that teammates were of high ability and had enjoyed working together, that communication had been of a high quality, that they had been open to new ideas, and that overall they had been satisfied with the group process. All because of the randomly assigned description of performance— nothing more. Like Staw, Downey and his colleagues found a strong tendency to make attributions on the basis of performance.

Surprising? It probably shouldn't be. Picture a group where people express their views vigorously and passionately, even arguing with one another. If the group performs well, participants might reasonably look back and say that open and forthright expressions of opinion were a key reason for success. They'll say: *We were honest, we didn't hold back—and that's why we did so well! We had a good process!* But what if the group's performance turned out to be poor? Now people might recall things differently. *We argued and fought. We were dysfunctional. Next time we should follow a respectful and disciplined process.* But now imagine a group where people are calm, polite, and respectful of one another. They speak quietly and in turn. If the group does well, participants might look back and credit their courteous and cooperative nature. *We respected one another. We didn't fight. We had a good process!* But if the same group's performance was poor, people might say: *We were too polite. We censored ourselves. Next time, we should be more direct and open, not so concerned about one another's feelings.* The fact is, a wide variety of behaviors can lead to good decisions. There's no precise way to engineer an "optimal" discussion process. We may try to avoid extremes, sure, but between those extremes is a wide range of behavior that might be conducive to success. And because we really don't know what makes an optimal decision process, we tend to make attributions based on other things that are relevant and seemingly objective—namely, what we're told about performance outcomes.

Halos on the People and for the People

The Halo Effect shapes many things, including the attributions we make about an organization's people. It's widely believed that companies that manage their human resources well will outperform those that don't. That was, after all, the idea behind O'Reilly and Pfeffer's book, *Hidden Value: How Great Companies Achieve Extraordinary Results with Ordinary People.* It makes good sense. A company that does an effective job of attracting people, provides them with an environment where they can be productive and creative, and motivates them to work hard for the common good, ought to do well. How could it be otherwise? But watch out for the Halo Effect. If we're not careful, any successful company can attribute its good results to its people.

Here's a memorable example. In 1983, *Fortune* published its first survey of *America's Most Admired Companies.* The winner was IBM. The following year, in 1984, IBM topped the list again. When asked to describe IBM's strengths, CEO John Opel gave credit to his company's people: "The fundamental thing is that the people who work in the company make it a good company. That's really the secret: the people. It's our good fortune to have superior people who work hard and support each other. They have adapted to our basic set of beliefs—the standard we expect of one another—and follow those standards in dealing with one another and with people outside the company. I know it sounds corny, but it's true, and there's no point in trying to analyze it much more than that." And what sorts of people did IBM look for? Opel explained: "We're a positive bunch of people, the kind who like to do creative things. I believe that like begets like. You look for people with the same qualities as other people who are building the company." Not only were IBM's people said to be great, they also guarded against feelings of self-satisfaction. Opel concluded: "If any of us in our company behave in any way that reinforces the idea of smugness of power or arrogance, then our image could be severely tarnished. The hero of today can become the bum of tomorrow."

That's the way it looked in 1984, and of course it seemed reasonable. Every day, John Opel came to work and found himself surrounded by smart, creative, hardworking people. It was only natural to think that IBM's great people were responsible for its success. But during those same years, IBM failed to see the growing commoditization of its main business lines—mainframe computer systems and minicomputers. By the end of the 1980s, IBM was slipping badly; and by 1992, it was awash in red ink. Opel's successor, John Akers, was replaced. How did observers explain IBM's poor performance? By pointing the finger at its people and company culture, of course. In *Big Blues: The Unmaking of IBM, Wall Street Journal* reporter Paul Carroll criticized the company's "button-down culture," its "rigid bureaucracy," and its "complacent executives." The same people who were praised in 1984 now were blamed for the decline of a great industrial enterprise. Had they suddenly changed their ways? Probably not. Had the CEO been blind about his people—had they been *complacent* and *rigid* all along? I don't think so. John Opel was probably entirely honest when he sensed that he was surrounded by hardworking, excellent people. And they *were* well-suited for IBM of the 1960s and 1970s. But when the industry changed and IBM missed the turn in the road, its people were on the receiving end of a very different attribution. Our evaluations depend on whether we think we're seeing a lady or a flower girl.

Halos on our Leaders

Perhaps nothing lends itself to the Halo Effect more than leadership. Good leaders are often said to have a handful of important qualities: clear vision, effective communication skills, self-confidence, personal charm, and more. Most people would agree these are elements of good leadership. But defining them is a different matter altogether, since several of these qualities tend to be in the eye of the beholder—which is affected by company performance. It's exactly what we saw at ABB. While his company was successful, people said that Percy Barnevik had a clear vision, excellent communication skills, impressive self-confidence, and great charm; and when ABB's fortunes turned, the very same man was demonized as arrogant, too controlling, and abrasive. Of course, it is possible that as ABB's fortunes fell, Barnevik became increasingly stressed and anxious, in which case causality runs in the opposite direction—from company performance to individual behavior. Yet that argument, plausible as it may be, was not advanced; no one said that Barnevik had changed.

Bill George, former CEO of Medtronic, advanced a similar list about leadership in his 2003 book, *Authentic Leadership: Rediscovering the Secrets to Creating Lasting Value.* George wrote that outstanding leaders share a handful of qualities, including steadfast courage, clear vision, personal integrity, and outstanding character. They are *authentic leaders.* Not surprisingly, all the examples came from successful companies. George also mentioned a handful of failed companies, and their leaders were always *inauthentic.* Well, you can *always* find good things to say about leaders at successful companies, and you can always find reasons to criticize leaders of failing firms. A critical reader ought to ask if any successful companies have *inauthentic leaders,* and if any unsuccessful companies are run by *authentic leaders,* because if not, it's quite possible we're just throwing around Halos. And very predictably—at least for a book written in 2003—listed among the *inauthentic leaders* was none other than Percy Barnevik. George recounted the secret pension payoff to Barnevik and Lindahl, described the resulting public outcry, and then observed: "Currently, ABB is operating at a loss, bleeding cash, and its $40 billion market [capitalization] has collapsed to $4 billion." The inference was clear: Barnevik was *inauthentic*—for which the secret pension deal was the smoking gun, the definitive proof—all of which helped explain why ABB had performed poorly. But of course, no one had suggested Barnevik was inauthentic while ABB was doing well.

George further explained that a quality of *authentic leaders* is "a burning passion for their missions" and "a laserlike focus on overcoming barriers." A prominent example? Microsoft's Bill Gates, who "believed so passionately in Microsoft's mission of unifying computing with an integrated set of software that he was willing to fight the U.S. Government with all his might to keep from being broken up." It was easy to applaud Gates's persistence in 2003, when it was clear that Microsoft would not be split apart. But just two years earlier, in 2001, things had looked very different. Microsoft had been found guilty of predatory behavior—hardly something that one normally associates with *authentic leadership*—and ordered to be broken up by Judge Thomas Penfield Jackson. Gates had been roundly criticized for stubbornly leading his company into an unnecessary and destructive confrontation with the U.S. government, something that could have been avoided with a bit of foresight and diplomacy. David Yoffie of Harvard Business School, writing in 2001, contrasted Gates's leadership style with that of Intel chief executive Andy Grove, whose company had also been the focus of a U.S. Department of Justice investigation but had taken a very different approach. Grove had carefully navigated Intel's position, admitting no wrongdoing but showing more cooperation with the Department of Justice and avoiding a bloody trial. Gates, meanwhile, had not given an inch, and the result was a mess. Yoffie wrote: "For years now, Microsoft has been mired in court, facing charges of predatory behavior by the U.S. Department of Justice and the attorneys general of more than a dozen states. It has seen its name and business practices dragged through the mud, its senior executives distracted and embarrassed, and its very future as a single company thrown into doubt. No matter how the litigation is ultimately decided, Microsoft will have suffered significant damage to its business and its reputation." Inviting conflict with the government is not good leadership, Yoffie observed: "Even if a company wins the verdict, it can still suffer large penalties in the form of wasted resources, distracted management, and a tarnished image. Just ask Bill Gates." And that wasn't all. A few months after Bill George applauded Gates's behavior, in early 2004, testimony in a new class-action lawsuit against Microsoft showed the company to be "combative and rude," using bullying and other "unfair tactics to compete in markets where its technology was inferior."

So which was Mr. Gates, *authentic* or foolhardy? I've been a Gates watcher for a long time now (I wrote my first case study about Bill Gates and Microsoft back in 1991, spending a week at the Redmond campus interviewing Gates, Steve Ballmer, and a dozen other Microsoft executives), and aside from a major philanthropic commitment to improving world health, he seems to have changed relatively little over the years. As Microsoft's chief executive, Gates was a highly ambitious, tough, uncompromising, and unapologetic competitor. Did that make him worthy of praise as a brilliant, visionary, and *authentic* leader? When Microsoft was doing well, that sort of description seemed justified. Was Bill Gates inflexible and obstinate, sometimes petulant, and occasionally exposing his company to needless risks? When times were tough, that sort of criticism seemed reasonable, too. The attributions we made depended on the company's fortunes.

None of this should be very surprising. A serious scholar of leadership, the late James Meindl at SUNY Buffalo concluded after a series of insightful studies that we have no satisfactory theory of effective leadership that is independent of performance. We think we know what good leadership is all about—clarity of vision, communication skills, good judgment, and more—but in fact a wide range of behaviors can be said to fit these criteria. Show me a company that delivers high performance, and I can always find something positive to say about the person in charge—about the clarity of his or her vision, about good communication skills, sound judgment, and integrity. Show me a company that has fallen on hard times, and I can always find some reason to explain why the leader failed. All of which brings to mind a 1964 Supreme Court case about free speech and pornography, in which Justice Potter Stewart memorably wrote that while he could not provide a good definition of hard-core pornography, "I know it when I see it." Since good leadership is usually difficult to identify in the absence of data about performance, it seems that leadership is even *more* difficult to recognize than is hardcore pornography—which at least Justice Stewart knew when he saw it. For all the books written about leadership, most people don't recognize good leadership when they see it unless they also have clues about company performance from other things that can be assessed more clearly—namely, financial performance. And once they have evidence that a company is performing well, they confidently make attributions about a company's leadership, as well as its culture, its customer focus, and the quality of its people.

Halos in our Surveys

The Halo Effect shapes how individuals think about decision processes, an organization's people, and leadership—and it doesn't go away when we conduct large-scale surveys, either. Quite the contrary. If we're not careful, surveys might be little more than large collections of Halos, much as we saw regarding the assessments of President Bush. Consider *Fortune* magazine's annual ranking of the *World's Most Admired Companies,* the one mentioned earlier that named IBM as *Most Admired* in 1983 and 1984. Every year, *Fortune* asks thousands of business executives and industry analysts to evaluate hundreds of companies in eight categories: quality of management, quality of products and services, value as a long-term investment, innovativeness, soundness of financial position, ability to attract, develop, and retain talented people, responsibility to the community and environment, and wise use of corporate assets. Mix the answers together and you get the *World's Most Admired Companies* in each of these categories—as well as the overall winner. It's an impressive effort, and it produces an eye-catching cover story every year. Over the years, *Fortune* has named not just IBM, but luminaries like General Electric, Wal-Mart, and Dell—a very impressive bunch.

But when some researchers took a closer look, they found that *Fortune*'s *Most Admired* ratings were heavily influenced by a Halo Effect. The scores on the eight different factors for a given company turn out to be highly correlated—much more than should be the case given variance within each category. Furthermore, many of the scores were very much driven by the company's financial performance, just what we would expect given the salient and tangible nature of financial results. Two different studies showed that a company's financial performance explained between 42 percent and 53 percent of the variance of the overall rating. In other words, when a company posts high profits and its stock price is moving upward, the people who fill out *Fortune*'s survey tend to infer that its products and services are of a high quality, that it is innovative and well managed, that it is good at retaining people, and so forth. Cisco offers a case in point. In 1997, the same year Cisco leapt onto the cover of leading business magazines, it made its first appearance on *Fortune*'s *Most Admired* list, entering the charts at number fourteen. Then it rocketed upward, reaching number four in 1999 before topping out at number three in 2000. It's no surprise that Cisco rated high for investment value—its stock value was, after all, going stratospheric. But Cisco was rated high for lots of other things, too: quality of management, innovativeness, quality of people, and more. When the tech bubble burst and Cisco's stock fell, in 2001, Cisco's rating as an investment value quite naturally fell. But with the Halo of financial performance tarnished, *its ratings fell across the boards.* Cisco was now *less admired* for innovativeness, for people, the whole works. Its overall rating dropped to number fifteen in 2001, then twenty-two in 2002 and twenty-eight in 2003. *Fortune*'s survey isn't the only one to be undermined by the Halo Effect. Remember the *Financial Times*'s survey of *Most Respected Companies*? In 1996, when ABB was at its peak, it was rated high across the boards, for business performance, corporate strategy, and maximizing employee potential, and its leader was applauded for his strategic vision and focus. Again, the pattern is entirely consistent with the Halo Effect.

And there's more. In 1984, an organization called the Great

Places to Work Institute made a big splash with a book called *The 100 Best Companies to Work for in America*. Every year since then, it has compiled the *Best Companies to Work For* index. Based on these findings, the *International Herald Tribune* claimed that being a *Great Place to Work* leads to high performance, noting that the companies on the 1998 list had a total market return (share price plus reinvested dividends) over the next five years of 9.56 percent, compared with a return of 3.81 percent for all the companies on the S&P 500. The inference was clear: Companies that care about creating a great place to work will attract good people and help them be more productive, leading to superior performance. It all makes good sense. But how did the institute determine what's a great place to work? Simple, they asked employees. Employees were asked to rate their companies on two attributes: trust and culture. The trust index had five elements: credibility, respect, fairness, pride, and camaraderie. Credibility, in turn, was measured by responses to statements like this: *Management keeps me informed about important issues and changes. People around here are given a lot of responsibility.* High agreement meant high credibility, which meant a *Great Place to Work.* Respect was measured by asking for responses to questions like this: *Management involves people in decisions that affect their jobs or work environment. I am offered training and development to further myself professionally.* Again, high agreement meant respect, which was associated with being a *Great Place to Work.* The website also gathered comments like this one, said to be from an employee in a sample company: "There is a high level of trust & empowerment here. We are not bound by any rules & we can do whatever we want at work. We receive encouragement & motivation from our team leaders. We have company events & wellness programs which allow us to balance our personal & professional lives."

At first glance, this all looks plausible, but it's undermined by the Halo Effect. Companies that are profitable, prosperous, and growing fast will often be perceived as desirable places to work. Again, look at Cisco. It debuted on the charts in 1998 at number twenty-five, then climbed to twenty-third place in 1999. In 2000, when Cisco was briefly the most valuable company in the world, it shot up to third place, where it stayed for two years. Once the lay-offs hit and the stock price tanked, how was Cisco rated as a *Great Place to Work*? It fell to fifteen in 2002, then to twenty-four, and fi-nally twenty-eight in 2004—not exactly tracking performance, but pretty close. Did Cisco become a *worse* place to work after 2000? Yes, if we think in terms of employee morale and the chance to get rich. But that's a *reflection* of performance, not a *cause* of it. If you *don't* believe the *Fortune* and *Best Places* lists are shaded by the Halo Effect, you have to believe that the people who filled out the sur-veys are *not* affected by the same tendency found in participants of Barry Staw's experiment or by journalists at *Business Week, Fortune,* and other news publications, which would seem doubtful.

Delusion One: *The Halo Effect*

In chapter 1, we asked why we know so little about company per-formance. For all the attention devoted to the question, why is it so hard to understand why some companies succeed and others fail? In fact, our thinking about business is shaped by a number of delusions, the first of which is the Halo Effect. So many of the things that we—managers, journalists, professors, and consultants—commonly think *contribute* to company performance are often at-tributions *based on* performance. And even when we try to gather data in large-scale samples, like the *Fortune* survey or the *Great Place to Work* study, we often do little more than multiply the Halo Effect.

The Halo Effect isn't the only delusion that distorts our think-ing about business. In the following chapters, we'll come across sev-eral more. But in many ways the Halo Effect is the most basic delusion of them all. It is a flaw—sometimes compounded by other errors—that turns up again and again, weakening the quality of our data and often diminishing our ability to think clearly about the fac-tors that shape company performance.

CHAPTER FIVE

Research to the Rescue?

A famous statistician once showed a precise correlation between arrests for public drunkenness and the number of Baptist preachers in nineteenth-century America. The correlation
is real and intense, but we may assume that the two increases
are causally unrelated, and that both arise as consequences of
a single different factor: a marked general increase in the
American population.

Stephen Jay Gould
Full House: The Spread of Excellence from Plato to Darwin, 1996

The Halo Effect shapes how we commonly talk about so many
topics in business, from decision processes to people to leadership and more. It shows up in our everyday conversations and in
newspaper and magazine articles. It affects case studies and large-
sample surveys. It's not so much the result of conscious distortion as
it is a natural human tendency to make judgments about things that
are abstract and ambiguous on the basis of other things that are
salient and seemingly objective. The Halo Effect is just too strong,
the desire to tell a coherent story too great, the tendency to jump on
bandwagons too appealing.

The Halo Effect shapes much of the way we think about business, yes, but by no means all of it. There's nothing inevitable about
the Halo Effect. If we're aware of the tendency to bestow Halos, we
can take corrective measures. For example, we know that one way to
evaluate a job candidate more accurately is to insist that some assessments are made without any knowledge of the applicant's school—to
use standardized tests or to conduct some interviews blind. Simi-

larly, we might expect that careful research conducted by serious scholars trained in scientific methods can avoid the Halo Effect. Maybe then we can find a satisfactory answer to the most fundamental of all business questions—*What leads to high performance?*

The good news is that there are many people at business schools and consulting firms who conduct very good research about company performance. They may not be able to run experiments with the rigor of natural science, but they can carry out solid research using quasi-experimental designs. That sort of study tries to isolate the impact that some variables, called *independent* variables, have on a given outcome, called the *dependent* variable. By carefully gathering data and then testing hypotheses with precise statistical tests, by isolating the effect of independent variables on dependent variables, these researchers can hope to distill the drivers of company performance.

What's needed, for starters, is good data about the dependent variable—namely, company performance. Luckily, that's usually not a problem. Every publicly traded company publishes its revenues and profits. There's plenty of information compiled neatly into databases like Compustat or DataStream, which can give us accounting measures of performance (profitability or return on assets) as well as market measures (cumulative stock returns, or Tobin's q, the ratio of asset replacement cost to market value). As for the drivers of performance, the data we need depends on what we're trying to test. For some hypotheses—say, diversification or research and development (R&D) spending or acquisition strategy—the same databases are relatively complete and not affected by Halos. Much trickier are studies about what goes on inside a company, like the quality of management, or levels of customer orientation, or company culture. Here, Compustat or DataStream aren't much help. Nor has Bloomberg put together a powerful online database that can tell you which companies are well managed, or innovative, or ethical, or environmentally responsible. These data have to be gathered by the researcher.

Since gathering data is hard work, a natural tendency is first to look to other studies whose data might serve as useful proxies. But be careful: If these studies are contaminated with Halos, they won't do much good. Want to study whether companies that are strong in corporate social responsibility outperform the rest? The temptation is to check *Fortune*'s *Most Admired* list for "responsibility to the community and environment" and see if it's related to performance. (Answer: *It is.*) Want to test whether the most innovative companies outperform the rest? Just check the *Fortune* list for innovativeness and see if it correlates with performance. (Same answer: *It does.*) *Of course they do.* But all we're really measuring is the strength of the Halo. What if we avoid proxies altogether and take the time to gather data directly? That's moving in the right direction, but even then we might have a problem with Halos—it all depends on how the data are gathered.

Halos of Customer Orientation

Suppose we want to test whether customer orientation leads to high performance. From what we saw at Cisco, we know to be wary of the Halo Effect. As long as sales and profits were up, Cisco was held up as a shining example of excellent customer orientation. It was described, at its pre-bubble peak in 2000, as having "extreme customer focus," and John Chambers was "the most customer-focused human being you will ever meet." A year later, as performance fell, Cisco was said to have exhibited "a cavalier attitude toward potential customers," and its sales tactics had been "irksome." Unless we believe that Cisco actually *got worse*—and no one suggested that was the case—all we have are changing attributions about customer orientation made on the basis of worsening financial performance. We know, therefore, to avoid relying on magazine and newspaper articles and to gather data in a different way.

One study, by John Narver at the University of Washington and Stanley Slater at the University of Colorado, set out to study the link between customer orientation and company performance. They defined *performance* as business unit profitability. No problem there. But to capture customer orientation, they asked managers to rate their companies on six criteria: overall customer commitment, creating customer value, understanding customer needs, setting customer satisfaction objectives, measuring customer satisfaction, and providing after-sales service. When they ran their statistical tests, they found that, sure enough, there was a significant correlation between performance and customer orientation. That's no surprise at all—it's exactly what we'd expect given the Halo Effect. If we want to test whether customer orientation leads to high performance, the *last thing* we should do is ask managers: "How customer oriented is this company?" We're likely to get an attribution based on performance. To have any validity at all, we need to rely on measures that are *independent* of performance. None of this, by the way, suggests that customer orientation *doesn't* lead to higher performance—I suspect that if we measure it carefully, we'll find that it does, at least to some extent. But passing out a survey where responses are likely to be shaded by the Halo Effect is not the way to go.

Halos of Corporate Culture

Corporate culture is something else that's widely thought to affect firm performance. Again, there's plenty of anecdotal evidence about the importance of a company's culture. We saw it at Cisco and at ABB, of course, and we find it at other companies, too. During the Tylenol crisis of 1982, when seven people died after ingesting capsules laced with cyanide, Johnson & Johnson took the unprecedented step of removing all bottles of Tylenol from all store shelves in the United States, even though the deaths had taken place only in the Chicago area. The recall cost $100 million, but it earned Johnson & Johnson a great deal of respect and admiration. How was Johnson & Johnson able to act so swiftly and decisively? Chief executive James E. Burke said: "Our culture is really it. That's what brought us together when the Tylenol tragedies hit. Without it, we never would have been able to manage the crisis as effectively as we did." According to Burke, Johnson & Johnson had been successful in this crisis because it had a strong corporate culture. Quick and coordinated action was possible only because Johnson & Johnson employees shared common values about customer health, about doing the right thing, and about integrity.

The story of Tylenol and Johnson & Johnson provides a memorable anecdote, but a good anecdote can be found to support just about anything. If we want to show that corporate culture has a major impact on business performance, we have to gather data across companies and look for patterns. That's exactly what John Kotter and James Heskett of Harvard Business School set out to do. Their findings were published in a 1992 book called, not surprisingly, *Corporate Culture and Performance.* Kotter and Heskett defined a strong corporate culture as one where "almost all managers share a set of relatively consistent values and methods of doing business." These companies were thought to have a "style, a way of doing things that provides internal cohesion, strong commitment to a common goal, high motivation, and consistency of behavior without the stifling formal rules and bureaucracy." That's the key—companies with strong cultures don't require lots of rules and formality because people share basic values and ways of doing things. So far, so good.

Kotter and Heskett first tested whether a "strong culture" was associated with high performance. How did they measure "strength of culture"? Did they find a way to capture corporate culture that was free of the Halo Effect? Not at all. They merely asked managers to rate the strength of their corporate culture on a scale of 1 to 5. Not surprisingly, they found a positive correlation between strength of culture and performance—just what we'd expect given the Halo Effect. But they didn't stop there. Even a strong culture, they reasoned, might not lead to high performance if it didn't "fit" the competitive environment, so Kotter and Heskett tested a second hypothesis: that a company's culture should "fit" its environment.

How did they test for "fit"? Again, by asking respondents to score their company, this time on a scale of 1 ("terrible fit") to 7 ("superb fit"). And once again, their analysis showed that high-performing companies had cultures that fit their environment, averaging 6.1 out of 7, while low-performing companies averaged just 3.7. These results are, of course, exactly what we'd expect from self-reporting. It's entirely predictable that when performance is high, managers perceive that their culture "fits" the environment, and when the company is struggling, they sense a mismatch. It would be surprising to find otherwise.

Then Kotter and Heskett took one step further. If a strong culture is good, and a culture that fits its environment is better, perhaps one that can adapt over time is the best of all. But how to measure cultural adaptability? The ideal way would be to study a company's culture over several years, watching as it evolves, all the while using measures that are not subject to the Halo Effect. But that takes quite a bit of time. Instead, Kotter and Heskett assumed that cultural adaptability was linked to two things. First was "leadership"—they claimed that a company with strong leadership should be more likely to adapt to changing circumstances. They asked respondents: "How much does the culture at [firm name] value excellent leadership from its managers?" with answers on a seven-point scale. High-performing firms received an average score of 6 out of 7, while low-performing firms scored less than 4, which is just what we'd expect—respondents tend to attribute good leadership to successful companies. And the second way they tried to capture adaptability? By measuring customer focus! The idea here was that if companies focus on their customers, they'll adapt more quickly and perform better. It sounds reasonable, but as we've already seen, asking managers to rate their companies on customer focus is likely to capture little more than a Halo. The results showed that high-performing companies scored 6 out of 7, while low performers scored just 4.6. But since there was no independent measure of customer focus at all, we really don't know if customer focus leads to cultural adaptability, which in turn leads to business performance, or whether employees at high-performing companies tend to infer that their companies are good at customer focus. From what we know about the Halo Effect, the latter is at least as plausible as the former.

Despite these basic flaws of logic and data validity, Kotter and Heskett were emphatic that they had demonstrated corporate culture has a *causal effect* on performance. Here's how they summarized their work:

> Corporate culture can have a significant impact on a firm's long-term economic performance. We found that firms with cultures that emphasized all the key managerial constituencies (customers, stockholders, and employees) and leadership from managers at all levels outperformed firms that did not have those cultural traits by a huge margin. Over an eleven-year period, the former increased revenues by an average of 682 percent versus 166 percent for the latter, expanded their work forces by 282 percent versus 36 percent, grew their stock prices by 901 percent versus 74 percent, and improved their net incomes by 756 percent versus 1 percent.
>
> Consider that final finding again: The companies that paid attention equally to customers, stockholders, and employees outperformed those that didn't in growth of net income over the 11-year period by a factor of 756. Paying attention to more than just returning profits to stockholders can have a huge payoff.

Note the words "have a strong impact on." That's a claim of science: *If you do this, here's what will happen.* The story line is appealing, and the findings might even be correct, but given the flaws in their research, we really don't know. The approach taken by Kotter and Heskett really doesn't let us conclude much about corporate culture and its impact on company performance at all.

Just to be clear, I think that strong customer orientation probably does lead to better performance. Companies that listen to their customers, that design products and services to meet customer needs, and that work hard to satisfy their customers should, all else equal, usually outperform companies that don't. But you don't discover these companies by asking: *Are you customer oriented?* All you'll get is the self-reporting Halo, cued by company performance. If you want to measure customer orientation, you have to rely on measures that are independent of performance. The same holds for corporate culture. It stands to reason that when employees share common values and don't need to be told what to do, decisions are made more quickly and people collaborate more easily. But you don't measure the strength or the fit or the adaptability of a corporate culture just by asking people who already have an opinion about company performance. Instead, you have to look for specific actions or policies or behaviors that are not shaped by perceptions of performance.

Delusion Two: *The Delusion of Correlation and Causality*

If we want to answer the mother of all business questions—*What leads to high performance?*—one thing is already clear: We have to avoid the Halo Effect. We have to gather data in ways that are unaffected by performance, so that independent variables are measured separately from the thing we're trying to explain. And the good news is that there are plenty of smart people who think deeply about problems of data independence and work very hard to conduct careful, disciplined research. Yet even if researchers avoid the Halo Effect, they may still not be able to say much about the drivers of high performance. Why? The example from Stephen Jay Gould at the start of the chapter gives the main idea: Arrests for public drunkenness and the number of Baptist preachers in nineteenth-century America may have been closely correlated, but we can't say much about whether one *caused* the other. Did the level of drunkenness lead to greater attention about morality in society and therefore a demand for preachers? Or did an abundance of preachers drive Americans to drink? Or were both of them the result of something different—namely, growth in the overall population? If all we have is a correlation, we really don't know.

Inferring causality from correlation trips up many studies about business. Take something as basic as, say, the relationship between employee satisfaction and company performance. It's logical to think that having satisfied employees ought to lead to high performance. After all, satisfied employees might be willing to work harder and longer, and might care more about keeping their customers happy. It *sounds* right. We know not to measure employee satisfaction simply by asking employees, "Are you satisfied?" since the answers will likely be colored by the Halo Effect. But suppose we look at a measure that is not tainted by Halos—say, the rate of employee turnover—and we find a high correlation with performance. Now the challenge is to untangle the direction of causality. Does lower employee turnover lead to higher company performance? Perhaps, since a company with a stable workforce might be able to provide more dependable customer service, spend less on hiring and training, and so forth. Or does higher company performance lead to lower employee turnover? That could be true as well, since a profitable and growing company might offer a more stimulating and rewarding environment as well as greater opportunities for advancement. Knowing which leads to which is critical if managers want to know what to do—how much they should invest in greater levels of satisfaction versus other objectives.

Or suppose we want to capture the impact of executive education on company performance. As a first step, we have to avoid the Halo Effect by measuring executive education in ways that are not shaped by perceptions of performance, like total spending on education, number of days of education per employee, range of educational opportunities available, and so forth. Suppose we find that companies that spend more on executive education also tend to be high performers. How do we interpret the results? Can we say that investing in executive education leads to high performance? No, because it could be that profitable companies have the funds to afford a greater investment in education. As long as we gather data at one point in time—*cross-sectionally*—we won't know. Psychologist Edwin Locke made the point emphatically: "While the method of correlation may be useful for the purposes of suggesting causal hypotheses, it is not a method of scientific proof. A correlation, by itself, explains nothing."

Would you imagine that consulting firms do a better job of distinguishing between correlation and causality? Guess again. In 2006, one of the leading consultants, Bain & Company, proclaimed on its website that "Bain's clients have outperformed the stock market 4 to 1." A chart showed that from 1980 to 2004, while the S&P 500 rose by a factor of about 15, the shares of Bain's clients grew by a factor of about 60—four times the rate of the market. The implication? That following Bain's advice leads to higher performance, in fact much higher performance. But there are two huge flaws in this claim. First, as a Bain spokesperson explained to me, the data in fact show the quarter-by-quarter performance of Bain's then-current clients relative to the S&P index in that quarter. A 400 percent gap over twenty-five years, or 100 quarters, translates to an average gap of somewhat more than one percent per quarter—1.4 percent, to be exact—which is not insignificant, but you'd have to enjoy that difference *every quarter for twenty-five years* in order to outperform your rivals by a four-to-one margin. Most consulting engagements last for a few years, not for two and a half decades, which means that the performance gap for a typical client is much less. But the second flaw, and the more important one for our present discussion, is that at best Bain has shown a correlation, not causality. Even if Bain's clients outperformed the market average by a little more than 1 percent each quarter, does that mean working with Bain leads to better performance? That's the suggestion, and maybe it's true. Or could it be that only profitable companies can afford Bain's services? That could be true, too, in which case working with Bain doesn't lead to higher profits; in fact, it might well be the other way around—only companies with high profits can afford Bain. Again, a simple correlation tells us very little.

One way to improve our ability to explain causality is to gather data at different points of time, so that the impact of one variable on some subsequent outcome can be more clearly isolated. This approach, called a *longitudinal* design, is more time-consuming and expensive to carry out, but it stands a better chance of avoiding mistaken inferences from simple correlation. That way we could, for example, tell whether the advice given by a consulting company in one time period led to better performance in subsequent periods. One recent study, by Benjamin Schneider and colleagues at the University of Maryland, used a longitudinal design to examine the question of employee satisfaction and company performance to try to find out which one causes which. They gathered data over several years so they could watch both changes in satisfaction and changes in company performance. Their conclusion? Financial performance, measured by return on assets and earnings per share, has a more powerful effect on employee satisfaction than the reverse. It seems that being on a winning team is a stronger cause of employee satisfaction; satisfied employees don't have as much of an effect on company performance. How were Schneider and his colleagues able to break the logjam and answer the question of which leads to which? By gathering data over time. It is far easier, of course, to rely on data from a single point in time and make an assumption about the direction of causality. But that way delusions lie.

Delusion Three: *The Delusion of Single Explanations*

Anyone with a solid training in research methods ought to know to avoid data sources that are tinged by the Halo Effect. The same goes for correlation and causality: The dangers of inferring causality from cross-sectional data are well-known. But even if we ward off these two problems, research about company performance sometimes runs smack into a different thorny issue, that of single explanations.

Let's come back to the question of customer orientation. We

know we can't measure customer orientation just by asking, "Is your company customer oriented?" because all we'll catch is the glow off the Halo. But there's a better way. A study by Bernard Jaworski at the University of Arizona and Ajay Kohli at the University of Texas–Austin looked into the link between market orientation and performance. They defined market orientation in terms of three elements—market intelligence generation, market intelligence dissemination, and business unit responsiveness to market intelligence—and then asked respondents to evaluate thirty-two separate statements. Most of these statements were not about perceptions, but about objective facts. That's a big step forward. For example, respondents were asked whether they polled end users at least once a year to assess the quality of products and services. Presumably that's something we can measure objectively and will not be answered differently based on performance. Respondents were also asked whether "data on customer satisfaction were disseminated at all levels in this business unit on a regular basis." Either that happens or it doesn't; the rating shouldn't be susceptible to the Halo Effect.

Jaworski and Kohli gathered data from a broad sample of companies in three different competitive environments—market turbulence, competitive intensity, and technological turbulence. That way, they could compare results across different environments and tell if any effect between market orientation and firm performance was explainable by things like market turbulence or competitive intensity. When they ran their calculations, they found that market orientation was strongly associated with higher performance. The effect was, in statistical terms, highly significant, meaning it wasn't just some random occurrence—something *real* was going on. Their model had an r^2 of .25, meaning that it could explain about 25 percent of the variance in company performance. Those are dramatic results! The authors brimmed with confidence: "The findings of this study suggest that the market orientation of a business *is an important determinant of its performance,* regardless of market turbulence, competitive intensity, or the technological turbulence of the environment in which it operates." (Italics mine.) According to Jaworski and Kohli, better market orientation leads to improved business performance. They don't claim that market orientation is everything, but they note that their model explained 25 percent of the variance of overall performance, which is pretty strong stuff. And they don't hesitate to tell managers what this means: "As such, it appears that managers should strive to improve the market orientation of their business in their efforts to attain higher business performance."

Hold that in your mind for a moment as we turn to another topic of current interest, corporate social responsibility (CSR). The idea here is that companies should do more than just pursue profits, but should think more broadly about the concerns of stakeholders— the community, the environment, the employees, and society at large. It sounds plausible, but is there evidence to show that CSR leads to better performance? We know not to rely on simple correlations, because even if we find that companies with strong positions on social responsibility also tend to perform well, we won't know which leads to which. It could be that such things as a good record on environmental protection, high product safety, and community investment do indeed lead to higher performance, but the reverse could be true as well, since successful companies might have greater funds to invest in socially responsible pursuits. Bernadette Ruf at the University of Delaware and four colleagues set out to test the impact of CSR on firm performance by gathering data from 488 companies—a good, large sample. They didn't simply ask managers, "How good are you at CSR?" but used an independent data set that measured CSR along eight dimensions—a good way to minimize the Halo Effect. To make sure they didn't confuse correlation with causality, Ruf and her colleagues gathered three years of data. That way, they could see if improvements in CSR in one year led to higher performance in later years. They also included control variables for industry and company size. No problems so far—this looked like a careful and rigorous study. When they ran their model, Ruf and her colleagues found that improving CSR led to higher company sales in year 2 and lifted profits by year 3. Again, the effect was statistically significant, and the r^2 was .415 for return on equity, and .425 for return on sales. That's an extraordinary finding—more than 40 percent of the change in a company's financial performance was linked to corporate social responsibility! The authors confidently declared: "The results of the current study suggest that improvements in [CSR] have both immediate and continuing financial impacts."

But wait. If market orientation explains 25 percent of firm performance, and corporate social responsibility explains 40 percent, does that mean that together they explain 65 percent? Are these *separate* effects and therefore *additive*? Or could it be that companies that are good at market orientation are also likely to be good corporate citizens? That's hugely important, because if these effects overlap, then we really can't say the improvement observed by Jaworski and Kohli was due to market orientation alone or that the performance rise found by Ruf and her colleagues was due to CSR alone. Maybe they're explaining the same thing, in which case the explanatory power of each one has been exaggerated. (And indeed, in a 2005 survey, *The Economist* suggested that many CSR initiatives were little more than examples of "good management." Just about *any* well-managed company is likely to do many of the things we call corporate social responsibility—we'd be surprised if they didn't.)

Now let's add another study to the mix. Mark Huselid at Rutgers University, collaborating with Susan Jackson and Randall Schuler of New York University, tested the impact of a company's human resource management (HRM) capabilities on firm performance. They asked managers to describe their companies on more than forty separate HRM items. They asked questions with an eye to minimizing the Halo Effect, and they also conducted their study over time to avoid problems of correlation and causality. Furthermore, they included control variables for firm size, capital intensity, union coverage, sales growth, and R&D intensity. They found that HRM was associated with firm performance, and that improving HRM effectiveness by one standard deviation led to increased sales of 5 percent, improved cash flow of 16 percent, and an increased stock market value of 6 percent. The authors were emphatic: "Taken as a whole, these estimates illustrate the impact of effective human resource management on three widely followed measures of firm performance." They went on: "Our results support the decade-old argument that investments in human resources are a potential source of competitive advantage."

But was this performance improvement due solely to HRM, quite apart from other things like market orientation and CSR? If so, would a company that had already bettered its performance by becoming more market oriented and by adopting strong CSR policies enjoy this further boost by improving its human resource management? Or do these effects overlap, maybe even to a great extent? The latter explanation seems more likely. In fact, it's entirely logical that a company that cares about its customers and the broader community should also care about its employees. Employees are, after all, one of the key stakeholders that Ruf and her colleagues included in measures of CSR. Market orientation, CSR, and human resource management very likely overlap to a great degree.

To show just how widespread this problem is, I'll give one more example, this time about leadership. It's often suggested that the person in charge—the chief executive—makes a big difference in a company's performance. Of course that makes sense. We can probably all think of examples where a new leader took actions that seemed to boost performance or, unfortunately, a new boss took the company in a wrong direction. One study tried to isolate the performance effect of the CEO by tracking the change in company performance immediately before and after a change in leadership. The data about firm performance and about CEO tenure are matters of public record, so there was no danger here of a Halo Effect from self-reporting or perceptions colored by performance. The authors found that 15 percent of the total variance in company performance was explained by a change in the CEO. "In other words," one of the authors concluded, "the choice of a chief executive is crucial."

Fine, but is this 15 percent *in addition* to what might be explained by improving customer orientation and CSR and HRM? Or does the leadership effect overlap with the others? Presumably the new CEO does more than just replace the nameplate and sit behind a big desk in the corner office. The new CEO *does something*—such as setting new objectives, or bringing about a better market focus, which may help improve the corporate culture, or overhauling the approach to managing human resources, and so on. The improved performance we attribute to the CEO almost certainly overlaps with one or more other explanations for company success.

Which brings us to the nub of the problem: Every one of these studies looks at a single explanation for firm performance and leaves the others aside. That would be okay if there were no correlation among them, but common sense tells us that many of these factors are likely to be found in the same company. Shouldn't we expect a company that was strong at one of these to *also* be good at many of the others? Occasionally, a researcher admits as much. The author of the HRM study just cited, Mark Huselid of Rutgers, writing with Brian Becker of SUNY Buffalo, noted that despite their best efforts to measure accurately the impact of HRM systems on firm performance, there were "unobserved firm-level characteristics, such as the quality of marketing or manufacturing strategies, that might bias the estimated HR strategy-firm performance relationship." They elaborated: "The typical concern in this literature is that unmeasured firm effects are positively correlated with HR strategy because of the adoption of such practices either contingent on firm success or simply a reflection of firms that are better managed across all functions." Exactly right. And they concluded: "There is considerable evidence in the business press that firm reputations for a wide range of management practices are highly correlated."

No wonder it's so difficult to know what drives firm performance. Even if we avoid the Halo Effect, and even if we conduct a longitudinal study, we *still* have the problem of alternate explanations. So many things contribute to company performance that it's awfully hard to know exactly how much is due to one particular factor versus another. Even if we try to control for many things *outside* the company, like environmental turbulence and competitive intensity and industry and firm size, we can't control for all the many different things that go on *inside* the company.

The problem of untangling rival alternatives is rarely given much attention. The article by Huselid and Becker is exceptional; most articles either touch on the subject briefly in a small section toward the end, when they discuss limitations of their research, or else they ignore it altogether. Why? Drawing attention to the limitations of the findings detracts from the power of the desired story—which is to demonstrate the importance of a given variable on company performance. Many academic researchers want to show strong conclusions about cause and effect. They want to demonstrate that leadership is hugely important, or that human resource management has a major impact on company success, or that strong customer orientation significantly raises performance. Readers, too, prefer clear stories. We don't really want to hear about partial causation or incremental effects or threats to validity. And there's a further problem compounding all of this. As Harvard psychologist Stephen Pinker observed, university departments don't always represent meaningful divisions of knowledge. Some of the most important questions come at the intersections among fields, such as the study of decision making, which rests at the convergence of cognitive psychology, sociology, and economics. The same holds for business performance, which is shaped by many different factors. Yet researchers often belong to one department or another. If you're a professor of marketing, you care a lot about market orientation and customer focus, and there's a natural tendency to want to demonstrate the importance of your specialty. Same for professors of human resource management or business ethics. There's no real incentive to explore correlations with other factors—better to leave them safely out of view. As for the journals that publish these articles, many use a "double-blind" review process where the reviewers don't know the name of the authors, and the authors never learn the names of the reviewers, in order to preserve impartiality. But almost everyone who reviews an article for the *Journal of Human Resource Management* believes in the importance of HRM—it's their field, it's their department, and it's their specialty. Of course they look favorably upon articles that show the importance of human resource management. Ditto for the *Journal of Business Ethics*—research that shows how investments in CSR boost firm performance is welcome news, a wonderful validation of their field. And who can blame the *Journal of Marketing* for publishing a study that demonstrates the importance of market orientation on firm performance? It would take an unusual amount of self-discipline to point out that market orientation is correlated with so many other things that its impact is small. Of course, the tendency for exaggeration isn't found just in academic articles—it's also found in business press articles like the one that told us how much a *Great Place to Work* contributed to performance. The bigger the claim, the larger the headline—and the greater the temptation to overlook rival explanations.

For a bit of perspective, I'll mention one last study. Anita McGahan at Boston University and Michael Porter at Harvard Business School set out to determine how much of a business unit's profits can be explained by the industry in which it competes, by the corporation it belongs to, and by the way it is managed. This last category, which they called "segment-specific effects," covers just about everything we've talked about in this chapter: a company's customer orientation, its culture, its human resource systems, social responsibility, and so forth. Using data from thousands of U.S. companies from 1981 to 1994, McGahan and Porter found that "segment-specific effects" explained about 32 percent of a business unit's performance. Just 32 percent. The rest was due to industry effects or corporate effects or was simply unexplained. So maybe all of the studies we've looked at make sense after all! It's just that, as we suspected, their effects overlap—they all explain the same 32 percent. Each study claims to have isolated an important driver of performance, but only because of *the Delusion of Single Explanations*.

CHAPTER SIX

Searching for Stars, Finding Halos

We had the sky, up there, all speckled with stars, and we used to lay on our backs and look up at them, and discuss about whether they was made or only just happened. Jim he allowed they was made, but I allowed they happened; I judged it would have took too long to *make* so many. Jim said the moon could a *laid* them; well, that looked kind of reasonable, so I didn't say nothing against it, because I've seen a frog lay most as many, so of course it could be done. We used to watch the stars that fell, too, and see them streak down. Jim allowed they'd got spoiled and was hove out of the nest.

Mark Twain
The Adventures of Huckleberry Finn, 1885

The first of the business blockbusters, the megahit that changed everything, was *In Search of Excellence: Lessons from America's Best-Run Companies* by Tom Peters and Bob Waterman, both at McKinsey & Co. The book has been widely read and endlessly discussed, but it deserves a fresh look in the context of the Halo Effect and other delusions that deceive managers. Curiously, for all its flaws, *In Search of Excellence* holds up fairly well. In fact, it's almost endearing in its simplicity, at least when compared with subsequent studies that became more complex but also more and more grandiose in the claims they made. But more about those studies in a little while.

The story of *In Search of Excellence* began in 1977 when McKinsey & Co, perhaps America's most prestigious consulting firm, undertook a study about organizational structure, which morphed into a broader study about managerial systems and skills, which eventually led to a project about managerial excellence. Peters and Waterman started with a broad question: *Why are some companies more successful than others?* They began by identifying the very best American companies through a rigorous process of careful selection. An initial sample of sixty-two strong companies was reduced to a very select group of forty-three excellent American companies. The very best of them, the cream of American business, included names like Boeing, Caterpillar, Delta Airlines, Digital Equipment, Emerson Electric, Fluor, Hewlett-Packard, IBM, Johnson & Johnson, McDonald's, Procter & Gamble, and 3M. To understand what made these companies so successful, Peters and Waterman talked to lots of people and gathered plenty of data. And then, as they described: "When we finished our interviews and research, we began to sift and codify our results. It was roughly six months after we had started, that we reached the conclusions which are the backbone of this book." The process was careful, systematic, logical, and objective. No fudging, no cutting corners.

Well, that's what they wrote in the preface of their 1982 book. Almost twenty years later, Peters told the tale a bit differently. In a 2001 article for *Fast Company,* titled "Tom Peters' True Confessions," he wrote:

> There's an official way that I tell the story now—and it's total bullshit. The way I tell it now is, "Americans were under attack by the Japanese, who were making good automobiles. So Bob Waterman and I set out to discover the real secrets of management." Usually when I tell that version of the story, I try to use my imitation voice-of-God way of speaking to convey the impression that what we set out to do was Very Important.
>
> Which is completely wrong.

What *really* happened? Peters recalls that at first his project wasn't given much attention at McKinsey—it was "the runt of the litter," a poor stepsister to a project about strategy. As for their research approach: "There was no carefully designed work plan. There was no theory that I was out to prove." Instead, they went around to McKinsey's partners and asked, "Who's doing cool work? Where is great stuff going on?" They talked to leading academics and managers; they spoke with "genuinely smart, remarkably interesting, first-rate people." They nosed around and asked lots of questions. And then they looked for patterns that might explain what the best companies had in common.

After some time, Peters and Waterman were asked to present their findings to the top management of Siemens. They gave a long and detailed presentation, with more than seven hundred slides. It was well received, and soon Peters was asked to give a similar presentation to the top management of PepsiCo. The head of PepsiCo was a hard-nosed fellow named Andrall Pearson. (I should know—some years later I taught with him at Harvard Business School, where he proudly displayed on his wall a 1980 *Fortune* article that named him one of the ten toughest managers in America.) Peters recalled: "We all knew that he'd go ballistic at the sight of a 700-slide presentation." So, with the clock ticking away, Peters sat at his desk, closed his eyes, and leaned forward. Then, as he recalled: "I wrote down eight things on a pad of paper. Those eight things haven't changed since that moment. They were the eight principles of *Search*."

Here they are:

The Eight Practices of America's Best Companies, from *In Search of Excellence*

A bias for action—a preference for doing something—anything—rather than sending a question through cycles and cycles of analyses and committee reports.

Staying close to the customer—learning his preferences and catering to them.

Autonomy and entrepreneurship—breaking the corporation into small companies and encouraging them to think independently and competitively.

Productivity through people–creating in all employees the awareness that their best efforts are essential and that they will share in the rewards of the company's success.

Hands-on, value-driven–insisting that executives keep in touch with the firm's essential business.

Stick to the knitting–remaining with the business the company knows best.

Simple form, lean staff–few administrative layers, few people at the upper levels.

Simultaneous loose-tight properties–fostering a climate where there is dedication to the central values of the company combined with a tolerance for all employees who accept those values.
Source: *In Search of Excellence*

In the context of its times, *In Search of Excellence* was a refreshing challenge to the old-fashioned model of command and control management, of time-and-motion precision, of organization men working together like so many parts in a smoothly running machine. And take a look at this list: *customers, values, people, focus.* It's not much different from the things we saw in chapter 5 that we often say drive firm performance. *Care about your customers. Have strong values. Create a culture where people can thrive. Empower your employees. Stay focused.* It may be hard to isolate exactly how much of a company's performance is due to culture versus leadership versus customer orientation, because they're probably correlated, and according to Peters and Waterman, *that's exactly right*–outstanding companies *do all of them.* That's what makes them excellent! The best companies don't do one or two of these things, they do them *all together!* The secret to success isn't rocket science but follows from a thorough attention to the basic elements of good management.

Peters and Waterman observed: "Far too many managers have lost sight of the basics, in our opinion: quick action, service to customers, practical innovation, and the fact that you can't get any of these without virtually everyone's commitment." *In Search of Excellence* was nothing less than an affirmation of basic principles of good management.

How good was their research? Peters admitted in 2001 that the quantitative data analysis came *after* they had reached their findings. He explained: "Because McKinsey is McKinsey, we felt that we had to come up with some quantitative measures of performance." And how did they reach their conclusions? Did they sift and codify, reducing pages and pages of interview notes into these eight principles? No, said Peters: "I confess, we faked the data." Well, I'm not exactly sure what Peters meant by faking the data, because I suspect he didn't need to fabricate anything. If he drew on retrospective interviews with managers, augmented by articles from publications like *Business Week, Fortune, Forbes,* and *Industry Week,* then the data were likely to be compromised by the Halo Effect from the beginning. It's no surprise that *Excellent* companies were thought to be good at managing people and listening to customers, or were said to have strong values or a good corporate culture. We've seen all that before. If you start by identifying a group of forty-three high-performing companies, it's hardly surprising that you'll find these sorts of results. Successful companies will almost always be described in terms of a clear strategy, good organization, strong corporate culture, and customer focus. But whether these things *drive* company performance, or whether they're mainly attributions *based on* performance, is a different matter. Peters and Waterman went searching for excellence, but they found a handful of Halos.

Of course, none of these finer points seemed to matter. *In Search of Excellence* arrived in bookstores in 1982, at a time when corporate America was worried sick by the rise of Japanese companies. We were surrounded by cars with names like Toyota and Honda, cameras from Nikon and Canon and Olympus, and televisions from Sony and Toshiba and Sharp. "Made in Japan" had become a mark of quality. Harvard professor Ezra Vogel declared that Japan was now the number one economic power—*ichiban*. Bookstore shelves bulged with titles like *The Art of Japanese Management*. Into this mix came Peters and Waterman's book with its headline: "There *is* an art of American management—and it works!" Rarely had a message been so timely or so well received. American managers, gripped by self-doubt, loved *In Search of Excellence*. It was the right story for the times. It made good sense. It was inspirational. It was even patriotic. The book sold by the truckload, zooming to the top of the bestseller charts and staying there for months on end. Phrases like *stick to the knitting* and *managing by wandering around* and *loose-tight coupling* became business buzzwords. As for Tom Peters and Bob Waterman, they were the first in a new generation of business gurus, traveling far and wide to give hundreds of speeches and conduct scores of workshops for thousands of managers. In 1982, with their book a titanic success, they were kings of the world.

Excellence plus Two

Part of the appeal of *In Search of Excellence* was that it wasn't just descriptive—it was *prescriptive.* The cover declared: "Learn how the best-run American companies use these eight basic principles to stay on top of the heap!" The implication? Go and do likewise, and success can be yours, too. That's the claim of science: *If you do this, here's what will happen.* But not everyone lived happily ever after. In 1984, *Business Week* ran a follow-up story under the title "Who's Excellent Now?" By their reckoning, at least fourteen of the companies highlighted by Peters and Waterman just two years earlier had "lost their luster." Many companies had "suffered significant earnings declines that stem from serious business problems, management problems, or both." Other companies were clinging tenuously to their status as *Excellent* companies but had been "humbled by blunders." What had gone wrong? *Business Week* criticized some companies for changing their winning formula: "The transgressors ran amok by walking away from the principles that had been key to their earlier success." *They didn't stick to their knitting!* Others were rebuked for their *inability* to change: "Of the 14 companies that had stumbled, 12 were inept at adapting to a fundamental change in their markets." And to top it off, *Business Week* reported: "Several excellent companies that fell by the wayside overstressed some attributes and ignored others." To help the reader understand how the mighty had fallen, a table identified which of the eight "commandments of excellence" each company had allegedly broken.

To find out just how well the *Excellent* companies fared in the years after 1980, I looked to Compustat, a leading business database run by Standard & Poor's, and calculated the total shareholder return (that is, the percent change in stock price with all dividends reinvested) for thirty-five of the *Excellent* companies, as well as for the S&P 500, for the five years after the study ended, 1980 to 1984, and for ten years after, 1980 to 1989. (Some of the companies were privately held, or were divisions of a larger company, and weren't publicly traded in 1984 and 1989, leaving data for only thirty-five.) How well did they do? Not very well. Between 1980 and 1984, while the S&P 500 almost doubled, growing by 99 percent, only twelve *Excellent* companies grew faster than the overall market. The other twenty-three failed to keep up. Some companies did very well (like Wal-Mart, which grew by a whopping 800 percent in those five years), but many well-known names like Caterpillar, Digital Equipment, Dupont, Johnson & Johnson, and Walt Disney didn't even match the market average. You would have been better off investing in a market index than putting your money on those *Excellent* companies. If we go out ten years, the record is about the same: Only thirteen companies outperformed the market, which was up 403 percent, while eighteen didn't match the market. Most of the companies weren't even *average*, never mind *Excellent*. *Sic transit gloria mundi*. (Full results are shown in the appendix, table 1A.)

Maybe there's a simple explanation for this sharp decline. Stock market performance is, after all, shaped by the expectations of investors. Suppose a company's stock has been bid up to very high levels, with price/earnings ratios of 40 or 80 or even more, very much as we saw earlier with Cisco or, in 2006, with Google. If the company continues to perform well and delivers the expected earnings, its stock price will stay steady but won't continue to rise, because those earnings are already reflected in the stock price. Through no fault of its own, the company's stock may underperform the market over the next years. Microsoft is a case in point: While its revenues and profits rose by more than 50 percent from 2001 through 2005, the price of its stock has been essentially unchanged, having been bid so high in the 1990s. Maybe that's what's going on here: The *Excellent* companies had their stock prices bid up to very high levels in the late 1970s, and a slide in stock price over the next years was due more to investors' earlier optimism than any real decline in performance. To remove the effect of expectations, I used a measure of performance that captured profitability: operating income as a percent of total assets. Again using data from Compustat, I found that for the five years after the study ended, fully thirty of the thirty-five *Excellent* companies showed a decline in profitability, some by a small amount and others by a lot. Only five improved their performance. These results make plain that Peters and Waterman's *Excellent* companies didn't decline just because they failed to meet market expectations. These companies, chosen precisely for their outstanding performance, actually became less profitable in the years after the study ended. (The results are shown in the appendix, table 1B.)

How should we interpret this flagging performance? When asked in 1984 to comment, Peters remarked: "There's no real reason to have ever expected that all of these companies would have done well forever and ever." Of course, no one had ever suggested these companies would be successful "forever and ever." Some regression is pretty much a fact of nature. But you would think that *Excellence* would last more than a few years! In fact, if you make the claim that you've discovered the elements that lead to success, you'd better have an explanation for failure, too. The door swings both ways—

Peters and Waterman can't pretend their principles explain the good times but overlook the bad ones.

So what's really going on here? A first explanation is that many of the *Excellent* companies really weren't excellent to begin with. *Business Week* suggested as much in its 1984 article: Maybe Peters and Waterman hadn't picked the right companies. But that explanation doesn't hold up very well. With the possible exception of Atari, a one-hit wonder in the early 1980s, the *Excellent* companies really were a solid and successful bunch by any standard measure. A second explanation is that companies faltered because they changed their winning ways. Maybe they stopped doing precisely those things that made them so good. Maybe they lost their desire. Or became self-satisfied and complacent. Or suffered from hubris, a classic theme as old as the Greeks. This explanation, where success contains the seeds of its own downfall, appeals to our sense of a good story, and it's the main explanation that *Business Week* offered. Of course, if we attribute great performance to a clear vision and brilliant leadership and a strong focus, it's natural to infer that poor performance is due to some error or mistake. Ex post facto, it's always easy to say that low performance was due to some blunder or to inept management. Like Huck and Jim trying to make sense of the heavens, we can always say that some stars got spoiled and was hove out of the nest. We can always say they did something wrong to deserve their punishment. It makes the world seem fair and just. Of course, it's possible that some companies fit this description, but it's not a good general explanation, because it would be stunning to find that so many of these *Excellent* companies so quickly lost their groove after doing so well—that two-thirds slumped in market performance and thirty out of thirty-five declined in profitability. It's unlikely that *so many* companies, selected precisely because of their strong values and discipline and culture and focus, could all falter *so quickly.* Contagious complacency? An epidemic of entropy? Probably not. (We could even—a *dreadful* idea—suggest these companies became self-satisfied *because* they were listed as *Excellent.* Hmm, maybe Peters and Waterman were to blame.) Rather, it's more likely that these *Excellent* companies carried on doing much the same things as before, but those things weren't enough to ensure success—because their success had been due to more than these eight principles in the first place. It's also possible that these eight principles reflect attributions made about successful companies, and in fact the drivers of success lie somewhere else. It's hard to know, since Peters and Waterman selected companies precisely for their success and gathered data by talking to managers at those companies, collecting perceptions and testimonials that were biased by the Halo Effect.

Delusion Four: *The Delusion of Connecting the Winning Dots*

Peters and Waterman's research method contained a pair of basic errors. First, of course, their data were very likely corrupted by the Halo Effect. Ask managers why their companies are successful, and we're likely to get attributions of the sort we've seen over and over. Read the business press and we'll get more of the same. There's no need to fake the analysis—because the data are suspect from the start.

But compounding the Halo Effect was a second mistake: Peters and Waterman studied a sample made up entirely of outstanding companies. The scientific term for this is sample selection based on the dependent variable—that is, based on outcomes. It's a classic error. Suppose we want to find out what leads to high blood pressure. We'll never find out if we only examine patients who suffer from high blood pressure; we'll only know if we compare them to a sample of people who *don't* have high blood pressure. The same applies to companies: By looking only at companies that perform well, we can never hope to show what makes them different from companies that perform less well. I call this the *Delusion of Connecting the Winning Dots,* because if all we compare are successful companies, we can connect the dots any way we want but will never get an accurate picture.

Under ideal conditions, of course, we might like to conduct an experiment where we assign different treatments to various subjects and compare results. That's the ideal way, but it's not easily done when we're trying to study company performance. We can't take 100 companies, ask half to manage according to one set of principles and the other half to manage by a different set, and then compare results. It's understandable that Peters and Waterman selected their sample after the fact, but if the only companies we study are successful, we have no way of knowing what distinguishes a successful company from an unsuccessful one. All we'll do is find out the sorts of Halos that people place on successful companies. Which is not a bad way to describe what *In Search of Excellence* is really all about.

But delusions or no, *In Search of Excellence* was a huge hit, the first of the modern business blockbusters. Why the appeal? Because it worked wonderfully as a *story*. It told the tale of successful American companies prevailing against stiff competition. It focused managers on a few key points: *people, customers, action*. It provided inspiration. And nothing was ever the same again. Twenty years after he shook up the business world, Tom Peters stood by his most famous work:

> Was our process fundamentally sound? Absolutely! If you want to go find smart people who are doing cool stuff from which you can learn the most useful, cutting-edge principles, then do what we did with *Search*: start by using common sense, by trusting your instincts, and by soliciting the views of "strange" (that is, nonconventional) people. You can always worry about proving the facts later.

The Quest for Corporate *El Dorado*

One of the McKinsey consultants who worked with Peters and Waterman, Jim Collins, later joined the Stanford Business School faculty and teamed up with a Stanford professor, Jerry Porras, on a new study about firm performance. Rather than focus on today's successful companies—many of which might soon falter—Collins and Porras turned their attention to companies that had been successful over the long term, that had stood the test of time. They hoped to find the "underlying timeless, *fundamental principles* and patterns that might apply across eras" (italics in the original). The title of their book said it all: *Built to Last: Successful Habits of Visionary Companies.*

Collins and Porras began by identifying 200 leading companies from a wide range of industries, then winnowed the field to include the most durable and successful of them all, the "best of the best." They found just eighteen companies worthy of this distinction—truly outstanding, enduring, *visionary* companies. Among Collins and Porras's eighteen *Visionary* companies were great names of American business: high-tech companies like IBM, Hewlett-Packard, and Motorola; financial services giants like Citicorp and American Express; health care companies like Johnson & Johnson and Merck; plus Boeing, General Electric, Procter & Gamble, Wal-Mart, Disney, and more. What a remarkable bunch they were. While a single dollar invested in the general market back in 1926 would have risen to $415 by 1990, a dollar invested in these eighteen companies would have grown to $6,356—fifteen times the market average over those sixty-four years!

Collins and Porras knew that *In Search of Excellence* had made a critical error in simply looking for commonality among successful companies—it had connected only winning dots. As they noted, if you look at a group of successful companies and try to find what they have in common, you might conclude that they all reside in buildings. Very true—but hardly something that distinguishes successful companies from less successful ones or that might conceivably lead to success. So Collins and Porras went a next step: For each of their *Visionary* companies, they identified a *Comparison* company from the same industry, of about the same vintage, and that was a *good* performer—not a "dog." Boeing was paired with McDonnell Douglas, Citicorp with Chase Manhattan, General Electric with Westinghouse, Hewlett-Packard with Texas Instruments, Procter & Gamble with Colgate-Palmolive, and so forth. This way, Collins and Porras might be able to isolate what made the most successful and enduring companies different from others that weren't quite so outstanding. One dollar invested in the eighteen *Comparison* companies in 1926 would have grown to $955 by 1990, twice the growth of the overall market, although nowhere near as good as the *Visionary* companies. Now they had two clearly different groups to compare. So far, so good.

"The Timeless Principles of Enduring Greatness"

The next step was to study these eighteen matched pairs. Collins and Porras recognized the special challenges of social science research. As they explained: "We cannot perform controlled, repeatable experiments where we hold all but one critical variable constant and assess various outcomes from tweaking that variable. We would love to make petri dishes of corporations, but we can't; we have to take what history gives us and make the best of it." And so, supported by a team of researchers, Collins and Porras undertook a long and arduous process of data gathering and analysis. They described it under the title "Crates of Data, Months of Coding, and 'Tortoise Hunting.'" First they devised a "systematic and comprehensive" framework for data collection. They read more than 100 books, including company histories and autobiographies. They consulted more than 3,000 documents, ranging from articles to company publications to video footage. They read Harvard and Stanford case studies. They performed "extensive literature searches" from sources including *Forbes, Fortune, Business Week, The Wall Street Journal, Nation's Business, The New York Times,* and so on. All together, the material filled three "shoulder-height storage cabinets, four bookshelves, and twenty megabytes of computer storage." The impression was clear: *We were very, very thorough.*

At the end of their research process, Collins and Porras distilled their findings into a series of "timeless principles." Here they are, the keys to enduring greatness, the things that set the eighteen *Visionary* companies apart from the eighteen *Comparison* companies:

- Having a strong core ideology that guides the company's decisions and behavior
- Building a strong corporate culture
- Setting audacious goals that can inspire and stretch people—so-called big hairy audacious goals, or *BHAGs*
- Developing people and promoting them from within
- Creating a spirit of experimentation and risk taking
- Driving for excellence

It's a nice list with a strong commonsense appeal. In fact, it's not very different from the list put forth by Peters and Waterman, as Collins and Porras themselves recognized. Many of the same major themes are present—*people, values, culture, action, focus*. The sample of companies may have been different, and the research methodology may have been different, but the findings were largely similar.

Built to Last was published in 1994 and became an immediate hit. *Inc.* magazine gushed: "The *In Search of Excellence* for the 1990s has arrived. It is *Built to Last*." Managers loved the book, and why not? It was immensely readable. It was filled with memorable anecdotes. And it claimed to offer the keys to lasting success. In its own words, *Built to Last* provided "a master blueprint for building organizations that will prosper long into the future." Collins and Porras didn't shy away from bold promises: "Just about anyone can be a key protagonist in building an extraordinary business institution. The lessons of these companies can be learned and applied by the vast majority of managers at all levels." They concluded: "You can learn them. You can apply them. You can build a visionary company." The *Chicago Tribune* agreed, declaring that *Built to Last* offered "no less than a revolution in our understanding of what makes companies successful over the long haul." *Built to Last* was named the best business book for 1995 by *Industry Week* and by 1996 had spent more than eighteen months on the *Business Week* bestseller list.

Yet for all their promises of exhaustive research, Collins and Porras didn't address a basic problem: the Halo Effect. Much of the data they gathered came from the business press, from books, and from company documents, all sources that are likely to contain, Halos. They also conducted interviews with managers, who were asked to look back on their experience and explain the reasons for success, a method likely to be tinged by Halos. And if your data contain Halos, it really doesn't matter how many cartons you fill. Pick any group of highly successful companies and look backward, relying either on self-reporting or on articles in the business press, and you may well find that they're said to have strong cultures, solid values, and a commitment to excellence. It would be remarkable if they *weren't* described in these terms. Pick a group of comparison companies that are good but not outstanding, and they're likely to be described in somewhat lesser terms. But unless the data were gathered in a way that was truly *independent of performance*—that is, unless Collins and Porras could avoid the Halo Effect—we really don't have an explanation of performance at all. Do these practices lead to high performance? Or do high-performing companies tend to be described in these terms? The latter explanation is at least as likely as the former.

Built to Last? Not So Fast!

Collins and Porras urge us not to "blindly and unquestioningly accept" their findings but ask that we subject their analysis to careful scrutiny. "Let the evidence speak for itself," they implore. So let's check the evidence. We may not be able to put companies in petri dishes and run experiments, but we can check how they fare over time. If the principles of *Built to Last* are indeed timeless and enduring explanations of performance, then we should expect these same companies to continue to perform well after the study ended. Conversely, if they can't keep up their high performance, well, that would lend support to the view that these so-called timeless principles were due mostly to the Halo Effect—a glow cast *by* high performance rather than the cause *of* high performance.

So how well did the eighteen *Visionary* companies fare in the years after the study ended on December 31, 1990? All eighteen were still up and running in 2000, so at least they were built to last for another ten years. But as for performance, the record wasn't so good. Using data from Compustat, I looked at total shareholder return for each company for the five years after the study ended, 1991–1995. The results? Out of seventeen companies, chosen specifically because they had outperformed the market by a factor of 15 for more than sixty-four years, only eight outperformed the S&P 500 market average; the other nine didn't even keep up. (One company, Marriott, was privately held and not included in the Compustat data set.) If we go out another five years, the picture is no better. In the ten years from 1991 to 2000, only six out of sixteen *Visionary* companies kept pace with the S&P 500; the other ten didn't even match the market. You would have been better off investing randomly than putting your money on Collins and Porras's *Visionary* companies. (Full results by company are shown in the appendix, table 2A.)

Again, it's possible that this decline mainly reflects a failure to meet exaggerated market expectations, not a decline in operating performance. Stock prices are a good indicator of performance in the long run but may be a poor measure in a shorter time frame. Yet if we look at company profitability, once again monitoring operating profit as a percentage of assets, the seventeen *Visionary* companies still don't fare well. For the five years after the study ended, only five companies improved their profitability while eleven declined, with one unchanged. Whether we look to market performance or profit performance, the picture is the same: Most of Collins and Porras's *Visionary* companies, chosen precisely because they had done so well for so long, fell back to earth. The "master blueprint of long-term prosperity" turns out to be largely a delusion. (These results are in the appendix, table 2B.)

And that's just the companies in the original study. The 1997 edition of *Built to Last*, written at the height of the book's success, promised that the study would soon be replicated in Europe, where Collins and Porras had already identified "eighteen European visionary companies: ABB, BMW, Carrefour, DaimlerBenz, Deutsche Bank, Ericsson, Fiat, Glaxo, ING, L'Oreal, Marks & Spencer, Nestlé, Nokia, Philips, Roche, Shell, Siemens, and Unilever." Quite a list, that. We've already read about ABB, but several other companies on this list soon fell on hard times, too. DaimlerBenz didn't fare well after it bought Chrysler in 1998; Ericsson tottered on the brink of bankruptcy in 2000; and Marks & Spencer fell out of favor with British shoppers. Then we have some whopping ethical problems: Roche was convicted of illegal price fixing in 1999, and Shell was exposed for exaggerating petroleum reserves in 2004. Strong values and culture indeed.

It really shouldn't surprise us that outstanding companies experience some regression in performance. As companies grow, they find it more difficult to sustain the same percentage growth (witness the current troubles of some of America's most successful companies, including General Electric, Microsoft, and Wal-Mart). The fact that some *Visionary* companies fell back would not by itself invalidate the overall findings. But the sheer amount of decline, so quick and so extensive, suggests that there's more going on here than Collins and Porras would have us believe. More likely, the very things Collins and Porras claimed to be drivers of enduring performance—strong culture, commitment to excellence, and more—were attributions based on performance. As for the *Comparison* companies, the picture is a bit cloudier since some were privately held, others were subsequently acquired, and a few went out of business. Of the twelve we can track from 1991 to 1995, seven outperformed the market while five trailed; and after ten years, the split was six above the market and three below. For profit performance, eight of twelve improved their profitability while four declined. (See the appendix, tables 3A and 3B.) These figures are somewhat better than those for the *Visionary* companies, contrary to what Collins and Porras would have us believe but very much what we'd expect from regression to the mean—the highest-performing companies tend to regress more sharply. The differences that Collins and Porras found between *Visionary* and *Comparison* companies were more likely attributions based on performance that had already taken place, rather than differences that led to performance.

Delusion Five: *The Delusion of Rigorous Research*

Built to Last made a good effort to avoid the *Delusion of Connecting the Winning Dots* by including *Comparison* companies, but it didn't shake off the basic problem we encounter again and again: the Halo Effect. We can do our best to select samples of high performers and low performers, but if the data are colored by the Halo Effect, we'll never know what drives high or low performance; instead, we'll merely find out how high and low performers are described. Of course, we don't see how problematic the research really is, thanks to another delusion: the *Delusion of Rigorous Research*.

Early in the book, Collins and Porras spent ten pages describing their research method, recounting how methodically they collected their data, how many cartons they filled, and how tirelessly they worked to code the data. Later, Collins and Porras devoted more than fifty pages to three separate appendixes, in which they set out their findings in a number of tables and summaries. Throughout the book there were repeated references to the sheer amount of data gathered—hundreds of books and thousands of articles, a database so extensive that it filled entire bookshelves and required vast computer storage. The effect of all this was to present *Built to Last* as *Very Serious Research*, carefully designed and meticulously conducted. The message came through clearly: *We were thorough. We were exhaustive. We speak with authority.* It all serves to intimidate the reader, for if you haven't done an equal amount of work, you don't dare question the findings. No wonder the *Chicago Tribune* gushed about a revolution in understanding—the study was presented with all the trappings of careful science. Most readers, including reviewers at *The Wall Street Journal* and *Harvard Business Review,* as well as members of the general public, were taken in by the *Delusion of Rigorous Research.* But of course, the *quantity* of data is entirely beside the point if the data aren't of a good *quality.* If your data sources are corrupted by the Halo Effect, it doesn't matter how much you've gathered. You can stack Halos all the way to heaven, but you've still only got Halos.

Delusion Six: *The Delusion of Lasting Success*

There's another delusion at work in *Built to Last,* and it calls into question the very premise of the study—that of finding the keys to enduring greatness. When two-thirds of Peters and Waterman's *Excellent* companies faded within just a few years, we might have been tempted to explain it as just a hiccup, a fluke. These companies were, after all, the cream of American business—surely so many couldn't go sour so soon. But when more than half of Collins and Porras's *Visionary* companies failed to match the S&P 500 over the next five years, after collectively outperforming the market by a factor of 15 over more than sixty years, we should have raised a few eyebrows. Two studies in a row? That would seem to be quite a coincidence. But in fact it's the norm. Lasting business success, it turns out, is largely a delusion.

It's hard to see how unusual lasting success really is when we pick a handful of companies precisely because they've done well for many years, then look back over time to explain what happened. But suppose we shift perspectives and look at the performance of a large sample of companies over time. One study, by McKinsey director Richard Foster and consultant Sarah Kaplan, did just that. Foster and Kaplan cast their net into the river at a few points in time and looked at the fish they caught. The results were striking. Guess how many companies on the S&P 500 in 1957 were still on the S&P 500 in 1997, forty years later? Only 74. The other 426 were *gone*—nudged aside by other companies, or acquired, or bankrupt. And of the 74 survivors, guess how many outperformed the S&P 500 over that time period? Only 12 out of 74. The other 62 survived, yes, but they didn't thrive. Foster and Kaplan wrote: "The last several decades we have celebrated big corporate survivors, praising their 'excellence,' their longevity, their ability to last." But companies that last longest usually *aren't* the best performers. Enduring greatness is neither very likely, nor, when we find it, does it tend to be associated with high performance.

How can this be, especially after Collins and Porras told us their eighteen *Visionary* companies had far outperformed the S&P 500? Well, sure, if we look for companies that have performed well over several decades, we'll find a few—and then if we gather data retrospectively, we can weave together enough Halos to tell a wonderful story about why they did so well. But that's an exercise in ex post facto selection—the *Delusion of Connecting the Winning Dots* coupled with the Halo Effect. That's like Huck and Jim looking up into the heavens and picking out those few stars that form the exact shape they want to see. But that's no way to understand the business world. What's missing is the flux and the dynamism of performance, the ebb and flow. We can tell ourselves that our handful of companies, selected by a rigorous and objective process, are a breed apart, somehow better than the rest (and the more rigorous the selection process appears to be, the more we can persuade ourselves these companies are somehow really better than the rest). But it's a delusion. We're kidding ourselves. If we start with the *full* data set and look objectively at many years of company performance, we find the dominant pattern is not one of enduring performance at all, but one of rise and fall, of growth and decline. Foster and Kaplan conclude: "McKinsey's long-term studies of corporate birth, survival, and death in America clearly show that the corporate equivalent of El Dorado, the golden company that continually performs better than the markets, *has never existed*. It is a myth. Managing for survival, even among the best and most revered corporations, does not guarantee strong long-term performance for shareholders. In fact, just the opposite is true. In the long run, the markets always win" (Italics in the original).

Looking for those few golden companies that succeed decade after decade may be a delusion, but it's one that managers are eager to grasp. After all, showing how companies tend to rise and fall over time doesn't make for a very compelling story. We prefer to read about *Excellent* and *Visionary* companies; we want to know the secrets of their success so we can try to do likewise. We yearn to find out how we can avoid the seemingly inevitable fate of decline and death. It's a far more appealing story than the one suggested by the facts: that success is largely transitory and that most companies that have done well in the past won't outperform the average in the future.

Does this mean that all company performance is just a matter of luck? Is it roughly equivalent to someone who flips a coin and gets heads ten times in a row, but stands no greater chance to flip heads on the eleventh try than anyone else? Not at all. Success is not random—but it is fleeting. Why? Because as described by the great Austrian economist Joseph Schumpeter, the basic force at work in capitalism is that of competition through innovation—whether of new products, or new services, or new ways of doing business. Where most economists of his day assumed that companies competed by offering lower prices for similar goods and services, Schumpeter's 1942 book, *Capitalism, Socialism and Democracy,* described the forces of competition in terms of innovation. He wrote:

> The fundamental impulse that sets and keeps the capitalist engine in motion comes from the new consumers, goods, the new methods of production or transportation, the new markets, the new forms of industrial organization that capitalist enterprise creates.
>
> Every piece of business strategy acquires its true significance only against the background of that process and within the situation created by it. It must be seen in its role in the

perennial gale of creative destruction; it cannot be understood
irrespective of it or, in fact, on the hypothesis that there is a
perennial lull. . . .

As some companies innovate and find new ways of doing
things, other companies fail—but their demise plays a role in a larger
pattern of improvement and progress. The dominant pattern is not
stability or endurance, but the "perennial gale of creative destruction" that Schumpeter talks about. It's entirely normal and very predictable that companies fall back after outstanding performance.

Several researchers have studied the rate at which company performance changes over time. Pankaj Ghemawat at Harvard Business
School examined the return on investment (ROI) of a sample of 692
American companies over a ten-year period, from 1971 to 1980. He
put together one group of top performers, with an average ROI of
39 percent, and one group of low performers, with an average ROI
of just 3 percent. Then he tracked the two groups over time. What
would happen to their ROIs: Would the gap persist, would it grow,
or would it diminish? After nine years, both groups converged toward the middle, the top performers falling from 39 percent to 21
percent and the low performers rising from 3 percent to 18 percent.
The original gap of 36 percent had shrunk to just 3 percent, a de-
crease of nine-tenths. Now, as Ghemawat pointed out, a persistent
difference of 3 percent isn't zero—it's nothing to sneeze at. But the
main point is that high performance is difficult to maintain, and the
reason is simple: In a free market system, high profits tend to decline thanks to what one economist called "the erosive forces of imitation, competition, and expropriation." Rivals copy the leader's
winning ways, new companies enter the market, consulting companies spread best practices, and employees move from company to
company. Another study, by Anita McGahan at Boston University,
examined thousands of U.S. companies from 1981 to 1997 and
found a similar pattern. Companies were placed into one of three
categories based on their profit performance during the first three
years (measured as operating income to total assets)—high (the top

25 percent), medium (middle 50 percent), and low (bottom 25 percent). Then they were tracked over the next fourteen years. How much movement was there among groups? Of the high performance companies, 78 percent were still in the high group at the end of the study, while 18 percent dropped to medium, and 5 percent fell all the way to low. Of the medium performance companies, 81 percent were still medium at the end, while 10 percent improved to high and 8 percent fell to low. As for the low performance companies, 78 percent were still in the bottom group at the end, but 20 percent moved up to medium and 2 percent moved all the way to high. These findings show that performance is not random but persists over time, yet there is also a tendency to move toward the middle, a clear regression toward the mean.

These studies, and others like them, all point to the basic nature of competition in a market economy. Competitive advantage is hard to sustain. Sure, if you want to, you can look back over seventy years of business history and pick out a handful of companies that have endured, but that's selection based on outcomes. On the whole, if we look at the full population of companies over time, there's a strong tendency for extreme performance in one time period to be followed by less extreme performance in the next. To revise a well-known phrase, *Nothing recedes like success.* Suggesting that companies can follow a blueprint to lasting success may be appealing, but it's not supported by the evidence.

CHAPTER SEVEN

Delusions Piled High and Deep

We people in organizationland are fascinated with science, I think, because we seek to minimize the feeling that our world is governed not by laws of nature but by mad, impetuous barbarians driven by greed, need, and the desire for maximum power and booty. In such a cosmos the stately dance of physical science is reassuring.

Stanley Bing
"Quantum Business," *Fortune,* 2004

Innovation, observed Joseph Schumpeter, is the basic force that drives market competition in just about every industry—and that holds for the industry of writing business books, as well. The huge success of *In Search of Excellence* and *Built to Last* was bound to spawn new competitors eager to tap the market of managers looking for the path to high performance. These new entrants, according to Schumpeter, would try to go beyond the standard set by the first two blockbusters, to offer something different and better, to be even more thorough and authoritative. And that's exactly what happened. But for all their claims of rigor and scientific precision, these studies got no closer to explaining what really drives company performance—if anything, they repeated some of the delusions we've seen so far, and then offered a few more of their own.

One study, called the Evergreen Project, was directed by a McKinsey & Co partner, Bruce Roberson, working with William Joyce at Dartmouth's Tuck School of Business and Nitin Nohria at Harvard Business School. They began by repeating the most basic of all business questions: "Business is full of mysteries, but none greater than this: What really works?" Companies rise and fall, fads come and go, but "the great question remains unanswered, and not even well asked: What really works?" Well, the authors assured us, help was on the way: "It is time for the first book identifying fundamental practices that create business success—the ones that do indeed really matter." This book, they declared, was "the world's most systematic, large scale study of the practices that create business winners. Instead of anecdotal evidence of personal intuition, it is based on a massive research project conducted with scientific rigor and verified by measured fact." Strong words! And the authors went further. *In Search of Excellence* was inadequate because it selected its sample based on outcomes, looking only at excellent companies but not comparing them with lesser firms. *Built to Last* was flawed, too, because it examined a long time period in a single gulp but could not show how actions taken at one moment led to results at a later time. There was no longitudinal dimension, no ability to show temporal causality. This study would do better. The Evergreen Project picked a ten-year period, 1986 to 1996, and then divided it into two blocks of five years. The result wasn't two categories but four: Companies that performed well in both five-year blocks were called *Winners; Climbers* were so-so in the first five-year block but showed dramatic improvement in the second; *Tumblers* did well in the first block but fell back to earth in the second; and *Losers* did badly in both blocks, racking up ten straight years of bad performance. The idea was to show how actions in the first time period led to better or worse results in the second, to show the causal impact of management decisions. It was a good idea but could work only if the data weren't shaped by performance—the very thing they were trying to explain.

The Evergreen Project described itself as the most massive and most systematic study of company performance of all time. On the very first page, it was said to be "an extraordinary collaborative effort" of academicians and consultants, and listed by name fourteen professors at prominent business schools who had lent their expertise to the project. The suggestion was clear: *This was serious, thorough, rigorous research.* Furthermore, the methodology was said to be "appropriate, honest, and effective—in short, as reliable as many good minds could make it." But regrettably, this study was no better than its predecessors. For starters, the Evergreen team conducted interviews with managers, asking them to look back over the ten-year period and recount their experiences. These sorts of retrospective interviews are likely to be full of Halos, as people take cues from performance and make attributions accordingly. The Evergreen Project also collected large amounts of documents about the companies— "newspaper and magazine articles, business school cases, government filings, and analysts' reports." A stack of paper three inches deep was collected for each of the 160 companies, adding up to 60,000 documents that filled fifty storage boxes. A prodigious amount of data indeed, but from the same sources we've seen over and over, sources that are frequently colored by the Halo Effect. Next, fifteen Brigham Young University graduate students spent months coding and classifying the data. Too bad, because it doesn't matter how many students spend how many years coding this sort of data—you'll just have a stack of Halos, piled high and deep. The authors claimed the result was "the biggest such content analysis ever undertaken." It may have been the biggest, but it was hardly the best.

After they analyzed their data, the Evergreen team identified eight practices that were highly correlated with total shareholder return, their measure of company performance. The best-performing companies—the *Winners*—had very high scores in four practices— *strategy, execution, culture,* and *structure.* They also had high scores in two out of four additional practices—*talent, leadership, innovation,* and *mergers and partnerships.* Together this produced a "4+2 Formula." You can mix and match, the authors said: The first four and any two of the next four will *really* work. Joyce, Nohria, and Roberson wrote that "the link between 4+2 practices and business success was astonishing." They were right—the numbers are remarkable. Take a look:

Table 7. 1 The Evergreen Project: *Winners* and *Losers*
on Four Primary Practices

		Highly Positive	Highly Negative
Strategy: Devise and maintain a	*Winners*	82%	7%
clearly stated, focused strategy	*Losers*	9%	77%
Execution: Develop and maintain	*Winners*	81%	4%
flawless operational execution	*Losers*	14%	56%
Culture: Develop and maintain	*Winners*	78%	3%
a performance-oriented culture	*Losers*	17%	47%
Structure: Build and maintain a	*Winners*	78%	3%
fast, flexible, flat organization	*Losers*	14%	50%

Source: *What Really Works*, p. 19.

For the first practice, *strategy,* fully 82 percent of the *Winners* were rated "highly positive" while just 7 percent were "highly negative." By contrast, only 9 percent of the *Losers* were rated "highly positive" while 77 percent were "highly negative." (*Climbers* and *Tumblers* were not reported on this table.) Regarding *execution,* 81 percent of *Winners* were rated "highly positive" and only 4 percent "highly negative"; for *Losers* it was 14 percent "highly positive" and 56 percent "highly negative." The findings for *culture* and *structure* were almost as dramatic. And if a company was "highly positive" on all four? The Evergreen team concluded: "A company consistently following the formula had a better than 90% chance of being a *Winner.*"

Given the doubts we have about data validity, the interpretation of these findings is open to question. Take, for example, the assessment of corporate culture. The Evergreen Project wanted to

assess whether a company had "a work environment that is challenging, satisfying, and fun" and "inspired all to do their best," and
it found that *Winners* had high scores on both items. Well, it's no
surprise that high-performing companies were perceived to have a
challenging work environment and that they were thought to inspire people to do their best. The same would have been said about
Cisco at its peak, about ABB in its heyday, and about IBM during
its glory years. Or take execution capabilities. The Evergreen Project
wanted to evaluate whether a company "delivers products and services that consistently meet customers' expectations" and whether it
"constantly strives to improve productivity and eliminate all forms
of excess and waste." Again, it's no surprise that successful companies were said to have high-quality products and to improve productivity and eliminate waste—at least as long as they were
successful! But given the way these data were gathered, it's not clear
at all that the "4+2 Formula" led to performance. In fact, a very different interpretation is more likely. High-performing companies
were *said to have* a clearly stated, focused strategy. They were *perceived to have* a performance-oriented culture. They were *seen to be*
good at execution. They were *said to have* fast and flat organizations. Taken together, *Winners* had a more than 90 percent chance
of being described as highly positive on these four criteria. All of
which is a world away from saying, *If you do these things, you will be
successful.*

The results on table 7.1 suggest a further speculation. Take a
close look at the figures. While 7 percent of the *Winners* were said
not to have followed a "clearly stated, focused strategy," only 3 percent of *Winners* were said not to have a "performance-oriented culture," and only 3 percent were said not to have a "flat, flexible
organization." What explains the difference between 7 percent and
3 percent? My hunch is that it has to do with the amorphous nature
of "corporate culture" and "organization." Our impression of
whether a company has a "clearly stated, focused strategy" is shaped
to a large degree by its performance, yes, but our perceptions about
a company's culture and organization are *almost entirely* shaped by

what we know of its performance. In our everyday conversations, we have almost no ability to evaluate whether a company has a "performance-based culture" or a "fast, flexible, flat organization" without knowing something about its performance. The ways we describe, mythologize, and sometimes speak rhapsodically about company culture and organization are almost entirely the result of performance.

Delusion Seven: *The Delusion of Absolute Performance*

In addition to presenting tables of data, *What Really Works* painted vivid portraits of two companies, one *Winner* and one *Loser*. The *Winner*, Dollar General, sounded like many of the successful companies we've read about: It had a clearly stated and laser-focused strategy, deep concern about its customers, a great company culture, plus an effective organization and outstanding leadership. The *Loser*, Kmart, was a company that seemingly got it all wrong: The strategy kept changing, the culture was miserable, execution was weak, and the organization was in disarray. Kmart made a wonderful whipping boy—imagine getting all four elements wrong at once! Think of the stunning incompetence that must have been present in such a company!

What could be wrong with this thinking? Well, two things. First is the *Delusion of Single Explanations,* which we talked about in chapter 5. These four elements might not be separate and independent at all but are very likely linked. Remember ABB in 2000. One explanation for its downward spiral was that a questionable shift in strategy led to declining performance, which led to a change in the top manager, who promptly reorganized the company, which hurt morale, leading to even worse performance. We can think of a similar scenario for Kmart. Imagine that at some point, Kmart's ability to execute began to slip, perhaps because of sloppy inventory management or problems in supply chain efficiency. As performance faltered, employee morale sagged and the company culture worsened. Seeking to pull out of its slump, Kmart executives responded by shifting the strategy, which in turn required a different organization design. In such a scenario, these four elements aren't independent at all—one leads to another. There are plenty of others we could imagine: For example, an ill-advised organizational redesign could have led to inefficiencies in execution, which led to worsened performance and a decline in morale, which caused managers to embark on a new strategy, and so forth, around and around. The mistake, once again, is to imagine these various elements are separate rather than closely linked.

Second, and more important, the example of Kmart shows up a delusion that is implicit in many of the studies we've seen so far, one that's very basic but often overlooked—indeed, a 2005 *Harvard Business Review* article that compared several studies of company performance missed the point entirely. I call it the *Delusion of Absolute Performance*. Companies are often described as succeeding or failing on the merits of their actions alone, as if performance were absolute. But in a competitive market economy, the performance of one company is always affected by the performance of other companies. Part of the problem is that we often think in terms of images from laboratory scientific research. Put a beaker on a stove and you'll find that water boils at 100 degrees Celsius, a bit less at high altitude. Line up a hundred beakers on a hundred stoves and you'll still find that water boils at 100 degrees Celsius. One beaker isn't affected by any other. But that's not the way it is in business.

To show how company performance is intrinsically relative, I'll present some data about a major U.S.-based retailer, a well-known company with hundreds of stores nationwide. I've made an effort to include only things that seem objectively verifiable and not shaped by the Halo Effect. To disguise the identity of this company, I'll give it a fictitious name: "Qual-Mart." According to the report of an independent industry analyst, Alex. Brown & Sons, during the early 1990s, "Qual-Mart" did these things:

- Installed point-of-sale terminals in its stores, which provided better information on sales by item and improved the inventory planning process.

- Expanded central buying to 75 percent of its merchandise, helping to reduce the costs of procurement.

- Modernized its inventory management and thereby significantly improved its "in-stock position." One result: better management of seasonal inventory, boosting Christmas and Halloween sales by 60 percent.

- Conducted physical inventory counts more frequently, not just once at year-end, resulting in greater accuracy and efficiency.

- Reduced its expense levels as a percentage of sales.

- Improved its merchandise assortment to match current demand trends, helping to raise sales.

- Installed a toll-free customer service number, which led to a sharp improvement in customer satisfaction.

- Implemented a sophisticated client/server technology that led to better merchandise management and savings of $240 million.

Thanks to these many steps, "Qual-Mart" saw an improvement in inventory turns—that is, how many times in a year it sold its inventory, a key measure of retailing efficiently—from 3.45 in 1994 all the way to 4.56 in 2002. That's a jump of 32 percent, not bad at all.

Table 7.2 Inventory Turns at "Qual-Mart" 1994–2002

	1994	1995	1996	1997	1998	1999	2000	2001	2002
"Qual-Mart"	3.45	3.75	3.66	3.85	3.98	4.01	4.22	4.75	4.56

Source: *Thomson One Banker.*

Would you say "Qual-Mart" improved its performance? Of course you would—it got significantly better at a number of important things, each one measured objectively. So you might be surprised to learn that the company we're talking about is Kmart. That's right: Kmart, the Evergreen Project's *Loser* with a capital *L*, the poster child of mismanagement, the guys who supposedly got everything wrong. How can a company seem to do so many things better and still wind up in the bone yard? Because its rivals improved at an even faster rate. Over the same eight years, Wal-Mart's inventory turns went from 5.14 all the way to 8.08, up 63 percent. Wal-Mart had faster turns at the *start* of the eight-year period than Kmart had at the *end*. Kmart got better in absolute terms and yet fell further behind at the same time—and the gap between the two retailers was growing ever wider.

Table 7.3 Inventory Turns at Kmart and Wal-Mart, 1994–2002

	1994	1995	1996	1997	1998	1999	2000	2001	2002
Kmart	3.45	3.75	3.66	3.85	3.98	4.01	4.22	4.75	4.56
Wal-Mart	5.14	4.88	5.16	5.67	6.37	6.91	7.29	7.79	8.08

Source: *Thomson One Banker.*

As for other measures of performance, Alex. Brown & Sons noted that Kmart improved in "the key areas of expense ratio reduction, in-stock position, and visual presentation," but its major rivals also got better—in fact, much better. It went on: "Both Wal-Mart and Target, by our estimate, continue to enjoy significant advantages on the expense ratio front—allowing them to be quite assertive on price and to post still higher financial returns than Kmart." And that wasn't all. By the early 1990s, while Kmart raised the amount of centrally purchased inventory to 75 percent, Wal-Mart reached 80 percent. Kmart installed point-of-sale scanning in its stores by 1990, but Wal-Mart had done the same two years earlier. No wonder Kmart was scrambling. Its rivals were driving down costs and improving logistics at an even faster rate. By 2002—just as its inventory turns were reaching an all-time high!—Kmart hoisted the white flag and shuffled off to bankruptcy court. It's irresistible to infer that a bankrupt company must have been poor at execution, but the evidence doesn't support that view at all, at least not if we're talking about execution in an absolute sense.

The difference between absolute and relative performance can be seen at other companies as well. Consider General Motors, another company with slumping sales and a falling share price. In 2005, GM's debt was reduced to junk bond status, hardly a vote of confidence from financial markets. Yet compared with the automobiles it produced in the 1980s, GM's cars are much better in so many respects: better quality, additional features, superior comfort, and improved safety. Owing to a myriad of factors, its share of the U.S. market keeps slipping, from 35 percent in 1990 to 29 percent in 1999 to 25 percent in 2005, as Japanese and Korean automakers continue to gain share. GM's declining performance has to be understood in relative terms. In fact, the rigors of competition from Asian automakers are precisely what stimulated GM to improve. Is GM a better automaker than it was a generation ago? Sure, by absolute measures. But try telling that to its employees or shareholders.

The *Delusion of Absolute Performance* is hugely important because it suggests that companies can achieve high performance by following a simple formula, regardless of the actions of competitors. If left unchecked, managers may pay attention to a misleading set of issues. The Evergreen Project wasn't alone in this basic misconception—the same delusion was implicit in *Built to Last*, where Collins and Porras claimed that following a handful of steps provided a "blueprint for enduring success" without any mention of rivals or any appreciation of the dynamics of industry competition. Yet once we see that performance is relative, it becomes obvious that companies can never achieve success simply by following a given set of steps, no matter how well intended; their success will always be affected by what rivals do. The greater the number of rivals, and the easier for new competitors to enter the market, and the more rapidly technology changes, the more difficult it is to sustain success. That's an uncomfortable truth, because it admits that some elements of business performance are outside of our control. It's far more appealing to downplay the relative nature of performance or ignore it completely. Telling a company it can achieve high performance, regardless of what competitors do, makes for a more attractive story.

The Evergreen Project had a good idea to break the ten-year time period into two blocks of five years but was undone by the reliance on data from retrospective interviews and from articles in the business press. Yet these failings didn't prevent the authors from claiming they had broken new ground in our understanding of company success. In fact, they made a stronger claim of scientific rigor and causal impact than either *In Search of Excellence* or *Built to Last*. As they presented their findings, the authors declared: "We can now say that improving upon specific practices virtually guarantees a company's superior performance." But they showed nothing of the kind. The correct title shouldn't be *What Really Works*—the use of the present tense is misplaced. More accurate would be *What Really Worked*, or perhaps even *What Was Said About Companies When They Really Worked*.

The Grand Delusions of *Good to Great*

At the same time the Evergreen Project was under way, one of the authors of *Built to Last*, Jim Collins, embarked on a new study of company performance. Whereas *Built to Last* looked at companies that had been, for the most part, always successful (well, at least until the study ended), most companies tend to muddle along, doing reasonably well but never achieving great success. What could be said to them? Collins's next project addressed this point directly. How, he wondered, did ordinary companies make the shift to outstanding performance? Why did some companies make the leap from *Good to Great* while others didn't?

Collins and his team of researchers began with a large sample—all the companies on the *Fortune 500* between 1965 and 1995, 1,435 in all. To find those that had gone from mediocre to magnificent, they undertook what they described as a "death march of financial analysis." Their objective was to find those companies that fit a specific pattern: fifteen years of stock market returns near the general average, "punctuated by a transition point," then followed by fifteen years of stock market returns well above the average. This image is commonly known as a "hockey stick," a flat blade and an upward shaft. It's well-known in the business world, as in: "Things aren't so good today, but don't worry, we're going to do great things in the future." Everyone in the business world wants to deliver a hockey stick, whether to their boss or to their investors. Everyone wants to find the key to sudden and sustained improvement. Collins had his finger on a hot button.

Of all the companies they examined, just eleven fit the stringent profile—fewer than one in a hundred. Here's the list: Abbot, Circuit City, Fannie Mae, Gillette, Kimberly-Clark, Kroger, Nucor, Philip Morris, Pitney Bowes, Walgreen's, and Wells Fargo. Some of these companies were well-known to the general public, but many were not. They were hardly the glamor companies of the day but a plain Jane assortment from everyday industries like retail, steel, consumer products, and financial services. Their headquarters weren't in Silicon Valley or Princeton or New York City, but in ordinary American cities like Dayton, Ohio, and Neenah, Wisconsin. They hadn't been born great but had languished in mediocrity for years. Collins wrote: "At first, we were surprised by the list. Who would have thought that Fannie Mae would beat companies like GE and Coca-Cola. Or that Walgreen's could beat Intel. The surprising list—a dowdier group would be hard to find—taught us a key lesson up front. It is possible to turn good into great in the most unlikely of situations." And these eleven *Great* companies did indeed have a terrific record of performance. A single dollar invested in each of these companies in 1965, with all dividends reinvested, would have grown to $471 by the end of 2000, compared to $56 for the overall market. Next, as he had done in *Built to Last,* Collins identified a suitable comparison for each *Great* company, picking a good company in the same industry and active at about the same time. Gillette was matched with Warner-Lambert, Kimberly-Clark with Scott Paper, Wells Fargo with Bank of America, and so forth. The *Comparison* companies were good but hardly *Great*—a dollar invested in each of them in 1965 would have grown to $93, about twice the overall market but far less than the *Great* companies. In the years after the study, most of the eleven *Good to Great* companies, selected because they had outperformed the general market by a torrid three-to-one margin over fifteen years, regressed somewhat, but that's not grounds to criticize Collins's study. His goal was not to predict anything beyond fifteen years of rapid growth, but to explain why those fifteen terrific years took place at all—why these companies became *Great* while others did not. If he could explain that transition, what transpired after the end of the study really wouldn't matter.

To explain the transition from *Good* to *Great,* Collins and his team of researchers labored for nearly five years. They devoted more than 15,000 hours to the project. They looked at a wide range of evidence, "everything from acquisitions to executive compensation, from business strategy to corporate culture, from layoffs to leadership style, from financial ratios to management turnover." They read dozens of books, reviewed more than 6,000 articles, and conducted scores of interviews. The data filled many crates and entire cabinets, and totaled 384 million bytes. By now we're used to these descriptions of rigorous research, and we know not to be impressed—the quality of data is what's important, not the quantity.

As for data quality, some appear to be free of the Halo Effect.

Measures of top manager turnover, for example, or the presence of major institutional shareholding blocks, or the extent of board ownership, are all matters of public record and not likely to be shaped by perceptions, whether by journalists, company spokespeople, or the recollections of the managers themselves. But much of the data was problematic. A great deal came from magazine and newspaper articles, the same sources we've seen time and again, and which are steeped in Halos. There was no effort to ensure that the data were free of Halos—in fact, there was not even a recognition that these data sources were potentially flawed. As for the interviews with managers, among the questions asked were these:

> What do you see as the top five factors that contributed to or caused the upward shift in performance during the years [ten years before transition] to [ten years after transition]?

> What was the process by which the company made key decisions and developed key strategies during the transition era— not what decisions the company made, but how did it go about making them?

> How did the company get commitment and alignment with its decisions?

Interview questions of this nature, where managers are asked to look back and explain what happened, rarely produce valid data, since retrospective self-reporting is commonly biased by performance.

As for coding and analyzing the data, Collins described a series of discussions and debates among members of his research team. They followed "an iterative process of looping back and forth, developing ideas and testing them against the data, revising the ideas, building a framework, seeing it break under the weight of evidence, and rebuilding it again." Why did Collins take a seemingly less formal approach than he had followed in *Built to Last*? He explained:

"We all have a strength or two in life, and I suppose mine is the ability to take a lump of unorganized information, see patterns, and extract order from the mess—to go from chaos to concept." As for the patterns that Collins and his team found, the fifteen years of average performance were described as a Buildup phase, characterized by strong yet humble leadership (known as "Level Five Leadership"), getting the right people on board ("First Who . . . Then What"), and facing reality directly and courageously ("Confront the Brutal Facts"). Then, without fanfare, sometimes with barely a notice, a point of inflection led to a Breakthrough phase, with the once good company now soaring onward and upward in a self-reinforcing virtuous circle of greatness, ascending to the glory of the brightness at an angle of forty-five degrees, launched like a shot off a shovel. Breakthrough was about focus ("the Hedgehog Concept"), about execution ("Culture of Discipline"), and finally, about using technology to reinforce progress ("Technology Accelerators)." The transformation was complete, and *Good* was now *Great*.

As with earlier studies, the presence of Halos forces us to question these findings. Does having "humble leadership" and "great people" lead to success? Or is it more likely that successful companies are described as having excellent leadership, better people, more persistence, and greater courage? Given the way the data were gathered, and given the widespread tendency to make attributions based on performance, the latter seems more likely than the former. Collins claimed to explain why some companies made the leap while others didn't, but in fact he did nothing of the kind. *Good to Great* documented what was written and said about companies that had made the leap versus those that had not—which is completely different. At the start of his book, Collins urges his readers to be honest, to "confront the brutal facts." Well, here's a brutal fact we may wish to consider: If you start by selecting companies based on outcome, and then gather data by conducting retrospective interviews and collecting articles from the business press, you're not likely to discover what led some companies to become *Great*. You'll mainly catch the glow from the Halo Effect.

Yet no one seemed to look closely at these shortcomings, because *Good to Great* had such an encouraging message: *You, too, can transform your good company into a Great one.* Collins was explicit on this point. He wrote: "Greatness is not a matter of circumstance. Greatness, it turns out, is largely a matter of conscious choice." It's a compelling story. People want to believe their good efforts will be rewarded, that good things come to those who wait, and that's exactly what Collins was saying: With vision and humility, by caring about people, through persistence and focus, you can become *Great.* As a tale of inspiration, there's hardly a better one than *Good to Great.*

Delusion Eight: *The Delusion of the Wrong End of the Stick*

The reliance on flawed data in *Good to Great* raises serious questions about the validity of its findings. But even if we set aside those questions and accept the data, we have a further problem, this one about the *interpretation* of findings. One of the central images in *Good to Great* is the Hedgehog Concept, drawn from Isaiah Berlin's famous essay "The Hedgehog and the Fox." Berlin wrote that many people fall into one of two basic categories. Foxes know many things—they are fleet and cunning, and they pursue many aims. Hedgehogs know one big thing—they look to be slow and methodical, but they stay focused on a single unifying vision. And this distinction, wrote Collins, has everything to do with achieving high performance, because the eleven *Great* companies were all Hedgehogs. They had a narrow focus and pursued it with great discipline. Foxlike companies, by contrast, scattered their attention and energy, often changed directions, but never became *Great.* There is, of course, a possibility that our classification is shaped by the Halo Effect—when viewed in retrospect, successful companies may tend to be described as more focused and persistent than less successful companies. But let's suppose that Collins got it right and the eleven *Great* companies really were more focused on a narrow core vision than the *Comparison* group. What then? Does it follow that companies perform better when they behave like Hedgehogs? Not quite. The story is a bit more complicated.

To see why, consider a somewhat different example. Imagine that a thousand people spend the day betting at the racetrack, and at the end of the day we select the ten bettors with the highest winnings—we'll call them our *Great* bettors. When we look closely at these most successful bettors, we're likely to find that all of them placed big bets on long shots—that's how they came out ahead of the other 990. They were Hedgehogs, focusing on a few big things. Very few Foxes will be among the top ten, because Foxes tend to diversify their positions. Yet even if the top ten bettors were all Hedgehogs, it does *not* follow that Hedgehogs, on average, outperformed Foxes, because some Hedgehogs may have done very well but many more may have gone home broke. In fact, overall Foxes probably did better than Hedgehogs—they took more prudent risks and avoided big losses. Now let's come back to companies. Because Collins selected eleven *Great* companies and then compared them with eleven that were only *Good,* we have no way of knowing whether, on average, companies did better when they behaved like Foxes or like Hedgehogs. We don't know how many of the 1,435 companies in the full sample were Hedgehogs and how many were Foxes, so we can't say which group performed better. Even if companies that racked up several years of consecutive growth were Hedgehogs, it doesn't follow that being a Hedgehog increased the chances of success—because lots of Hedgehogs might have wound up as roadkill.

As a point of comparison, consider a study about expert political judgment by Philip Tetlock at the University of California. Using the same categories drawn from Isaiah Berlin, Tetlock compared the predictive accuracy of Hedgehogs, experts who have a clear and strongly held worldview, with that of Foxes, experts who take a more flexible view. Which group made more accurate predictions of future events? *The Foxes.* They factored in a wider range of information and modified their beliefs in the face of changing circumstances, and as a result were consistently more accurate in their judgments about future events than Hedgehogs. Tetlock found that a few Hedgehogs were extremely accurate in their judgments, but many more were considerably off the mark, and on average scored less well. (Tetlock's study, by the way, examined the accuracy of predictions over the course of fifteen years—this was not a study about a fifteen-year window that was conducted in retrospect and therefore prone to hindsight biases, but a study that was conducted from 1988 to 2003, over a fifteen-year period!)

My guess is that Tetlock's findings about individual predictive judgment are about right for companies, too: On average, companies that are resilient and can adjust to changing circumstances tend on average to outperform less flexible companies. Yes, a few Hedgehogs will turn out to be spectacularly successful, but Hedgehogs will also fail in large numbers. Which group does better is an empirical question that hasn't yet been the subject of careful study, and until we have solid answers we can only speculate. But until then, we're on shaky grounds if we infer that because a handful of extremely successful companies were Hedgehogs, it follows that companies ought to act like Hedgehogs, pursuing one big thing.

One might counter that a Hedgehoglike focus is a risky but necessary gamble when striving for *Greatness*. We know, after all, that performance is relative, not absolute. Perhaps it makes sense to follow a Hedgehog approach, because although the average result may be lower, the potential payoff of winning big is so much greater. That's a reasonable argument, and it could be correct. If that were Collins's point, fine. But Collins does *not* argue that companies ought to adopt a Hedgehog focus in spite of its inherent risks. He does *not* suggest that the payoff of hitting it big is so great that companies should accept a correspondingly higher risk of failure. Not at all. The overarching lesson of *Good to Great* is that any company can become *Great* if it is focused and persistent, that success is not a matter of circumstance, and that the Buildup phase inexorably leads to Breakthrough. Nowhere does *Good to Great* talk about the need to take calculated but sometimes considerable risks, to pursue a course of action that could lead to glory but even more likely lead to the gutter. Collins urges managers to be Hedgehogs by pointing out the upside while overlooking the attendant risks. Which is dangerous, because you can't have it both ways.

These errors aren't too surprising, given that Collins's understanding of the Fox-Hedgehog parable is questionable from the start. He suggests that people who have had the greatest impact on humanity—including Darwin, Marx, and Einstein—were Hedgehogs, consumed with a single and simple idea, then pursuing it with dogged focus. But Isaiah Berlin made no such claim, observing only that Foxes and Hedgehogs were two different ways of looking at human experience. There have been great people in both categories. According to Berlin, Plato was a Hedgehog but Aristotle a Fox; Dante a Hedgehog but Shakespeare a Fox; Dostoyevsky and Nietzsche were Hedgehogs while Goethe and Joyce were Foxes. Collins's assertion about Darwin is also doubtful: After all, Charles Darwin was raised as a conventional Christian and arrived at his revolutionary ideas about natural selection after decades of careful observation and reflection—challenging conventional dogma is not the sort of thing a Hedgehog normally does. It's not even clear that Marx was a Hedgehog, as his favorite epigram—*De omnibus disputandum* (Everything must be doubted)—has a distinctly Foxlike ring. Many so-called Marxists may be Hedgehogs, but of course that's a different matter.

Delusion Nine: *The Delusion of Organizational Physics*

The emphasis on certainty, on clear causal relations rather than contingency and uncertainty, illuminates one final misconception. It pervades many of the business bestsellers that offer steps to guaranteed success, but it's most clearly seen in *Good to Great*. In the opening pages, Jim Collins describes his ambition: to discover "timeless, universal answers that can be applied by any organization." He writes:

> While the practices of engineering continually evolve and change, the laws of physics remain relatively fixed. I like to think of our work as a search for timeless principles—the enduring physics of great organizations—that will remain true and relevant no matter how the world changes around us. Yes, the specific application will change (the engineering), but certain immutable laws of organized human performance (the physics) will endure.

The reference to physics is no accident. Of all the sciences, physics is the most elegant, the most sublime feat of pure intellect, the most able to reduce the workings of the universe to simple yet precise mathematical equations. As physicist-turned-finance-expert Emanuel Derman explains: "Theoretical physicists are accustomed to the success of mathematics in formulating the laws of the universe and elaborating their consequences. The universe does indeed seem to run like some splendid Swiss clockwork: We can predict the orbits of planets and the frequency of light emitted by atoms to eight or ten decimal places." The prestige of physics is such that lesser mortals in biology and chemistry are said to suffer from "physics envy." Comparing the study of business with the study of physics flatters both the writer and the reader.

If the business world really did run with clocklike precision, then perhaps the promise of *Good to Great* would be reasonable. We can predict the movements of the planets, so why not the performance of companies, too? Perhaps there really are universal principles of good management that can be applied by any company, at any time, in any industry. Small company or large? The laws of gravity surely apply to them all. Incumbent or challenger? The same principles govern their motion. Growing rapidly or steady in size? Companies are all made of the same atoms. It's an appealing image. In the words of *Fortune*'s resident wit, Stanley Bing, at the start of this chapter, we find the stately image of science to be reassuring. We like to believe that some cosmic order makes the business world a just and predictable place, ruled by precise laws. Yet as we saw in chapter 1, the most important questions in the business world don't lend themselves to the predictability or replicability of physics. They never have and never will, and for the reasons that Porras and Collins themselves admitted: We can't put companies in petri dishes and run neat experiments. And since even the best studies of business, ones that carefully follow stringent research methods, ones that make sure to avoid Halos and that control for rival variables and make sure not to confuse correlation with causality, can never achieve the precision and replicability of physics, then all the claims of having isolated immutable laws of organizational performance are unfounded.

CHAPTER EIGHT

Stories, Science, and the Schizophrenic Tour de Force

We are story-telling creatures, products of history ourselves. We are fascinated by trends, in part because they tell stories by the basic device of imparting directionality to time, in part because they so often supply a moral dimension to a sequence of events: a cause to bewail as something goes to pot, or to highlight as a rare beacon of hope. But our strong desire to identify trends often leads us to detect a directionality that doesn't exist, or to infer causes that cannot be sustained.

Stephen Jay Gould
Full House: The Spread of Excellence from Plato to Darwin, 1996

Start with *In Search of Excellence*, draw a line to *Built to Last*, link it to *What Really Works*, and then extend it all the way to *Good to Great*. What pattern do we see when we connect these dots?

Each successive study made a bolder set of claims—to have gathered more data, to have consulted more experts, to have been more exhaustive in its research and more thorough in its analysis than previous studies. Each one claimed to boldly go where no research had gone before, to do what had never been done, and to have a greater claim to the truth. By the time we get to the last two, there are grandiose claims about virtual guarantees of success and immutable laws of physics. The one that started it all, Peters and Waterman's *In Search of Excellence*, seems almost modest by contrast, a quaint throwback to a less pretentious age. But for all their claims of rigor and science, not one of these studies cracked the nut at the center of the puzzle. Not one of them recognized the central problem that robs them of validity—namely, that by relying on articles from the popular press, on business school case studies, and on retrospective interviews, their data were compromised by the Halo Effect.

Yet for all their similarities, these books fared rather differently in the marketplace. *In Search of Excellence* was a huge success, as was *Built to Last,* while *What Really Works* was only moderately successful. Why the difference? I suspect it's not because of analytical rigor, because none of these studies is likely to win a blue ribbon at your local high school science fair. Rather, *In Search of Excellence* and *Built to Last* were better *stories.* Their imagery was more compelling. Peters and Waterman gave us memorable phrases like *a bias for action, sticking to the knitting, managing by wandering around,* and *loose-tight coupling. Built to Last* talked about *big hairy audacious goals, clock building, the genius of the "and,"* and *cultlike cultures.* These were memorable phrases that sparked curiosity and stimulated discussion. By contrast, *What Really Works* relied on conventional terms like *strategy, execution, culture,* and *structure.* There was little original or engaging here, no surprising metaphors or captivating images. The fact is, whatever their shortcomings may have been as researchers, Tom Peters and Bob Waterman, and Jim Collins and Jerry Porras, shared one great strength: *They were terrific storytellers.* Because that's really what we have here: stories that help managers make sense of their world, that direct their actions, and that give them confidence in the future.

As for *Good to Great,* well, it was the best story of them all. Jim Collins's book was released with great fanfare in late 2001 and went straight to the top of the charts. Since then it has been a phenomenal success, spending years on the *New York Times* Best-Seller List. By 2005, sales had passed 3 million copies and were still going strong. It's not hard to see why. By its own description, *Good to Great* reads "as well as a fast-paced novel." It has engaging ideas, like Level-5 Leadership and the Stockdale Paradox. It offers intriguing metaphors like *rinsing cottage cheese.* It speaks of *Hedgehogs* and *Foxes.* It talks about *Flywheels* and *Doom Loops*—we can almost feel the momentum as companies surge upward to glory or spiral downward to their death. Jim Collins wrote that one of his skills was finding patterns in chaos, and he's right. In fact, *Good to Great* follows a form that's rooted in a classic narrative structure. In *The Seven Basic Plots,* British author Christopher Booker identified a handful of plots that recur in stories across cultures and eras. One of them goes by the name of *Rags to Riches.* Booker explained: "Few things have more consistently appealed to the fantasies of mankind than the dream of emerging from obscurity to fame and fortune. We see it in people's perennial dream of having their humdrum lives miraculously transformed by a lottery win, or conceiving some idea that will bring fabulous riches, or simply by being plucked out from the anonymous crowd to become the focus of attention or celebrity." The *Rags to Riches* story almost always involves a humble character, unremarkable in any way, who undergoes a series of adventures that brings about a miraculous transformation in fortunes. Examples go as far back as Joseph in the book of Genesis and include everything from the legend of King Arthur pulling the sword from the stone, to Aladdin and the magic lamp, to Cinderella and her glass slipper, and of course to Shaw's *Pygmalion.* Sound familiar? Start with a humble little firm, preferably in a dowdy industry, then show how it became one of the great performers of its day thanks to persistence and honest effort, and you've got the basic ingredients of *Good to Great.* Collins didn't have to look far to find a proven archetype that taps into our fondest hopes. Why, even the title *Good to Great* is an echo of *Rags to Riches.* No wonder the book has been such a hit—it speaks to a perennial dream and appeals to our deepest fantasies. None of which would matter much if the picture that Collins paints were accurate, if humility and persistence and focus do indeed lead to success with the predictability of physics. But that's not the case. And while most reviewers took Collins's work at face value—accepting its claims to be rigorous, scientific, and exhaustive—a few saw it for what it is: a trip to feel-good fantasyland. George Anders of *The Wall Street Journal* wrote that *Good to Great* offered a picture of the business world somewhere between Norman Rockwell and Mister Rogers—a simple and reassuring place of homespun values and old-fashioned virtues, where everyone feels safe and secure. In Mr.

Collins's neighborhood, the simple story with the positive message is paramount. And if that story could be made to look like rigorous science, well, it would be all the more convincing.

And the Hits Just Keep on Coming

The quest for the business Holy Grail didn't end with *Good to Great*. There was no reason to imagine that Jim Collins would kill the genre—quite the contrary, the huge success of *Good to Great* would likely lead to more books in the same vein, claiming to reveal the secrets of business success. The latest one to cross my desk, published in 2006, was called *Big Winners and Big Losers: The 4 Secrets of Long-Term Business Success and Failure*. The author? Alfred Marcus, professor of strategy and technology at the University of Minnesota. The publisher? Wharton School Publishing. Cover endorsements? Glowing praise from eminent business school professors at Dartmouth, Duke, Northwestern, and MIT. Why, it would be hard to imagine a book with better credentials.

I opened the book wondering if someone finally got it right—if at last someone had cast aside business delusions in favor of a more sensible view of company performance. But it didn't take long to see that there's not much different here. The title, which claims to reveal the secrets of long-term success, is hardly an auspicious beginning. After that, the book offers a review of previous studies, from Peters and Waterman, to Joyce, Nohria, and Roberson, and on to Jim Collins. According to Marcus, each of those studies contained a major flaw—each one erred by stressing the importance either of adaptability or of focus, but failed to show the importance of both at the same time. This study, he promises, will go a step better. It will show that the real secret to lasting success is the ability to be adaptable *and* focused—and at the same time.

Mercifully, there are no claims of having discovered the laws of organizational physics. But after that, it's déjà vu all over again. Again, there's a claim of rigorous research—thousands of companies studied carefully over ten years, 1992–2002. Once again, there's a sample of high performers and a sample of low performers, selected based on outcome. To study these companies, Marcus assigned students in his part-time executive MBA program to conduct analyses, then used his students' reports as his data. Now, there's nothing necessarily wrong with enlisting managers as researchers, provided their findings are based on valid data and of comparable quality. Managers aren't necessarily less capable researchers than graduate students or professors themselves—in fact, managers may be open to follow the facts where they find them and not shade their findings to support a preferred outcome. Rather, the question has to do with the quality of their data, and that's where the problem lies. What were the data for this study, said to be the product of rigorous analysis and careful detailed research? Most of it was based on the same flawed sources we've seen over and over—managers' ex post facto recollections, company statements, and articles from the business press. As for the "secrets of long-term success," Marcus found that *Big Winners* had discovered an attractive industry position—a *sweet spot*—and were well managed—they were *adaptive, disciplined,* and *focused.* The *Big Losers*? They were stuck in a *sour spot* and were *rigid, inept,* and *diffuse.* But as we know by now, a successful company can always be described as *disciplined* while the same company, in times of trouble, can be seen as *inept;* companies that change successfully can always be described as *adaptive* while those that don't will naturally be seen as *rigid.* Unless those terms are defined in ways that aren't shaped by performance, all we're doing is stacking Halos. We're collecting attributions about successful and unsuccessful companies but not identifying the drivers of success or failure. The effect, once again, is to tell managers that companies can succeed by following a simple formula, never mind what other companies do. Nowhere is there an appreciation of the relative nature of performance, of the need for managers to take calculated risks if they hope to outdo their rivals. The years of study may change, and the companies examined may be different, but the delusions remain the same.

Perhaps the most interesting finding in *Big Winners and Big*

Losers is mentioned as a brief aside but not examined closely: Marcus points out that large companies show up more frequently among the *Big Losers,* while almost all the *Big Winners* are small or midsize companies. This observation ought to spark one's curiosity, because large companies got that way in the first place by doing things well—they didn't grow by being *Losers*—yet something seemed to prevent them from maintaining that high performance. Did they abandon their winning ways? Did they suffer from hubris? Or did they continue to do largely the same things but, quite naturally, regressed to the mean as they got bigger, due mainly to the erosive effects of competitive pressures? Extreme performance, for better and for worse, is more common among small companies. One company, in particular, might have caught Marcus's eye. One of the *Losers,* a low performer for the ten-year period of 1992–2002, was Campbell Soup. Guess where Campbell Soup figured in *What Really Works,* the ten-year study by the Evergreen Project? For the years 1986–1996, it was listed among the *Winners,* having racked up strong performance in both five-year blocks. Did Campbell Soup so quickly change its winning ways—did it foolishly venture into new markets or change the formula for its famous tomato soup? Or was its performance eroded by market forces, improved competition, or changing customer tastes? What drove the lower performance of Campbell Soup isn't carefully explored; we're given only a collection of attributions based on its lower performance, with predictable results. Regrettably, for all its claims to be new and improved, this latest effort to crack the code of business success has many of the same flaws as its predecessors and comes no closer to offering a satisfying explanation of company performance.

Good Science, Bad Stories?

Of course, not all that's written about business and management works primarily at the level of storytelling. Many studies of company performance try hard to avoid the Halo Effect and other delusions. They're carefully designed and well executed. One such study, by Marianne Bertrand at the University of Chicago and Antoinette Schoar at MIT, investigated whether company performance was affected by the chief executive's personal managerial style. It's easy to find anecdotal evidence that CEOs of successful companies have effective personal styles—given the Halo Effect, that much is almost inevitable. But Bertrand and Schoar knew better than to gather cartons of magazine articles or to ask managers to rate the style of their chief executives—methods that would do little more than capture Halos. Instead, they defined "managerial style" in terms of two specific policies: *investment policies* (captured by levels of capital expenditures and administrative costs, and the frequency of mergers and acquisitions) and *financial policies* (captured by levels of debt and of dividends). These policies were objective and measurable, not ambiguous and hard to define. Next, they gathered data from audited financial statements so there could be little chance of a Halo Effect. As additional steps, they controlled for a number of other variables, and they also looked at the actions of specific managers over time, examining their tenure at more than one company. This was good, solid social science research. And the results? Bertrand and Schoar found that individual managers indeed have preferred personal styles when it comes to investment and financial policies, and that these preferences explain about 4 percent of the variance of company performance. In other words, after controlling for several other factors, the impact of a manager's personal style on company performance was about 4 percent. That's a statistically significant finding, but it's hardly a seductive story. You won't excite many managers by saying: *If you do these things, all else equal, you might improve company performance by about 4 percent.* But rigorous science doesn't always lead to a riveting story.

Here's a second example. Nick Bloom at the London School of Economics and Stephen Dorgan at McKinsey set out to test the association between specific management practices and company performance. It's similar to the question Peters and Waterman asked—*What leads to excellent performance?*—and it's also close to the Evergreen Project's question—*What really works?* But Bloom and Dorgan took a very different approach. Did they begin by selecting a list of high performers, then look backward to see what they had in common? No, they began by selecting a wide sample of more than 700 medium-size manufacturing companies in Europe and the United States, a mix of high performers and low performers. Did they ask respondents to evaluate things like corporate culture or management quality or customer orientation, all of which are likely to be shaped by performance? No, they asked managers to describe specific practices, wording their questions in such a way as to ensure the answers were not colored by the Halo Effect. To further improve the validity of their data, they used a "double blind" method of gathering and coding the data: Respondents were told only that the research was about practices, not that it was concerned with company performance; and the person who gathered the data did not know the performance of the company, removing a potential source of bias. Finally, since the study gathered data at a single point in time—it was cross-sectional, not longitudinal—the authors were careful to point out they had found correlation only, not causality. They even suggested that causality could run in the *opposite* direction—that is, high-performing companies might have the funds or resources to adopt certain management practices. They deliberately *understated* their findings. So after all that, what did Bloom and Dorgan find? Their study showed that specific management practices were indeed associated with differences in performance and explained about 10 percent of the total variance in firm performance. That is, a company that adopted the best practices across the boards—from manufacturing and customer service to human resource management and finance—tended to outperform a laggard company by about 10 percent. That's a statistically significant result, and it's a useful finding, but it falls far short of promising that a company that adopts a given set of management practices will be successful. It's good social science research—

careful, clear, and rigorous—but it doesn't claim to virtually guarantee anything.

Both of these studies, and plenty more like them, meet the test of good science, but they don't exactly sizzle as stories. In fact, if the hallmark of a story is to provide some guidance for action, they're really not stories at all. To say that 700 companies showed, on average, a 10 percent difference in performance doesn't say anything about what will happen at my company—the impact could be more or less or nothing at all. There's no guarantee, no promise that inspires me to take action. Is it any wonder that more attention is paid to books that claim to reveal the secrets of high performance? Those books provide simple and definitive advice, they help people make sense of a complex world, and they hold out the promise that humility and persistence lead to lasting success, that greatness beckons if only one is patient and determined. The result, according to James March and Robert Sutton of Stanford University, is that studies of organizational performance stand in two very different worlds. The first world speaks to practicing managers and rewards speculations about how to improve performance. Here we find studies whose main desire is to inspire and comfort. The second world demands and rewards adherence to rigorous standards of scholarship. Here, science is paramount, storytelling less so. March and Sutton explain: "In its efforts to satisfy these often conflicting demands, the organizational research community sometimes responds by saying that inferences about the causes of performance cannot be made from the data available, and simultaneously goes ahead to make such inference." The result is a "schizophrenic tour de force" in which "the demands of the roles of the consultant and teacher are disassociated from the demands of the role of the researcher." These two worlds operate on different logics, follow different sets of rules, and speak to audiences with different needs, but they rarely intersect.

Two separate worlds operating on their own logic would be complicated enough, but what's going on is even more troublesome than that. Stories about company performance appear to be all the more persuasive when they're dressed up to look like science, when they're said to be based on exhaustive research, backed up by cartons of documents and gigabytes of data, blessed by a roster of experts from well-known universities, and claiming to reveal underlying principles with the accuracy of science. We're back to the *Delusion of Rigorous Research*. The bestsellers we've reviewed spent considerable time discussing their methodology and data analysis, and reviewers and readers alike were hugely impressed by how extensive and exhaustive the research appeared to be. By now, of course, we know that the data were flawed and that explanations of improved performance were highly questionable. Yet the rewards for an appealing story, made all the more impressive by claiming to be science, are considerable. According to *The Economist,* Tom Peters can charge corporate clients up to $85,000 for a single appearance, and Jim Collins commands a fee of $150,000. There's a lucrative market for spinning stories of corporate success. Will anyone hire Bertrand and Schoar at $85,000 or $150,000 a pop to talk about a statistically significant 4 percent difference in performance? Somehow it seems doubtful.

Chapter 1 borrowed a line from a Frank Sinatra song: *"How little we know, how much to discover."* Yet if what's really vital is the ability to weave a compelling and inspiring tale, then perhaps scientific rigor isn't so important after all. Maybe the last lines of the song are the most revealing ones: *"How little it matters, how little we know."*

Satisfying Stories or Dangerous Delusions?

One might imagine that a way forward is to reject stories and insist on a purely scientific approach to business and management. But I'm not so sure. Stories will always be with us. They're an important part of life, providing coherent explanations of complex events. They help people act by conferring a moral dimension to events. By offering what Stephen Jay Gould called "a rare beacon of hope," stories can inspire people to action. Some of the people I've enjoyed quoting, like Gould and Richard Feynman, were scientists, professors at universities. They could take their time and refine their research, running additional experiments or gathering more data until they were satisfied with their answers. Managers, on the other hand, have to act. Endless debate about alternative courses of action can't be conducive to success when, as we know, performance is relative and companies that stand still are rarely successful. Another chief executive, Harry S. Truman, famously complained that he wanted one-armed advisers—he was tired of advisers who continually said, "on one hand . . . and on the other hand . . ." Executives have to act, which may be one reason the image of the Hedgehog, focusing on one thing rather than having to know many things, is so appealing.

The test of a good story is not whether it is entirely, fully, scientifically accurate—by definition it won't be. Rather, the test of a good story is whether it leads us toward valuable insights, if it inspires us toward helpful action, at least most of the time. By that yardstick, perhaps we should be more charitable about the popular business books we've reviewed here, because most return again and again to the same fundamentals. From Tom Peters through Jim Collins, the same themes are sounded: Companies do well when managers live by deeply held values, pursue a clear vision, care about their employees, focus on their customers, and strive for excellence. Surely it can't be such a bad thing if a manager navigates by those few basic principles, can it? Surely a dose of Norman Rockwell optimism can't be harmful, can it?

And truth be told, I find a lot of good in these basic principles. In the 1980s, I worked for six years at Hewlett-Packard, a company that was featured prominently in *In Search of Excellence* and *Built to Last*. Strongly shared values, empowered people, a culture of innovation—those were all bedrock principles at Hewlett-Packard, one of the most progressive and successful companies in American business history. Furthermore, the chief executive I've admired most in my career is David Packard—a wise and pragmatic man, direct and unpretentious, committed to his company but also willing to serve in government—indeed, an exemplar of what Jim Collins calls Level

Five Leadership. So overall, I'm sympathetic to much of what these bestsellers have to say. Most companies can benefit from their basic principles—and if the authors have been able to present them in a way that's accessible and vivid, so that millions of managers read these ideas and take them to heart, perhaps that's not such a bad thing.

Yet there's a bit more to it. Our desire to tell stories, to provide a coherent direction to events, may also cause us to see trends that do not exist or infer causes incorrectly. We may ignore facts because they don't fit into our story. (In *The Man Who Shot Liberty Valance*, John Ford's 1962 elegy to the passing of the Old West, the editor of the local newspaper, *The Shinbone Star*, decides not to print a story that would reveal who really shot the town villain. He explains: "This is the West, sir. When the legend becomes fact, print the legend!" Well, many of the studies we've looked at do just that: They print the legend, over and over, until we think it's the truth.) Therefore, we need to ask whether stories about company performance, although comforting and in many ways good, might also be harmful. Do they paint a simple picture when a more complex one would be more helpful? Because if *that's* the case, we should be careful not to be seduced, however pleasant they may seem. So is there reason to believe that the delusions we've encountered in the previous chapters can be harmful? I suspect the answer is *yes*. Here's why.

The Delusion of Lasting Success promises that building an enduring company is not only achievable but a worthwhile objective. Yet companies that have outperformed the market for long periods of time are not just rare, they are statistical artifacts that are observable only in retrospect. Companies that achieved lasting success may be best understood as having strung together many short-term successes. Pursuing a dream of enduring greatness may divert attention from the pressing need to win immediate battles.

The Delusion of Absolute Performance diverts our attention from the fact that success and failure always take place in a competitive environment. It may be comforting to believe that our success is entirely up to us, but as the example of Kmart demonstrated, a company can improve in absolute terms and still fall further behind in relative terms. Success in business means doing things better than rivals, not just doing things well. Believing that performance is absolute can cause us to take our eye off rivals and to avoid decisions that, while risky, may be essential for survival given the particular context of our industry and its competitive dynamics.

The Delusion of the Wrong End of the Stick lets us confuse causes and effects, actions and outcomes. We may look at a handful of extraordinarily successful companies and imagine that doing what they did can lead to success—when it might in fact lead mainly to higher volatility and a lower overall chance of success. Unless we start with the full population of companies and examine what they all did—and how they all fared—we have an incomplete and indeed biased set of information.

The Delusion of Organizational Physics implies that the business world offers predictable results, that it conforms to precise laws. It fuels a belief that a given set of actions can work in all settings and ignores the need to adapt to different conditions: intensity of competition, rate of growth, size of competitors, market concentration, regulation, global dispersion of activities, and much more. Claiming that one approach can work everywhere, at all times, for all companies, has a simplistic appeal but doesn't do justice to the complexities of business.

These points, taken together, expose the principal fiction at the heart of so many business books—that a company can choose to be great, that following a few key steps will predictably lead to greatness, that its success is entirely of its own making and not dependent on factors outside its control. We're not far off from self-help books that tell people they can be millionaires in five easy steps, or lose twenty pounds in two weeks, or awaken the power of greatness in them. Furthermore, if one accepts all of this, then the converse holds, too: If a company never becomes great, its managers must have failed somewhere along the line. They must have disregarded the right steps or wavered from the true path. If greatness is within our power to achieve, then failure to become great is our responsibility, too.

Lego, Redux

Which bring us back, once again, to Lego. Remember that in January 2004, after a dismal holiday season, Poul Plougmann was *sacked, ousted, removed,* and *dismissed*—and deservedly so, all the newspapers told us, because Lego's sales and profits had fallen sharply. The press explained that Lego had *strayed from the core,* which meant that Plougmann had blundered, which meant it was time for him to go. The real question isn't whether Lego had a bad year in 2003—we *know* that it did. The question we should ask is a different one: Did the company falter because of decisions taken by Plougmann or because of other factors? Of course, it's possible that he was an ineffective leader and that Lego would be better off without him. But it's also possible that Lego's situation was already grim, far above Poul Plougmann's poor powers to add or detract. Perhaps the company's problems had to do with choices made long before Plougmann arrived in 1999, as his predecessors repeatedly failed to break out of a doomed niche, in effect staying too long in a narrow core. If that were so, then firing the manager might be little more than a knee-jerk reaction, a simplistic response to hold someone accountable, but not a sound business decision. And Plougmann's successor, instructed to go back to basics, might find himself with an even tougher job as Lego tries to reverse course once again. If the company continues to flounder and the new executive is eventually *dismissed* or *canned* or *replaced,* one day someone will write that Lego, just like Kmart, made the classic errors: It shifted its strategy, it failed to execute, it had a slow culture, and it suffered from a cumbersome organization.

Just for the record, what happened to Lego after Poul Plougmann was fired? Lego's sales continued to decline, from 6.8 billion kroner in 2003 to 6.3 billion kroner in 2004. Operating losses continued for another year. Then a new chief executive turned his attention to cutting costs. In 2005, Lego sold its Legoland amusement parks and began to reduce its manufacturing activities in Denmark, Switzerland, and the United States, shifting capacity to low-cost countries in Eastern Europe and Asia. More than 1,200 jobs were lost, a 20 percent drop in employees. The result? By 2005, Lego was back in the black. However, this was mainly the outcome of a drastic and painful reduction in expenses, not because it had found a way to generate profitable growth in its core. Would Lego have done better or worse had Plougmann remained in charge? I can't say, and I'm not sure that anyone can. We can't turn back the clock, change one variable, and then run the experiment again. Assessing the performance of a chief executive doesn't easily lend itself to scientific experimentation. But my guess is that Lego's problems went well beyond the short tenure of any single executive. It's easy to blame one man for a company's woes, but these sorts of attributions, while appealing for their simplicity, may not provide the best basis on which to manage a company.

CHAPTER NINE

The Mother of All
Business Questions, *Take Two*

> The job of supposed intellectuals is to combat oversimplification or reductionism and to say, well, actually, it's more complicated than that. At least that's part of the job. However, you must have noticed how often certain complexities are introduced as a means of obfuscation. Here it becomes necessary to ply with glee the celebrated razor of old Occam, dispose of unnecessary assumptions, and proclaim that, actually, things are *less* complicated than they appear.

> Christopher Hitchens
> *Letters to a Young Contrarian*, 2001

Exposing delusions that cloud our thinking about company performance is essential for discerning managers, but it's not entirely satisfying, because it doesn't answer the mother of all business questions: *What leads to high performance?* In fact, it may seem as if we've been going backward. We may seem to know even less than we did at the start of this book. Does *employee satisfaction* lead to high performance? Probably, but it's hard to say how much, and it turns out the reverse effect is stronger: Company performance is a more important determinant of employee satisfaction. Well then, a strong *corporate culture* leads to high performance, right? Managers should strive to build strong values that are shared by all, shouldn't they? Perhaps, but just how much culture affects performance is hard to say, and once again the reverse effect may be greater, as successful companies are usually said to have strong cultures. What about *customer focus?* Isn't it vital for companies to be close to their customers? Yes, but if we're not careful, just about any high-performing company can be said to have good customer focus, and any company with sluggish sales or falling margins can be said to have lost its way with customers. *Leadership* isn't a more satisfying explanation, either, because we can always claim that successful companies have effective leaders, who seem to be endowed with clear vision and good communication skills; and we can always say that the leader of a failing company somehow lost the plot.

But all of this begs a deeper question: If so many of the things we observe are not drivers of performance but attributions based on performance, then what brought about high performance in the first place? We may agree with George Bernard Shaw that the difference between a lady and a flower girl isn't how she acts but how she's treated, but that doesn't explain how she came to be a lady to begin with. To say she was born into a wealthy family only pushes the question back a generation—how, we should want to know, did her family become wealthy while another did not? So we have to return to the question that started it all: *What leads to high performance?*

If we believe management gurus and consultants and many business school professors, high performance can be achieved with enough care and attention to a precise set of elements—these four factors or those six steps or these eight principles. Do those things, and success is just around the corner. But to paraphrase Christopher Hitchens, all the emphasis on steps and formulas may obscure a more simple truth. It may further the fiction that a specific set of steps will lead, predictably, to success. And if you never achieve greatness, well, the problem isn't with our formula—which was, after all, the product of rigorous research, of extensive data exhaustively analyzed—but with you and your failure to follow the formula. But in fact, the truth may be considerably simpler than these formulas suggest. They may divert our attention from a more powerful insight—that while we can do many things to improve our chances of success, at its core business performance retains a large measure of uncertainty. Business performance may actually be simpler than it is often made out to be, but may also be less certain and less amenable to engineering with predictable outcomes.

Here's the way I like to think about company performance. According to Michael Porter of Harvard Business School, company performance is driven by two things: *strategy* and *execution*. Strategy is about performing different activities from those of rival companies, or performing similar activities in different ways. A strategy is not a goal or an objective or a target. It's not a vision or mission or a statement of purpose. It's about being different from rivals in some important way. In turn, *execution* is all about carrying out those choices. It refers to the way that people, working together in an organizational setting, mobilize resources to deliver on the strategy. Building high-quality products, providing customer service, managing working capital, developing and deploying talent—these usually aren't matters of strategy because almost every company wants to do these things well. Rather, these things are the stuff of day-to-day management. They're all about effective operations. Explaining high performance in terms of just two things—strategy and execution— may at first raise our hopes. Just two items rather than some lengthy list! Surely managers ought to be able to get two things right! But a closer look shows that both are fraught with uncertainty, and makes plain why all the talk about blueprints and guarantees and immutable laws is a delusion.

Strategy : being different in an important way.

The Risky Business of Strategic Choice . . .

All companies face a handful of basic strategic choices. In what products and markets shall we compete? What activities shall we perform—and what shall we decide to leave to suppliers or partners? How shall we position ourselves against our rivals—shall we take a premium position, or shall we be known for low cost? These are choices in the sense that a company can't hope to be all things to all customers at all times, but has to choose to compete in *this* product line and not in *that* one; to enter *this* market and stay out of *that* one; to perform *these* activities but not *those;* and to position itself relative to competitors in *this* way but not *that* one. These sorts of choices aren't bland statements of aspiration, but fundamental decisions that set a company apart from its rivals. And choosing to be different implies risk.

You wouldn't appreciate the risky nature of strategic choice if you read most business books. For example, the Evergreen Project advised companies to "devise and maintain a clearly stated, focused strategy." The exact nature of that strategy wasn't important. If a company desires to grow, the authors explained, "it doesn't matter how you achieve this growth. You can do it by organic expansion, mergers and acquisitions, or a combination of both." They went on: "Whatever your strategy, whether it is low prices or innovative products, it will work if it is sharply defined, clearly communicated, and well understood by employees, customers, partners, and investors." Which is, of course, sheer nonsense. It may be true that if we pick a group of highly successful companies, we can find some that grew by organic expansion and others by acquisition, some that offered low prices and others that emphasized innovation, but it doesn't follow that one strategy is just as good as another provided it's well-defined and clearly communicated. All we've done is grab the wrong end of the stick. In a given market setting, some choices may be foolish, even suicidal. Try, for example, pursuing capacity expansion in an industry that already has overcapacity—that's rarely a wise move, and even the best communication and sharpest definition won't help. Likewise, *Good to Great* underplayed the risky nature of strategic choice. At the outset, Collins wrote: "We expected that good-to-great leaders would begin by setting a new vision and strategy." Instead, his team found that successful companies first assembled a team of great people, and a successful strategy followed. *Great* companies got "the right people on the bus, the wrong people off the bus, and the right people in the right seats—and then figured out where to drive it." That's the extent of attention paid to strategic choice in *Good to Great*. There's nothing about competitors or positioning or risk. Strategy isn't even a topic that's listed in the index.

Neither of these books recognized a central fact: Strategy always involves risk because we don't know for sure how our choices will turn out. There are several reasons why strategic deci-

making best decision — in advance of knowing.

sions are so uncertain. A first reason has to do with customers. Will customers embrace or reject a new product or service? How much will they be willing to pay? It's hard to tell for sure. Market research is often useful, and as we said with regard to Harrah's in chapter 1, some businesses lend themselves to scientific experimentation— they offer natural laboratories where variations can be tested in carefully controlled settings. But many major initiatives, like the launch of a new product or a new business model, don't easily lend themselves to experiments. There are, in fact, legendary examples where mountains of market research didn't help at all. Sam Phillips, the legendary Sun Records producer, once cautioned: "Any time you think you know what the public's going to want, that's when you know you're looking at a damn fool when you're looking in the mirror." Market reaction is always uncertain, and smart strategists know it.

A second source of risk has to do with competitors. Even if we can accurately predict what customers will do, we still have to contend with rivals, some of whom have made equally good predictions about customers and may pursue a similar set of choices—or may leapfrog us entirely with a revolutionary product or service. Predicting a rival's moves is hardly an exact science—especially when that rival is also trying to predict our behavior. An entire branch of economics, game theory, has grown up around a simple form of competitive intelligence that involves just two players, called the Prisoner's Dilemma. Expand the game to include multiple players, each with somewhat different resources and capabilities and risk preferences, and the complexity of the game grows in exponential leaps.

A third source of risk comes from technological change. Some industries are relatively stable, with products that don't change much and customer demand that remains steady for long periods of time. If you're Kellogg's and you sell cornflakes, you might be able to crank out a steady profit year after year. People still need to eat breakfast, no one has invented a much better cornflake, and you have a well-known brand, all of which may translate into steady revenues and profits (at least until generic cornflakes and private labels erode market share and margins or until large retailers squeeze our profits—nothing is forever, as Schumpeter would tell us). But in other industries, technology changes rapidly and strategic choices can come one after another with life-and-death consequences. In his groundbreaking research, Clayton Christensen at Harvard Business School showed that in a wide range of industries, from earth-moving equipment to disk drives to steel, successful companies were repeatedly dislodged by new technologies. They didn't fail because they were badly managed—the problem was more insidious than that. Rather, it was because they kept doing everything *right*—they focused on the needs of their customers and invested in new products that had a high likelihood of success—that they became vulnerable to new technologies. These so-called disruptive technologies at first didn't look attractive to established players—they didn't meet the needs of existing customers and didn't promise substantial sales—and therefore tended to be ignored, yet they improved over time and eventually displaced the existing technology, spelling disaster for market leaders. It is, after all, very hard to know which new technologies will lead nowhere and can be safely ignored, and which will transform the industry and pose a mortal threat.

Add together these three factors—uncertain customer demand, unpredictable competitors, and changing technology—and it becomes clear why strategic choice is inherently risky. And nowhere have the risks been higher than in high-technology industries. Remember in chapter 7 when Jim Collins expressed surprise that the eleven *Great* companies came from ordinary, unspectacular industries like consumer retailing, consumer products, financial services, and steel? He offered a powerful implication: *You don't have to be a glossy high-tech or biotech company to become Great. If these run-of-the-mill companies can become Great, well, then so can you!* But I suspect a different interpretation is more accurate. These industries can be described as *dowdy,* but a better word might be *stable.* They were less subject to radical changes in technology, were less susceptible to shifts in customer demand, and may have had less intense competi-

tion. All of which meant that companies in these industries had a
better chance of racking up consistent performance, year after year,
than did companies in more turbulent industries. High tech companies, by contrast, were much less likely to string together fifteen
years of high performance. Among the thirty-five darlings of corporate America featured in *In Search of Excellence* were several high-tech
companies: computer makers Amdahl, Data General, Digital Equipment, IBM, Hewlett-Packard, and Wang Labs, plus semiconductor
firms like Intel, National Semiconductor, and Texas Instruments. In
the ten years after the study ended, not one of them kept pace with
the overall market, as shown on table 1A in the appendix. *Not one.* It
makes a wonderful story to claim that anyone can become *Great,*
but the only companies that met Collins's criteria of fifteen years
above the market average happened to be active in consumer products like cigarettes and razor blades and toilet paper, or consumer retailing like drugstores, or financial services like retail banks and
mortgages. Collins remarked that companies can become *Great* even
in unlikely places, but a fresh look at the evidence suggests that he
got it backward. If the criterion is fifteen consecutive years of high
performance, it may be more accurate to say that *only* companies in
stable industries are likely to achieve *Greatness.*

A final source of risk comes not from all the things outside the
company—customers, rivals, and technologies—but from uncertainties surrounding internal capabilities. The fact is, managers can't tell
exactly how their company—with its particular people and skills and
experiences—will respond to a new course of action. Strategy professors describe this with the phrase "causal ambiguity," meaning that
the many and subtle interrelationships inside a company make it
hard to know exactly what will be the outcome of a given set of actions. Take all of these together, and the inherent riskiness of strategic choice is clear.

What should a manager do in the face of all this uncertainty? Is
it better to take a Foxlike view of the world and ceaselessly factor in
a wide range of information, making adjustments and shifting plans
accordingly? Or is better to pursue Hedgehoglike simplicity and

focus? The latter is certainly easier to explain to employees and easier for them to follow with confidence. And, according to some, it may also be more effective. Peters and Waterman spoke about the value of *sticking to the knitting;* the Evergreen Project emphasized the importance of a clearly stated, sharply focused strategy; and Collins's eleven *Great* companies were all said to have a Hedgehoglike focus. And they're not alone. In a study that I mentioned briefly in chapter 1, Chris Zook of Bain & Co looked at 1,854 companies over ten years and found that of those companies that had achieved high performance—defined as *sustained, profitable growth*—fully 78 percent had focused on one core business. The implication: Companies that focus on their core outperform those that do not. But let's be careful. It may be true that 78 percent of high-performing companies had a single core business, but it doesn't follow that having a single core improves your chances of success, because we don't know the proportion of companies in the total population that had one core versus those that had more. We need to make sure we grab the right end of the stick. The key question is not how many successful companies have a focused profile; rather, it's whether companies with a focused profile are more likely to be successful. A change in strategy might not be the *cause* of bad performance as much as the *result*, since companies normally stick with a winning formula. A more interesting question, which so far hasn't been answered, goes like this: What should a company do when its core comes under pressure? Will it improve its chances of success by becoming more Hedgehoglike, by redoubling its focus on a narrow core? Or will it benefit from Foxlike improvisation and adaptation? That's a tougher question, but it's one that managers face in their daily jobs. It's the question that Nokia faced in chapter 1 when its handsets came under pressure from new rivals, and it's also the question Lego faced as demand for traditional toys faltered. So far, there's little conclusive research on the subject, perhaps because the question cannot be answered by taking a long sweep of time and looking at overall patterns. The question has to be studied in a different way, isolating specific moments of decision and comparing the fortunes of companies that followed different paths. As of now, we have little in the way of persuasive answers to this question.

In the meantime, we're left with the brutal fact that strategic choice is hugely consequential for a company's performance yet also inherently risky. We may look at successful companies and applaud them for what seem, in retrospect, to have been brilliant decisions, but we forget that at the time those decisions were made, they were controversial and risky. McDonald's bet on franchising looks smart today, but in the 1950s it was a leap in the dark. Dell's strategy of selling direct now seems brilliant but was attempted only after multiple failures with conventional channels. Or, recalling companies we discussed in earlier chapters, remember Cisco's decision to assemble a full range of product offerings through acquisitions or ABB's bet on leading rationalization of the European power industry through consolidation and cost cutting. The managers who took those choices appraised a wide variety of factors and decided to be different from their rivals. We remember all of these decisions because they turned out well, but success was not inevitable. As James March of Stanford and Zur Shapira of New York University explained, "Post hoc reconstruction permits history to be told in such a way that 'chance,' either in the sense of genuinely probabilistic phenomena or in the sense of unexplained variation, is minimized as an explanation." But chance *does* play a role, and the difference between a brilliant visionary and a foolish gambler is usually inferred after the fact, an attribution based on outcomes. The fact is, strategic choices always involve risk. The task of strategic leadership is to gather appropriate information and evaluate it thoughtfully, then make choices that, while risky, provide the best chances for success in a competitive industry setting.

. . . And the Uncertainties of Execution

In recent years, increasing attention has been paid to the second pillar of company performance, execution. A few prominent business leaders have trumpeted its importance. In the view of Larry

Bossidy, former head of Honeywell and before that a senior executive at General Electric, execution isn't merely one of the important elements of company performance, but ranks right at the top. "Execution," he wrote, "is the great unaddressed issue in the business world today. Its absence is the single biggest obstacle to success and the cause of the disappointments that are mistakenly attributed to other causes. No strategy can deliver results unless it's converted into specific actions—and those specific actions are the stuff of execution." That might seem like good news, because if execution is not only very important, but also involves less uncertainty than strategic choice, then perhaps managers can make predictable improvements to company performance after all. And it is true that execution isn't as risky as strategic choice, and for an obvious reason. Strategic choice depends on customer preferences and the actions of competitors and the prospects of some new technology—all of which are in the messy world outside. By contrast, execution takes place entirely within the company. It happens on our premises, with our people, working together to achieve an agreed-upon strategy that we formulated. There are fewer unknowns.

Yet execution still involves a number of uncertainties. After all, an organization isn't a system of mechanical parts, interchangeable and replaceable. It's better understood as a *sociotechnical system,* a combination of men and machines, of people and things, of hardware and software, but also of ideas and attitudes. Some technical elements can often be copied and applied with predictable results. For example, manufacturing methods, production formulas, inventory management, and computer systems can often be shared across business units with similar effect. But when we begin to examine how those technical systems interact with social systems, with people and values and attitudes and expectations, the results are harder to predict. Take, as an example, human resources management practices. Mark Huselid and Brian Becker, authors of a study we read about in chapter 5, found that human resource management systems have an important impact on company performance and concluded that managers would be well-advised to identify leading HR practices and apply them to their company. But they warned that what works at one organization, with its people and norms and traditions, may not lead to the same result in another. The way human resource policies affect performance reflects an "idiosyncratic contingency." Effective execution remains uncertain.

"Idiosyncratic contingency" is a bit like "causal ambiguity"–it's how a PhD says *"I don't know."* But it's the truth. Despite our best efforts, the ways that people and processes work together in complex organizations are very hard to untangle and even harder to transplant elsewhere with the same results. Even if we set out with the best of intentions to improve operational effectiveness, we can never predict exactly how a given set of practices will shape a company's performance. Which helps explain why the explanatory power of the study by Nick Bloom and Stephen Dorgan, reviewed in the previous chapter, was rather modest. They found that adopting certain business practices could explain about 10 percent of the variance in company performance. Why not more than 10 percent? Because those same practices will lead to somewhat different results depending on a whole host of factors: an organization's people, their skills, their expectations, and the organizational context in which those practices are used. None of this suggests that some practices aren't, on balance, better than others, nor does it mean that they won't be generally useful for most companies much of the time. It means only that execution, like strategy, doesn't lend itself to predictable cause-and-effect relationships. Our best efforts to isolate and understand the inner workings of organizations will be moderately successful at best.

Given its importance as a contributor to company performance, it's good that execution has received a growing amount of attention. Countless books and articles now talk about the need to get things done. A phrase we hear over and over is "flawless execution." One of the four elements in *What Really Works* used exactly this term: Successful companies were said to "develop and maintain flawless operational execution." A recent book titled *Flawless Execution* claimed to offer companies a way to achieve peak performance and "win their battles of the business world." *Business Week* used the same phrase to describe the challenges facing Nissan in its battle with Toyota: "Nissan's execution must be flawless." All of this ought to be a good thing—not just to recognize the importance of operational effectiveness, but to set the target high, to talk about *flawless execution*.

Yet in my experience, good intentions about execution are often undermined by a few basic errors. Let me explain. Recently I attended a presentation by a senior executive of a well-known multinational company who spoke to forty of his managers from around the world. The company is a high performer, a leader in its industry, not a troubled firm. At the beginning of his talk, as he described the challenges facing the company, the executive said emphatically: "We have the right strategy. We just need to execute better." Everyone in the room nodded in agreement, and the discussion moved on, covering a wide range of topics over the next hour. What could be wrong with that? Only this: There are dozens of dimensions of execution, and the forty people in the room may well have been thinking about forty different things. When the session ended, they had no greater understanding of the most difficult challenges facing their company, nor were they any closer to agreement on specific actions that they should take—which made it unlikely that much would change for the better. Saying, "We need to execute better," is about as helpful as saying, "Let's all do a better job." It's just motherhood and apple pie.

Rather than merely state the importance of flawless execution— after all, who could be *against* flawless execution?—managers would do better to identify those few elements of execution that are most important to deliver on the chosen strategy. For one company, it could be the reduction of manufacturing cycle time. Or lowering defect levels. For another, it could be improving speed to market for new products. Or achieving higher levels of customer retention. Or improving the rate of on-time delivery. Of course, it's tempting to say that everything is important, but that's too easy. The key is to ask: For *our* company, at *this* time, competing against *our* rivals, which of the many dimensions of execution are *most* important? Which ones are most vital for *us* at *this* time? That's a tougher question, but it's necessary if we want to develop a shared sense of priorities. And it can be done. When Larry Bossidy was CEO of AlliedSignal, he didn't just talk about the importance of execution in a general way, he focused attention on four specific dimensions: accelerating new product development, improving the order-fill rate, superior inventory management, and better working capital management. It was a short list that everyone in the company could understand and everyone could focus on.

A second challenge is our old friend, the Halo Effect. If we're not careful, *any* successful company can be said to execute well, and *any* failure can be explained, after the fact, as a failure to execute. By now, we know how to avoid Halos—we have to rely on measures that aren't shaped by performance. We have to separate inputs from outcomes. For the last decade, Dell Inc. has been a leading example of great execution. While it's natural to look at Dell's success and make an attribution of outstanding execution, a closer look makes clear that Dell rigorously measured many aspects of its operations, from the speed of its build-to-order production process, to its ability to squeeze time out of every step of the production cycle, to its superior inventory turnover (more than eighty times per year!). Dell also collected money from its customers before it paid suppliers—meaning, in accounting terms, that it had negative days of working capital, a rather remarkable achievement. Dell didn't just talk about the importance of flawless execution, it focused on a number of key elements and then measured them with precision. And the results have been, objectively measured, superb.

There's another reason I question the value of broad pronouncements about *flawless execution*—which is that it can divert attention from *strategy*. Remember when all forty managers nodded in agreement at the importance of execution? Of course they did—who could disagree? But by putting the attention on execution, the topic of strategic choice was neatly sidestepped. This happens all the time.

When my old company, Hewlett-Packard, announced disappointing results in August 2004, CEO Carly Fiorina stated, "The strategy is the right one. What we failed to do is execute the strategy." Her explanation sounded reasonable, and no one questioned her when she swiftly replaced a few key executives—it looked like an appropriate step to improve execution and raise company performance. Curiously, when Fiorina herself was fired just six months later in February 2005, a company spokesperson repeated the same line: HP was following the right strategy, but the chief executive was replaced because the board of directors wanted better execution! Again, it all sounded reasonable, and no alarms were raised about the company's basic choices. Six weeks later, when Mark Hurd was hired as the new CEO, Hewlett-Packard stuck to its message, announcing that it had "picked Mr. Hurd because of his execution skills." And therein lies the problem: It's *always* easier to bang the drum about execution than to address fundamental questions of strategy. It's always easier to insist we're going in the right direction but just need to run a little faster; it's far more painful to admit that the direction may be flawed, because the remedies are much more consequential. On closer inspection, Hewlett-Packard was beset on all sides by strategic worries. It enjoyed a strong position in printing and imaging products, but in personal computers it was locked in a losing battle with Dell; in corporate computers it was squeezed between Dell and IBM; in corporate data storage systems it trailed EMC; its information technology services lagged behind IBM, Accenture, and EDS; and in consumer electronics, HP faced a range of tough competitors from Kodak to Sony. In fact, there were plenty of reasons to question HP's strategy, but doing so raised serious issues that had far-reaching consequences. Managers quite naturally find it easier to keep the attention on execution, which everyone will always agree can be done better. And not even Dell is exempt: When it announced disappointing quarterly results in mid-2005, CEO Kevin Rollins explained away the problems as an "execution issue." In fact, there were ample reasons to question Dell's strategic choices regarding target markets and competitive positioning, but those discussions invariably have more troubling implications. It's far simpler to point the finger at execution. Which leads to an observation: Whenever someone says, "We have the right strategy, we just need to execute better," I make sure to take an extra-close look at the *strategy.*

And that brings us to the best answer I can provide to the question *What leads to high performance?* If we set aside the usual suspects of leadership and culture and focus and so on—which are perhaps better understood as attributions based on performance rather than causes of performance—we're left with two broad categories: strategic choice and execution. The former is inherently risky since it's based on our best guesses about customers, about competitors, and technology, as well as about our internal capabilities. The latter is uncertain because practices that work well in one company may not have the same effect in another. In spite of our desire for simple steps, the reality of management is much more uncertain than we would often like to admit—and much more so than our comforting stories would have us believe. Wise managers know that business is about finding ways to improve the odds of success—but never imagine that success is certain. If a company makes strategic choices that are shrewd, works hard to operate effectively, and is favored by Lady Luck, it may put some distance between itself and its rivals, at least for a time. But even those profits will tend to erode over time. Success at one moment doesn't ensure success in the next moment, because success invites new challengers, some of them willing to take greater risks than the incumbents. All of which helps explain why, seductive stories notwithstanding, there's simply no formula that can guarantee success. As Tom Peters observed: "To be excellent, you have to be consistent. When you're consistent, you're vulnerable to attack. Yes, it's a paradox. Now deal with it."

CHAPTER TEN

Managing Without Coconut Headsets

Once you've internalized the concept that you can't prove anything in absolute terms, life becomes all the more about odds, chances, and trade-offs. In a world without provable truths, the only way to refine the probabilities that remain is through greater knowledge and understanding.

Robert E. Rubin
In an Uncertain World: Tough Choices from Wall Street to Washington, 2003

It's no wonder that managers, under pressure to deliver ever higher revenues and profits, are attracted to books that claim to reveal the secrets of success. Even some well-known business leaders occasionally look to bestsellers for help. In September 2005, *Business Week* wrote about Microsoft chief executive Steve Ballmer and his efforts to fend off challengers like Google and Yahoo!, to reinvigorate the company and return Microsoft to its former greatness. Among other things, Ballmer was said to have looked for inspiration to Jim Collins's *Good to Great.*

Now, Steve Ballmer is a smart fellow and I don't imagine he seriously thought that Collins's book held many answers for Microsoft. The problems facing the world's leading software company as it tries to maintain a dominant position in a highly dynamic industry, with challenges ranging from open-source software to a blizzard of online innovations with names like wikis and blogs and mash-ups, are light-years away from the problems that face midsize companies in consumer finance or retailing. But if Ballmer had tried to implement Collins's self-described immutable laws, he would have been disappointed: Since he became CEO, Microsoft's annual revenue growth fell from 36 percent to 8 percent and its stock price dropped by 40 percent. None of that should be very surprising. We know that high-performing companies usually fall back over time because of competitive forces. The core ideas in *Good to Great—have great people, stay focused,* and *be persistent—*are probably helpful for many companies in many circumstances, but there's no reason to believe they're sufficient to restore a mammoth software company to its glory days.

Unfortunately for Ballmer and every other manager, there's no magic formula, no way to crack the code, no genie in the bottle holding the secrets to success. The answer to the question *What really works?* is simple: *Nothing* really works, at least not all the time. That's not the nature of the business world. But that insight, however accurate, isn't of much comfort. Management is about taking action, about *doing things.* So what can be done? A first step is to set aside the delusions that color so much of our thinking about business performance. To recognize that stories of inspiration may give us comfort but have little more predictive power than a pair of coconut headsets on a tropical island. Instead, managers would do better to understand that business success is relative, not absolute, and that competitive advantage demands calculated risks. To accept that few companies achieve lasting success, and that those that do are perhaps best understood as having strung together several short-term successes rather than having consciously pursued enduring greatness. To admit that, as Tom Lester of the *Financial Times* so neatly put it, "the margin between success and failure is often very narrow, and never quite as distinct or as enduring as it appears at a distance." By extension, to recognize that good decisions don't always lead to favorable outcomes, that unfavorable outcomes are not always the result of mistakes, and therefore to resist the natural tendency to make attributions based solely on outcomes. And finally, to acknowledge that luck often plays a role in company success. Successful companies aren't "just lucky"—high performance is *not* purely random—but good fortune does play a role, and sometimes a pivotal one.

If all of this seems discouraging, it need not. The fact that business performance depends on so many things outside our control is no cause for despair. And fortunately, there are several good examples of managers who see the world clearly, accurately, without delusions. They don't write self-congratulatory accounts of their victorious careers or offer platitudes about authenticity and integrity and humility, as if those things—important though they may be—were sufficient to guarantee success. They don't cling to an idealized view of the business world. Rather, they are thoughtful managers who recognize that success comes about from a combination of shrewd judgment and hard work with a dose of good luck mixed in, and they're well aware that if the breaks of the game had gone just a bit differently, the results could have been vastly different. The executives we'll look at—Robert Rubin, Andy Grove, and Guerrino de Luca—have all been very successful, so it may seem that I'm selecting my sample based on outcomes, and to some extent that's true. We wouldn't know of them if they hadn't enjoyed some success. But I feature them here not for their successes—for the outcomes—but for the way they made decisions, for how they managed their companies, the way they made risky strategic choices with eyes wide open and then pushed for great execution. That sort of approach is an example to managers everywhere.

Robert Rubin and the Management of Probabilities

Robert Rubin is perhaps best known for his eight years in the Clinton administration, first as director of the White House National Economic Council and later as secretary of the Treasury. Before that, Rubin spent twenty-six years at the investment bank Goldman Sachs, eventually serving as co–senior partner. In his memoirs, Rubin described: "What has guided my career in both business and government is my fundamental view that nothing is provably certain. One corollary of this view is probabilistic decision making. Probabilistic thinking isn't just an intellectual construct for me, but a habit and discipline deeply rooted in my psyche." It was a view first developed in college, where he studied philosophy and learned never to take propositions at face value, but to approach what he read and heard with a skeptical mind. Rubin's thinking was further honed on Wall Street, where he saw there were no sure things, no formulas for success. Rather, "success came by evaluating all the information available to try to judge the odds of various outcomes and the possible gains and losses associated with each. My life on Wall Street was based on probabilistic decisions I made on a daily basis."

Many of Rubin's years at Goldman Sachs were spent in the field of risk arbitrage, which involves buying securities that are subject to a major event—a merger, for example, or a divestiture or a bankruptcy. It was highly complicated but also, if done well, highly profitable. Make the right bet and you come out far ahead. Make the wrong bet and *whoosh,* all gone. Risk arbitrage didn't lend itself to exact calculations but always involved a measure of risk. As Rubin recalled: "Flux and uncertainty made risk arbitrage quite nerveracking for some people. But somehow or other, I was able to take it in reasonable stride. Arbitrage suited me, not only temperamentally but as a way of thinking—a kind of mental discipline. . . . Risk arbitrage sometimes involved taking large losses, but if you did your analysis properly and didn't get swept up into the psychology of the herd, you could be successful. Intermittent losses—sometimes greatly in excess of your worst-case expectations—were a part of the business."

One memorable deal was the proposed 1967 acquisition by Becton Dickinson of a rival company in the medical products industry, Univis. Under the terms of the stock-swap merger, one share of Univis would rise from its current market price of $24 1/2 to about $33. When the deal was announced, Univis shares rose partway, from $24 1/2 to $30 1/2, reflecting the market's uncertainty about whether the deal would come to pass. That was the question Rubin's department had to answer. If Goldman Sachs believed the merger would succeed, it would buy Univis at $30 1/2 and enjoy the further rise to $33; but if it expected the deal to fall through, it might sell Univis short. After much calculation, Goldman Sachs bought shares in Univis. It stood to gain $125,000 if the merger went through, a tidy chunk of change in 1967. But some weeks later, a disappointing earnings report at Univis caused Becton Dickinson to withdraw its bid, and Goldman Sachs ended up losing $675,000—more than five times what it had hoped to gain. Naturally there was a fair amount of second-guessing and finger-pointing along the corridors of Goldman Sachs, a normal reaction since many people infer that a bad outcome is the result of a bad decision. But even though the result turned out badly, Rubin knew the decision hadn't necessarily been wrong. He explained: "Even a large and painful loss doesn't mean that we had misjudged anything. As with any actuarial business, the essence of arbitrage is that if you calculate the odds correctly, you will make money on the majority of deals and on the sum total of all your deals. If you take a six-to-one risk, you will lose money every seventh time. . . . To an outsider, our business might have looked like gambling. In fact, it was the opposite of gambling, or at least of most amateur gambling. It was an investment business built on careful analysis, disciplined judgments—often made under considerable pressure—and the law of averages." As a veteran of deal making at Goldman Sachs, Robert Rubin knew that roughly one deal out of seven was likely to go bad. He and his colleagues tried to improve their success rate, sure, but they knew from experience that one loss out of seven was likely—and acceptable. (If the loss rate went much lower, it might signal that Goldman was not taking enough risks—which would also be a serious problem. The optimal rate of failure wasn't zero, any more than the optimal number of defaults on banks loans is zero. Just make sure that one loss doesn't break the bank!) This view of the world is based on an appreciation of probability, not a search for certainty.

If even a large and painful loss doesn't necessarily mean a bad decision, then what does? To answer that question, we have to get beyond the Halo Effect. We have to take a close look at the decision process itself, setting aside the eventual outcome. Had the right information been gathered, or had some important data been overlooked? Were the assumptions reasonable, or had they been flawed? Were calculations accurate, or had there been errors? Had the full set of eventualities been identified and their impact estimated? Had Goldman Sachs's overall risk portfolio been properly considered? This sort of rigorous analysis, with outcomes separated from inputs, isn't natural to many people. It requires an extra mental step, judging actions on their merits rather than simply making ex post facto attributions, be they favorable or unfavorable. It may not be an easy task, but it's essential. Only with such a sober assessment could Goldman Sachs hope to learn from this episode and do better next time. For Robert Rubin, this sort of thinking was natural. His view of the world was based on probabilities and uncertainty. He wrote: "Some people I've encountered in life seem more certain about everything than I am about anything. That kind of certainty isn't just a personality trait I lack. It's an attitude that seems to me to misunderstand the very nature of reality—its complexity and ambiguity—and thereby to provide a rather poor basis for working through decisions in a way that is likely to lead to the best results."

Rubin's attitude, which showed a respect for complexity and ambiguity, coupling humility in good times with an insistence on learning from bad times, served him well not only at Goldman Sachs but also in government service, where he faced decisions that were just as uncertain and for which there were no easy formulas. On his first day as secretary of the Treasury—the very day in 1995 that he was sworn in—Rubin faced a critical decision related to the Mexican peso crisis. With Mexico facing imminent default, should the United States intervene and support Mexico or not? As he had with arbitrage decisions, Rubin thought through the different options. What were the risks of intervention—what signals would it send, what precedents would it establish? What were the risks of *not* intervening—would Mexico default, and if so, with what repercussions for the United States and the global monetary system? There were no formulas to follow, just careful judgment of options and probabilities and consequences, each one with approximate odds, jotted down on a mental yellow pad, and forming the basis for an eventual judgment—not taken with any assurance of certain success, but aimed at improving the chances for success to as great a degree as possible. Based on as much sound information as it could gather, the Clinton administration provided much-needed financial support for the Mexican peso—which helped stabilize the market and begin the process of economic recovery. It was not without substantial risks and was hardly guaranteed to succeed, but it was based on the same dispassionate thinking and assessment of probabilities that had helped Robert Rubin do so well over the course of his career.

Andy Grove and the Gamble of New Technologies

Risk arbitrage at Goldman Sachs involved many transactions, none of which was large enough to break the bank—at least not if risks were managed properly. But companies also face strategic decisions where the risks are not known and where one bad outcome cannot be offset against other favorable outcomes. There are no base rates to consult and few guidelines about the potential magnitude of gains or losses. Some companies face these sorts of decisions only occasionally, but others—especially in industries where technology changes rapidly—have to confront them with regularity.

One manager who has navigated this uncertainty as well as anyone is Andy Grove of Intel. Born Andraz Graf in Hungary, he survived both Hitler and Stalin before immigrating to the United States in the late 1950s, and never lost a deeply held sense that success was never assured, that failure could strike at any time. After studying chemical engineering at the University of California,

Grove went to work in the booming electronics industry. In 1968, he moved from Fairchild along with Gordon Moore and Robert Noyce to found Intel Corporation, a new semiconductor company. This was no dowdy industry. Semiconductor technology was advancing rapidly, with the capacity of chips doubling roughly every eighteen months, as Moore had famously observed.

In 1969, when Intel was just one year old and competing with tough, established players like Texas Instruments and Mostek, a major computer company called for proposals to build a new chip with a 64-bit memory. Intel was one of seven bidders, and after intense development efforts—working as if their life depended on it, Grove recalled—it came out on top. The 64-bit chip was a huge success for a young company, but there was no time for complacency. Rivals were aiming to build a chip with four times the memory, with 256 bits. Again, developing the new product was seen as a matter of life and death, and once again Intel met the challenge, coming up with the best design. And once again, rivals were busy at work, intent on developing the next generation beyond the 256-bit chip. To break clear of the pack, Intel decided to forgo the logical next step, a 512-bit device, and set its sights on leapfrogging its competitors with a chip that held 1,024 bits, four times the previous chip. That was a choice—a deliberate decision to do something very different but potentially beneficial. It was also very risky. It demanded Foxlike thinking: agility, a bit of cunning, sensing opportunities but also recognizing dangers. Recalled Andy Grove: "This required taking some big technological gambles." Once the decision was made, employees pulled together—engineers and technicians and manufacturing experts working under intense pressure to execute the strategy. And this time, Grove recalled: "We hit the jackpot. This device became a big hit." Note the words. Grove spoke about "gambles" and the need to "hit the jackpot." There was no talk about blueprints for enduring greatness or guaranteed success. Grove recognized the risks and uncertainties involved, and knew that Intel had to take bold chances that might let the company enjoy a temporary advantage, then leverage that advantage in new fields. It was a calculated gamble, but a gamble nonetheless.

The decision to press ahead with the 1,024-bit chip was one of many risky choices that Intel made over the years. As CEO, Grove continuously scanned the environment to learn of changes in technology and competitors and customers, gathering information that could be useful for Intel. He wrote: "Think of the change in your environment as a blip on the radar screen. You can't tell what the blip represents at first but you keep watching radar scan after radar scan, looking to see if the object is approaching, what its speed is and what shape it takes as it moves closer. Even if it lingers on your periphery, you still keep an eye on it because its speed and course may change." Grove's accounts of his years at Intel are full of instances where survival called for choices made under uncertainty. They weren't guaranteed to succeed—strategic bets never are. But as Robert Rubin said, you try to improve your chances of success by looking clearly and carefully at the odds, at your own capabilities, at the motives and abilities of your rivals, and make the best judgment you can, with the full knowledge that even the best decisions won't always turn out well, but that failing to take measured risks ensures that in a competitive marketplace you won't win. Yet once bets had been placed, Grove was also a believer in disciplined execution. He explained: "How can you hope to mobilize a large team of executives to pull together, accept new and different job assignments, work in an uncertain environment and work hard despite uncertainty in the future, if the leader of the company can't or won't articulate the shape of the [future]?" Now the Fox made way for the Hedgehog.

Building on its early successes, Intel became a powerhouse in the semiconductor industry during the 1970s and early 1980s, commanding a large share of the memory chip market. But by the mid-1980s, Intel was under attack again, this time from Japanese firms. Intel hadn't declined in any absolute sense but was slipping relative to its surging Japanese rivals. In 1985, Noyce and Grove made another gutsy call: to get out of memory chips entirely and shift the company into microprocessors, which were less cyclical and offered higher margins. It was hugely risky, but it paid off brilliantly. Over the next years, Intel's sales and profits soared, thanks in part to its partnership with Microsoft. Under Andy Grove's leadership, Intel maintained a dominant market share in microprocessors, releasing generation after generation of fast and powerful chips—the 286, 386, Pentium, and beyond.

Was Intel just lucky? I don't think so. Throughout these and other decisions, Grove knew that company performance is relative. It's not enough to do something well; you have to do it better than others—and that means you have to take chances. Grove's 1996 book, *Only the Paranoid Survive,* is a thoughtful primer for managers about strategic inflection points—moments of extreme risk when the company's life is at risk. He showed a keen understanding of industry dynamics, of changing technology, and of the necessity for making calculated bets. Grove had no delusions about following blueprints that claim to guarantee success. A willingness to take risks is essential—and not for the faint of heart. It's stimulated in part by a measure of fear. Grove commented:

> The quality guru W. Edwards Deming advocated stamping out fear in corporations. I have trouble with the simplemindedness of this dictum. The most important role of managers is to create an environment where people are passionately dedicated to winning in the marketplace. Fear plays a major role in creating and maintaining such passion. Fear of competition, fear of bankruptcy, fear of being wrong and fear of losing all can be powerful motivators.

Business bestsellers don't normally talk about fear. Fear has no place in the rosy world of rags to riches or in the cozy confines of *Mister Rogers' Neighborhood,* where good always triumphs and a handful of simple rules are said to lead predictably to success, regardless of what anyone else does. Fear doesn't make a comforting bedtime story. But by now, we know that this sort of simpleminded confidence is based on delusions and not likely to lead to the best results.

I'm not alone in my admiration for Andy Grove. In 2004, he was named the most influential CEO of the previous twenty-five years by the Wharton School. Jeffrey Garten, former dean of the Yale School of Management, went a step further, calling Grove "a superb model for future generations of CEOs." Why the accolades? Not just because of Intel's superb results—other companies have done as well if we rely on measures of stock performance—but because of Grove's ability to respond to change, to rebound from crises. Garten wrote that Grove's genius was to align strategy and execution even as forces of globalization were causing massive shifts in the business environment. He made calculated strategic choices, never overlooking the huge risks involved. As for execution, Grove allowed his managers room for initiative, but "he was brutal in demanding that they measure their performance every step of the way." He demanded that his managers think for themselves, not accept bromides because others say they happen to be true. More recently, Grove has been the subject of a full-length biography by Richard Tedlow of Harvard Business School, who called his subject "the best model we have for leading a business in the 21st century," not because Grove followed a blueprint for long-term success and followed it with the tenacity of a Hedgehog, but because he was vigilant about changes to the competitive landscape and adapted to new circumstances—technological, competitive, regulatory, and consumer. As Tedlow wrote: "Grove has escaped natural selection by doing the evolving himself. Forcibly adapting himself to a succession of new realities, he has left a trail of discarded assumptions in his wake."

Even as Intel prospered in the 1990s, Grove never took success for granted, never lost his Hungarian refugee's apprehension about the risk of imminent failure. He worked closely with Clayton Christensen of Harvard Business School in an effort to avoid the trauma of disruptive technologies. He also collaborated with Robert Burgelman of Stanford Business School, whose 2002 book, *Strategy Is Destiny*, detailed Intel's strategy-making process. If any company has shown the industry awareness, the management savvy, the track record of innovation, and the combination of deep talent as well as deep pockets, it would be Intel. *The New York Times* observed: "For two decades, Intel has been the most sure-footed of Silicon Valley companies." In 2005, it was the seventh largest American company in market capitalization, worth more than $180 billion, and ranked eighteenth in profits.

So for all of that, was Intel assured of continuing success? Not at all. Like every successful company, Intel struggled to find new avenues for profitable growth. A competitor, AMD, made important inroads into Intel's dominance in microprocessors, and the market for personal computers was slowing down. Intel's early efforts to expand into new markets hadn't been successful. Its entry into the digital television market had sputtered. It had also been slow to recognize a shift in the chip market away from an emphasis on speed and toward the integration of microprocessors with other technologies. In 2005, the *Financial Times* reported: "Intel's confidence, built on its dominance of the PC market, where its chips are inside four out of five machines sold, has been shaken over the past year."

What was needed to improve performance? Strategic choice, of course—which always involves risk. In 2006, new CEO Paul Otellini announced that Intel would move well beyond its traditional core of microprocessors and toward a new emphasis on chips and software, combining them into platforms aimed at a variety of fields—from the laptop to the living room to wireless applications. Along with this shift came a redesign of Intel's brand and new company tagline—Leap Ahead. It was a bold redirection, a break from the past, and to some observers seemed almost a repudiation of the course steered by Andy Grove. So how did Grove react? Did he denounce Intel's new approach as an example of *straying from the core?* Quite the contrary. At a meeting of top Intel managers, Grove signaled his strong approval, proclaiming Intel's new direction as "one of the best manifestations incorporating Intel values of risk taking, discipline, and results orientation I have ever seen here." Was success assured? Hardly—Intel's new strategic thrust was fraught with risk. But once again, Intel was forced to reinvent itself or accept declining growth and shrinking margins. Smart companies assess their options and do their best to raise the probabilities of success, but even then their fortunes are *still* uncertain, and the wisest managers, like Andy Grove, know it.

A Look at Logitech

For a last example, we'll look at a company that doesn't have a famous CEO or a thirty-five-year record of success. Logitech is one of the world's leading producers of computer interface devices—mice, keyboards, peripherals, speakers, and more. It was founded in Switzerland and is now headquartered in Fremont, California, with design and manufacturing operations in Europe, North America, and Asia. In a tough market with very intense competition, some of it coming from Microsoft—and now, perhaps Intel as well—Logitech has done very well. From 1999 through 2005, sales tripled and profits grew by even more.

How can we explain Logitech's success? It's appealing to say that Logitech has great people, and by any objective measure it probably does, but we know that it's easy to say favorable things about a company's employees as long as it's successful. We might also guess that Logitech has a great corporate culture, and if we asked Logitech employees, they would probably say that it does, but that's not an adequate explanation, either. Successful companies are usually said to have great cultures—because employees like to play on a winning team and feel confident about their future. As for customer orientation, that's an easy one, too, because Logitech's rapid sales growth must mean that customers like their products (like the cordless mouse I'm using right now). We might also claim that Logitech is successful because it has followed a focused strategy, and it's true that Logitech has focused on a fairly narrow range of products, but we can debate whether Logitech has been successful because of its focus or whether it has remained focused because of its success. And let's not forget leadership. We can always find reasons to infer that a rapidly growing and profitable company has a brilliant leader. We can always find evidence of a CEO's strong vision, ability to inspire, and personal integrity. But by now we know more. Success is relative, never absolute. Competitors imitate and advantages erode. Even good decisions sometimes turn out badly—which doesn't mean they were mistakes or blunders. The practices that work at one company won't have quite the same effect at another. So how should we explain Logitech's success?

In 2005, I attended a talk by Logitech's president and CEO, Guerrino de Luca. A native of Italy, de Luca has lengthy U.S. experience, serving for many years as a senior marketing manager for Apple Computer. I was curious: Would he try to explain Logitech's success in terms of great people and strong values and employee morale? In fact, de Luca described Logitech's success—and its challenges—explicitly in terms of strategy and execution, and did not shy away from addressing the intrinsic uncertainty of each. First he reviewed the conscious strategic choices that Logitech had made. It focused on a single segment: products that provide the interface between people and technology. Within that segment, it emphasized design, functionality, and technology. It cared about the user experience—and wanted to build products that people love to use and were proud to show friends. Logitech explicitly avoided commodity products—"The minute you think your product is a commodity, it will be," warned de Luca. And while Logitech refused to compete on price, it deliberately maintained affordable price points so that people could make buying decisions without lengthy consultation. Recognizing the speed of technological change, Logitech also aggressively replaced its own products. De Luca pointed out that Logitech had repeatedly "killed the golden goose that brought eggs more quickly than the market would have." It also refrained from pursuing new products that didn't seem to offer a chance for competitive advantage. De Luca noted: "You have to choose your playing field very carefully, and be the best there. We've said 'no' many, many times to opportunities that seemed obvious, to markets that grew fast. The reason why we said no? Either because we could not differentiate, or we felt we could not be a reasonably sized fish in those markets." This was an ever vigilant manager, scanning the competitive environment and making choices accordingly. Logitech's emphasis on innovation called for massive spending on research and product development, which de Luca described as "a fundamental choice that we make consciously." Did these choices involve risk? Yes. You read the marketplace, you study the competition, you examine trends, you look at your skills and capabilities—and you make a bet. Was Logitech, to use Andy Grove's phrase, a bit "paranoid"? Absolutely. In this industry, given the intensity of competition and rapidity of change, it had to be.

De Luca also emphasized the importance of execution. Once strategic choices were made, the focus shifted to getting things done. "We learned many times," he said, "modestly defined strategies have given dramatic success through great execution." But de Luca didn't just invoke the word "execution," he identified key elements that were most important for his company to succeed in its competitive environment. One was new product development, conducted through explicit methods and processes. Another was supply chain management, which used distribution centers in North America and Europe. Logitech also invested heavily in state-of-the-art manufacturing sites, recently opening a new facility in China. Yet for all of its attention to strategy and execution, de Luca also recognized that success is never guaranteed. There was, he said, a concerted effort at Logitech to avoid arrogance and complacency: "We force ourselves to try to avoid the syndrome of 'If it ain't broke, don't fix it.' We are constantly making changes to the way we run our business. We make changes to our organization. We make changes to our system. Resistance to change in successful companies is very high, and yet we have to drive that change." Did Logitech's CEO think he was following a blueprint for enduring success? No. But he made thoughtful decisions about strategic choices—deciding what *not* to do as much as what to do—followed up with disciplined execution based on clear priorities and explicit measures.

And Last

Will Logitech always thrive? Probably not. The brutal nature of market competition means that for Logitech, and for just about every other company, getting to the top is hard—it's a mix of shrewd strategy, superb execution, and good luck. Staying at the top is even harder, because success attracts imitators, some of which are willing to take risks that appear foolish to incumbents—but a few of which may turn out spectacularly well, even disrupting established players. Sooner or later, the forces of competition, coupled with technological change, will erode Logitech's position. And when its performance falters, whether in two years or twenty, it's inevitable that someone will say the company blundered or that the chief executive blew it. Monday morning quarterbacks will say that Logitech should have done more of this or less of that, that it erred by straying from the core, or perhaps that it failed by staying too long in its core. Decisions that turned out badly will be castigated as bad decisions. There will always be a temptation to tell a neat story that makes everything sensible and logical and that suggests why the deserving succeeded while the wicked or arrogant failed.

There will always be, as well, books that try to discover the elements that separate the best companies from the rest of the pack and that advise managers on what they might do to lead their companies to loftier heights, to join the ranks of the great, the winners, the outstanding successes. Some of these books will be good, some not. Managers will continue to read them, eager to learn any new insights, hoping to discover new things they can apply. That's not only inevitable, that's healthy.

The central idea in this book has been that our thinking about business is shaped by a number of delusions. My hope is that managers will read business books a bit more critically, free from delusions, their deepest fantasies and fondest hopes tempered by a bit of realism. I would hope in particular that managers would remember:

- If independent variables aren't measured independently, we may find ourselves standing hip-deep in Halos.

- If the data are full of Halos, it doesn't matter how much we've gathered or how sophisticated our analysis appears to be.

- Success rarely lasts as long as we'd like—for the most part, long-term success is a delusion based on selection after the fact.

- Company performance is relative, not absolute. A company can get better and fall further behind at the same time.

- It may be true that many successful companies bet on long shots, but betting on long shots does not often lead to success.

- Anyone who claims to have found *laws of business physics* either understands little about business, or little about physics, or both.

- Searching for the secrets of success reveals little about the world of business but speaks volumes about the searchers—their aspirations and their desire for certainty.

Once we've swept away these delusions, what then? When it comes to managing a company for high performance, a wise manager knows:

- Any good strategy involves risk. If you think your strategy is foolproof, the fool may well be you.

- Execution, too, is uncertain—what works in one company with one workforce may have different results elsewhere.

- Chance often plays a greater role than we think, or than successful managers usually like to admit.

- The link between inputs and outcomes is tenuous. Bad outcomes don't always mean that managers made mistakes; and good outcomes don't always mean they acted brilliantly.

- But when the die is cast, the best managers act as if chance is irrelevant—persistence and tenacity are everything.

Will all of this guarantee success? Of course not. But I suspect it will improve your chances of success, which is a more sensible goal to pursue. And you won't find yourself on the shore of a tropical island, wondering why, despite all your earnest efforts to follow the formula of success, the cargo planes still haven't landed.

Appendix

The tables on these next pages support the analysis of financial performance of companies profiled in *In Search of Excellence* and *Built to Last*, as discussed in chapter 6.

Table 1A

This table shows the total shareholder return (change in stock price with all dividends reinvested, all values shown in percent) of thirty-five *Excellent* companies for five years and ten years after the end of Peters and Waterman's study. The Standard & Poor's 500 market index grew by 99.47 percent from 1980 to 1984 and by 403.40 percent from 1980 to 1989. The growth of each company is stated for each time period and indicated with a "+" if greater than the S&P 500 and with a "–" if less than the S&P 500. In all, twelve companies surpassed the S&P 500 from 1980 to 1984 while twenty-three trailed the market; for 1980 to 1989, thirteen companies did better than the market average, while eighteen did less well.

Total Shareholder Return of Thirty-five *Excellent* Companies
1980–1984 and 1980–1989
(All Values in Percentage)

		1980–1984		1980–1989	
	S&P 500	99.47%		403.40%	
1	3M	99.06	–	380.79	–
2	Allen-Bradley	206.89	+	460.36	+
3	Amdahl	11.38	–	149.76	–
4	Avon Products	–15.35	–	95.32	–

		1980–1984		1980–1989	
5	Bristol-Meyers	235.09	+	750.96	+
6	Caterpillar Tractor	−29.62	−	40.61	−
7	Chesebrough-Pond's	94.47	−		
8	Dana	104.46	+	225.68	−
9	Data General ·	114.12	+		
10	Digital Equipment	60.80	−	138.11	−
11	Dow Chemical	15.92	−	438.65	+
12	Dupont	66.79	−	408.84	+
13	Eastman Kodak	90.70	−	203.55	−
14	Emerson Electric	141.69	+	478.65	+
15	Flour	−34.76	−	72.64	−
16	Frito-Lay (PepsiCo)	114.06	+	967.85	+
17	Hewlett-Packard	135.08	+	237.46	−
18	Hughes Aircraft	−39.80	−		
19	IBM	141.02	+	119.70	−
20	Intel	65.93	−	206.68	−
21	Johnson & Johnson	56.45	−	476.32	+
22	Kmart	83.99	−	227.08	−
23	Levi Strauss	−11.39	−		
24	Maytag	156.85	+	459.34	+
25	McDonald's	189.85	+	822.66	+
26	Merck	53.57	−	750.88	+
27	National Semiconductor	54.33	−	−5.78	−
28	Procter & Gamble	95.17	−	474.78	+
29	Raychem	1.81	−	91.94	−
30	Schlumberger	0.27	−	52.10	−
31	Standard Oil (Indiana)	74.75	−	368.07	−
32	Texas Instruments	48.91	−	45.74	−
33	Wal-Mart	800.28	+	4269.51	+
34	Walt Disney	46.90	−	1038.73	+
35	Wang Laboratories	213.97	+	−34.2	−

Above S&P 500	12	13
Below S&P 500	23	18

Source: Compustat

Table 1B

This table compares the profit performance (operating income as a percent of total assets) of thirty-five *Excellent* companies in the five years before the end of Peters and Waterman's study, 1975–1979, with the five years after the study ended. Thirty of the thirty-five companies declined in profitability after the study ended, consistent with the idea that companies selected on the basis of high performance will tend to regress in subsequent times. Only five companies—Allen-Bradley, Hewlett-Packard, IBM, McDonald's, and Wal-Mart—increased their profitability.

Profit Performance of Thirty-five *Excellent* Companies
1975–1979 and 1980–1984
(All Values in Percent)

		1975–1979	1980–1984	
1	3M	21.9 %	21.0 %	–
2	Allen-Bradley	9.3	10.3	+
3	Amdahl	21.2	5.7	–
4	Avon Products	33.8	20.4	–
5	Bristol-Meyers	21.6	21.2	–
6	Caterpillar Tractor	18.1	3.2	–
7	Chesebrough-Pond's	20.7	19.5	–
8	Dana	18.2	11.6	–
9	Data General	20.6	9.4	–
10	Digital Equipment	14.9	11.9	–
11	Dow Chemical	14.5	6.5	–
12	DuPont	14.0	13.8	–
13	Eastman Kodak	21.6	16.9	–
14	Emerson Electric	24.1	22.8	–
15	Flour	16.1	7.3	–
16	Frito-Lay (PepsiCo)	16.6	14.8	–
17	Hewlett-Packard	18.8	19.4	+
18	Hughes Aircraft	17.5	10.6	–
19	IBM	23.4	23.7	+
20	Intel	29.8	10.1	–
21	Johnson & Johnson	20.1	17.4	–
22	Kmart	16.2	9.7	–

		1975–1979	1980–1984	
23	Levi Strauss	29.4	20.0	–
24	Maytag	37.3	27.5	–
25	McDonald's	17.8	18.1	+
26	Merck	24.4	18.5	–
27	National Semiconductor	16.1	5.0	–
28	Procter & Gamble	18.3	17.4	–
29	Raychem	15.0	13.2	–
30	Schlumberger	23.2	20.2	–
31	Standard Oil (Indiana)	19.4	15.8	–
32	Texas Instruments	15.4	8.4	–
33	Wal-Mart	18.4	19.8	+
34	Walt Disney	15.7	10.0	–
35	Wang Laboratories	15.3	13.8	–

Increase	5
Decrease	30

Source: Compustat

Table 2A

This table shows the total shareholder return (change in stock price with all dividends reinvested, in percent) of seventeen *Visionary* companies for five years and ten years after the end of Collins and Porras's study. (Note: Collins and Porras's study ended at year end 1990, so the subsequent period of study begins January 1991; by contrast, Peters and Waterman's study ended year end 1979, so the subsequent period begins January 1980.) The Standard & Poor's 500 market index grew by 115.44 percent from 1991 to 1995 and by 399.78 percent from 1991 to 2000. Eight companies surpassed the S&P 500 from 1991 to 1995 while nine trailed the market; for 1991 to 2000, six companies did better than the market average while ten did less well.

Market Performance of Seventeen *Visionary* Companies, 1991–1995 and 1991–2000
(All Values in Percent)

		1991–1995		1991–2000	
	S&P 500	115.44%		399.78%	
1	3M	82.32	–	290.10	–
2	American Express	168.03	+	1027.59	+
3	Boeing	92.96	–	245.81	–
4	Citicorp	480.49	+		
5	Ford	167.66	+	611.18	+
6	General Electric	76.61	–	152.42	–
7	Hewlett-Packard	456.53	+	884.07	+
8	IBM	–4.95	–	266.39	–
9	Johnson & Johnson	163.71	+	593.59	+
10	Merck	149.37	+	675.95	+
11	Motorola	352.69	+	399.69	–
12	Nordstrom	91.10	–	82.12	–
13	Philip Morris	114.53	–	302.09	–
14	Procter & Gamble	114.28	–	338.25	–
15	Sony	65.26	–	283.58	–
16	Wal-Mart	51.11	–	643.67	+
17	Walt Disney	139.46	+	264.76	–
	Above S&P 500	8		6	
	Below S&P 500	9		10	

Source: Compustat

Table 2B

This table compares the profit performance (operating income as a percent of total assets) of seventeen *Visionary* companies in the five years before the end of Collins and Porras's study with the five years after the study ended. Five of the *Visionary* companies increased their profitability while eleven declined and one was unchanged.

Profit Performance of Seventeen *Visionary* Companies
1986–1990 and 1991–1995
(All Values in Percent)

		1986–1990	1991–1995	
1	3M	20.3	16.9	–
2	American Express	5.0	1.5	–
3	Boeing	5.2	8.3	+
4	Citicorp	2.5	3.8	+
5	Ford	9.7	5.3	–
6	General Electric	6.3	3.7	–
7	Hewlett-Packard	12.6	12.2	–
8	IBM	12.5	5.5	–
9	Johnson & Johnson	19.4	19.4	unch
10	Merck	28.2	24.5	–
11	Motorola	9.3	11.4	+
12	Nordstrom	15.4	13.1	–
13	Philip Morris	17.4	18.6	+
14	Procter & Gamble	11.8	13.3	+
15	Sony	5.1	3.1	–
16	Wal-Mart	20.1	13.4	–
17	Walt Disney	16.6	13.1	–

Increase	5
Decrease	11

Source: Compustat.

Table 3A

This table, similar to table 2A, shows the total shareholder return (change in stock price with all dividends reinvested, in percent), but for the *Comparison* companies in Collins and Porras's study. Fewer companies are included here than for the *Visionary* companies, as some were privately held and others were acquired, making a direct comparison between the two groups difficult. Nevertheless, the data show that seven *Comparison* companies surpassed the S&P 500 from 1991 to 1995 while five trailed the market; for 1991 to 2000, six did better than the market average while three did less well.

Market Performance of Thirteen *Comparison* Companies
1991–1995 and 1991–2000
(All Values in Percent)

		1991–1995		1991–2000	
	S&P 500	115.44 %		399.78 %	
1	Wells Fargo	269.00	+	1288.97	+
2	McDonnell Douglas	683.86	+		
3	Chase Manhattan	630.98	+		
4	General Motors	76.61	–	152.41	–
5	Westinghouse	–32.41	–	148.94	–
6	Texas Instruments	192.22	+	2112.43	+
7	Burroughs/Unisys	120.00	+	485.00	+
8	Bristol Meyers	57.63	–	500.09	+
9	Pfizer	250.94	+	1521.54	+
10	Zenith	3.77	–		
11	Melville	–12.43	–	310.21	–
12	Colgate Palmolive	115.65	+	755.90	+

Above S&P 500	7	6
Below S&P 500	5	3

Source: Compustat

Table 3B

This table, similar to table 2B, compares the profit performance (operating income as a percent of total assets) of twelve *Comparison* companies in the five years before the end of Collins and Porras's study with the five years after the study ended. All values are in percents. The data show that eight of the companies increased their profitability in the five years after the study ended while four showed a decline in performance.

Profit Performance of Twelve *Comparison* Companies
(All Values in Percent)

		1986–1990	1991–1995	
1	Wells Fargo	2.1	3.0	+
2	McDonnell Douglas	5.1	8.2	+
3	Chase Manhattan	1.3	1.7	+
4	General Motors	5.3	4.1	−
5	Westinghouse	9.1	5.9	−
6	Texas Instruments	4.5	9.6	+
7	Burroughs/Unisys	4.4	6.2	+
8	Bristol Meyers	22.8	26.2	+
9	Pfizer	13.6	16.6	+
10	Zenith	−0.8	−7.4	−
11	Melville	21.6	13.1	−
12	Colgate Palmolive	11.3	14.5	+

Increase	8
Decrease	4

Source: Compustat

Notes

Preface

xvi   Herbert Simon's Travel Theorem is from Simon, Herbert A., *Models of My Life*, New York: Basic Books, 1991, pp. 306–307.

xviii   "If they'd explain that this is their best guess." Feynman, Richard P., *The Pleasure of Finding Things Out: The Best Short Works of Richard P. Feynman*, London: Penguin Books, 1999, p. 195.

Chapter One

1   "How Little We Know (How Little It Matters)." Words by Carolyn Leigh, music by Philip Springer, © 1956, Edwin H. Morris & Company. © Renewed 1984, EMI Carwin Catalog Inc. and Tamir Music. All rights reserved. Used by permission.

1   "the attractive potential of our core products." Clare MacCarthy, "Deputy Chief Sacked as Lego Tries to Rebuild," *Financial Times*, January 9, 2004, p. 25.

3   Zook, Chris, with James Allen, *Profit from the Core: Growth Strategy in an Era of Turbulence*, Boston: Harvard Business School Press, 2001, p. 74.

5   Hjelt, Paola, "The World's Most Admired Companies," *Fortune*, March 14, 2005, pp. 41–45; Coggan, Philip, "World's Most Respected Companies," *Financial Times, Special Report*, November 18, 2005.

6   All quotes about what Lego might do come from Doonar, Joanna, "Brand MOT: Lego," *Brand Strategy*, February 10, 2004.

7   I came across this anecdote about Ted Williams many years ago but have been unable to trace the exact source. The likely focus of Ted's discontent was Joe Cronin, manager of the Red Sox

from 1935 to 1947. In a 2000 article titled "Pitching in the Big Leagues the Underhand Way," by Jim Sargent, former Red Sox pitcher Eldon Auker wrote: "Every time I walked on the pitcher's mound to pitch a ball game, [Cronin] spent most of his time out on the mound telling me how to pitch. He'd say, 'Don't give him anything good to hit, but don't walk him.'" Anyone with the exact source of Williams's comment can contact a grateful author at phil@the-halo-effect.com.

7   The quotes about Mattel and its troubles with Barbie come from Moore, Angela, "Mattel Earns Rise, but Barbie Sales Snag," Reuters, July 19, 2004.

8   "made itself vulnerable to competition." Clark, Nicola, "Fraying Brand Image at Britain's WH Smith," *International Herald Tribune,* April 26, 2004, p. 9.

9   "even complex wireless systems for corporations." Andy Reinhardt, "Can Nokia Get the Wow Back?," *Business Week,* May 31, 2004, pp.18–21.

11   Wal-Mart's power as a censor of social taste was seen in November 2004, when it refused to carry George Carlin's book *When Will Jesus Bring the Pork Chops?,* claiming it would not be of interest to Wal-Mart customers. The book opened at number two on the *New York Times* Best-Seller List and sold millions. A highly irreverent book? Yes. Profane? Sure. But not of interest to Wal-Mart's millions of customers? Unlikely.

11   "so much as *rationalizing* beings" is from Eliot Aronson, *The Social Animal,* 5th ed., New York: W. H. Freeman & Company, 1988, p. 119.

12   The two quotes from Richard Feynman, "questions which can be put into the form: *If I do this, what will happen?*" and "put together a large amount of information from such experiences," come from Feynman, 1999, p. 255.

13   "Scientific progress owes a great deal to the careful and incremental refinement of experiments." Physicist John R. Platt wrote that scientific progress is most rapid when a certain method of reasoning is followed, "an accumulative method of inductive inference that is so effective that I think it should be given the name of 'strong inference.'" The core of strong inference is a four-step process of devising alternative hypotheses; designing experiments with alternative possible outcomes that can exclude one or more of the hypotheses; conducting the experiments; and repeating the process with newly refined hypotheses. Platt, John R., "Strong Inference," *Science* 146, no. 3642 (October 1964): 16.

13   The passage about Harrah's comes from Loveman, Gary, "Dia-

monds in the Data Mine," *Harvard Business Review,* May 2003, pp. 109–113.

14 "business schools are professional schools–or should be." Bennis, Warren, and James O'Toole, "How Business Schools Lost Their Way," *Harvard Business Review,* May 2005.

16 "better described as *pseudoscience.*" John Platt, using similar terminology, wrote that the results of these efforts are "not science, but faith; not theory, but theology." See Platt, 1964.

16 Feynman's anecdote about Cargo Cult Science is from Feynman, 1999, p. 209.

Chapter Two

19 Market capitalization values from "Fortune 500 Largest U.S. Corporations," *Fortune,* April 18, 2005.

20 "five hundred yards away at the computer science lab." Waters, John K., *John Chambers and the Cisco Way: Navigating Through Volatility,* New York: John Wiley & Sons, 2002.

21 "And all they do is smile, smile, smile." Flower, Joe, "The Cisco Mantra," *Wired* 5.03, March 1997.

22 "and Intel is to computer chips." Reinhardt, Andy, and Peter Burrows, "Crunch Time for the High Tech Whiz," *Business Week,* April 28, 1997, p. 80.

22 "lightning quick acquisitions." Schlender, Brent, "Computing's Next Superpower," *Fortune,* May 12, 1997, pp. 64–71.

22 "a massive 80 percent share of the high-end router market." Quick, Rebecca, "Tiny Dogs and a Dream: Beating Cisco," *Wall Street Journal,* June 4, 1998.

22 "riding on a smile and a shoeshine" is a line from Arthur Miller's 1949 play, *Death of a Salesman:* "He's a man way out there in the blue, riding on a smile and a shoeshine."

22 "Saw its market capitalization roll past $100 billion." Gomes, Lee, "Cisco Tops $100 Billion in Market Capital–Passing Milestone in 12 Years May Be Speed Record," *Wall Street Journal,* July 20, 1998.

23 "closest thing to a sure bet in the technology business" and "give them a lead they're nearly impossible to catch." Kupfer, Andrew, "The Real King of the Internet," *Fortune,* September 1998.

23 "They're just getting started." Thurm, Scott, "Cisco Profit Before Charges Rises 33% as Revenue Growth Keeps Accelerating," *Wall Street Journal,* February 3, 1999.

24 "I don't ever want to go through that again." Schlender, 1997.

24   "to handle vast surges of Internet traffic." Goldblatt, Henry, "Cisco's Secrets," *Fortune*, November 8, 1999.

24   The Harvard Business School case was "Cisco Systems, Inc.: Acquisition Integration for Manufacturing (A)," by Nicole Tempest and Christian G. Kasper, Harvard Business School Case Study 9-600-015, 1999.

25   "'repot'" start-ups into the larger company." Schlender, 1997.

25   "managing the experience of acquired employees." Tempest and Kasper, 1999, p. 4.

25   "a scant 2.1% vs. an industry average of 20%." Goldblatt, 1999.

25   "including the merger of information systems and adoption of manufacturing methods." Tempest and Kasper, 1999, p. 8.

25   The Best Practices client survey was quoted in Thurm, Scott, "Joining the Fold: Under Cisco's Systems, Mergers Usually Work," *Wall Street Journal*, March 1, 2000.

26   All quotes from O'Reilly and Pfeffer come from O'Reilly, Charles III, and Jeffrey Pfeffer, *Hidden Value: How Great Companies Achieve Extraordinary Results with Ordinary People*, Boston: Harvard Business School Press, 2000, pp. 49–77.

27   All quotes from the May 2000 *Fortune* article are from Serwer, Andy, "There's Something About Cisco," *Fortune*, May 15, 2000.

28   *Fortune*'s annual poll: "Global Most Admired: The World's Most Admired Companies," *Fortune*, October 2, 2000.

28   "sought more lucrative opportunities." Thurm, Scott, "Superstar's Pace: Cisco Keeps Growing but Exactly How Fast Is Becoming an Issue—As Debate over Its Stock Mounts, the Outcome Could Have Big Ripples," *Wall Street Journal*, November 3, 2000.

29   All quotes in this section come from Manette, Nicole, "Cisco Fractures Its Own Fairy Tale," *Fortune*, May 14, 2001.

30   "as vulnerable as any other company to an economic slowdown." Weber, Joseph, Peter Burrows, and Michael Arndt, "Management Lessons from the Bust," *Business Week*, August 20, 2001.

31   "the most valuable corporation on the planet." Byrne, John A., and Ben Elgin, "Cisco Behind the Hype," *Business Week*, January 21, 2002.

32   All quotes are from Burrows, Peter, "Cisco's Comeback," *Business Week*, November 2003.

33   "I think there is a pendulum effect, and that we all may get too caught up and perhaps overaccentuate what's going on." Correspondence by e-mail with Andy Serwer, March 15, 2004.

34   "never more than during the biggest boom of them all, in the late 1990s." Correspondence by e-mail with Peter Burrows, August 27, 2004.

Chapter Three

35   An early version of this chapter was published as "What Do We Think Happened at ABB?: Pitfalls in Research About Firm Performance," Philip M. Rosenzweig, *International Journal of Management and Decision Making* 5, no. 4 (2004): 267–81.

36   "the new model of competitive enterprise." Taylor, William, "The Logic of Global Business: An Interview with Percy Barnevik," *Harvard Business Review*, March–April 1991, pp. 91–105.

37   "swift, confident decisions is paramount." Kennedy, Carol, "ABB: Model Merger for the New Europe," *Long Range Planning* 25, no. 5 (October 1992): 10–17.

37   "the most successful cross-border merger since Royal Dutch linked up with Shell in 1907." Rapoport, Carla, and Kevin Moran, "A Tough Swede Invades the U.S.," *Fortune*, June 29, 1992, pp. 76–79.

37   "Call it Planet Barnevik. The hard charging executive of ABB . . ." and subsequent quotes are from Schares, Gail E., "Percy Barnevik's Global Crusade," *Business Week*, December 6, 1993, pp. 56–59.

37   "coloring our chat with the occasional American profanity." Karlgaard, Rich, "Interview with Percy Barnevik," *Forbes*, December 5, 1994, pp. 65–68.

38   "remarkably fresh, dynamic, and engaging." McClenahen, John S., "Percy Barnevik and the ABBs of Competition," *Industry Week*, June 6, 1994, pp. 20–24.

38   "He continually played down his own contribution to the success of ABB." Kets de Vries, Manfred, "Making a Giant Dance," *Across the Board* 31, no. 9 (October 1994): 27–32.

38   "paperwork in the sauna." Kennedy, Carol, "ABB's Sun Rises in the East," *Director*, September 1996, pp. 40–44.

38   "voted "CEO/Chairman of Europe's most respected company." Tomlinson, Richard, and Paola Hjelt, "Dethroning Percy Barnevik," *Fortune*, April 1, 2002, pp. 38–41.

38   Mention of the Korean Management Association naming Barnevik "the world's best honored top manager" was reported in the ABB annual report, 1997.

39   "Not to take action (and lose opportunities) is the only unac-

ceptable behavior." Bartlett, Christopher A., "ABB's Relays Business: Building and Managing a Global Matrix," Harvard Business School Case Study 9-394-016, 1993.

39   "The only thing we cannot accept is people who do nothing." Tomlinson and Hjelt, 2002.

39   a simultaneous need to be "global and local, big and small, and radically decentralized with central reporting and control." Barham, Kevin, and Claudia Heimer, *ABB: The Dancing Giant*, London: FT Pitman Publishing, 1998.

39   "so power technicians in Sweden can make design changes, and so factories in India can alter production methods on their own." ABB annual report, 1988.

40   "make more difficult the maintenance of a sharp customer focus." McClenahen, 1994.

40   "and profits soon took off." Schares, 1993.

40   "critical to making the ABB structure work." Peters, Tom, *Liberation Management: Necessary Disorganization for the Nanosecond Nineties*, London: Pan Books, 1992.

40   Bartlett, Christopher A., "ABB's Relays Business: Building and Managing a Global Matrix," Harvard Business School Case Study 9-394-016, 1993.

40   ABB as an organization to emulate is from Kets de Vries, Manfred, "Making a Giant Dance," *Across the Board* 31, no. 9 (October 1994): 27–32; describing ABB as a "prototypical post-industrial organization" is from Kets de Vries, Manfred, "Leaders Who Make a Difference," *European Journal of Management* 14 , no. 5 (1996): 486–93.

41   "particularly praised for strategic vision and focus." De Jonquieres, Guy, "Europe's Most Respected Companies," *Financial Times*, September 18, 1996, p. 1 of survey.

41   "to (twice) boss of Europe's most respected company." Micklethwait, John, and Adrian Wooldridge, *The Witch Doctors: What the Management Gurus Are Saying, Why It Matters, and How to Make Sense of It*, London: Heinemann, 1996, p. 243.

42   Reference to a "new form of global organization" and ABB's "five guiding lights" is from Barham, Kevin, and Claudia Heimer, "Creating the Globally Connected Corporation," *Financial Times Mastering Management*, June 1997, pp. 12–14.

43   "reduce its exposure to some of the cyclic swings to which it has been vulnerable in the past." ABB annual report, 1999.

44   "one such analyst observed." Morosini, Piero, "ABB in the New Millenium: New Leadership, New Strategy, New Organization," IMD Case Study 3-0829, 2000.

44   The new organization design was described in Woodruff, David,

"ABB Unveils New Board, Overhaul–Structural Plan Aims to Shift Focus from Products to Corporate Customers," *Wall Street Journal Europe*, January 12, 2001.

44   Speculation about the reasons behind Lindahl's departure are from Woodruff, David, "Shares of ABB slide 8.5% in Zurich on Disappointing Report of Results–New Chairman Vows to Boost Earnings, Revenue at Industrial Conglomerate," *Wall Street Journal Europe*, February 14, 2001.

45   "high technology fields appeared to go awry as profits fell." Fleming, Charles, "New Chairman of ABB Aims to Tighten Business Focus," *Wall Street Journal Europe*, November 23, 2001.

45   Background on the transition from Centerman to Dormann is from Bilefsky, Dan, Goran Mijuk, and Brandon Mitchener, "In a Surprise Move, ABB Replaces CEO–Appointment of Successor to Centerman Raises Questions on Management," *Wall Street Journal Europe*, September 6, 2001; and Fleming, Charles, "New Chairman of ABB Aims to Tighten Business Focus," *Wall Street Journal Europe*, November 23, 2001.

46   Speculation that the company was close to bankruptcy is from Tomlinson and Hjelt, 2002.

47   "The company wasn't disciplined enough," "communication problems between departments," sharing data had become a "nightmare," and the alleged obsession with matching the size and success of General Electric are all from Bilefsky, Dan, and Anita Raghavan, "How ABB Tumbled Back Down to Earth," *Wall Street Journal Europe*, January 23, 2003.

47   "vast duplication of effort." Tomlinson and Hjelt, 2002.

48   "vicious circle of narcissism." Woodruff, David, and Almar Latour, "Barnevik Gets Harsh Verdict in Court of Public Opinion–Former ABB Chief Is Disgraced in Pension Row," *Wall Street Journal Europe*, February 18, 2002.

48   "His successors are questioning his business legacy." Tomlinson and Hjelt, 2002.

48   "should have seen 13 years ago risks nobody else saw." Bilefsky and Raghavan, 2003.

49   "how much of the blame he should shoulder." Tomlinson and Hjelt, 2002.

49   Dropping the investigation about Barnevik and Lindahl is from Mijuk, Goran, "Pensions Case Against Ex-CEOs of ABB Is Ended," *Wall Street Journal Europe*, October 6, 2005.

Chapter Four

50 Thorndike, Edward L. "A Constant Error in Psychological Ratings," *Journal of Applied Psychology* 4 (1920): 469–77. Thorndike also observed that soldiers thought to be inferior overall were also judged to be bad on specific criteria and called this the Devil Effect.

50 For a thorough review of the Halo Effect and associated research, see William H. Cooper, "Ubiquitous Halo," *Psychological Bulletin* 90, no. 2 (1981): 218–44. Cooper describes several sources of Halos: "undersampling, engulfing, insufficient concreteness, insufficient rater motivation and knowledge, cognitive distortions, and correlated true scores." The two that seem most germane to the examples in this book are "insufficient concreteness," whereby perceptions of things that are vague and ambiguous but not concretely defined are shaped by more concrete variables, such as financial performance; compounded by "insufficient rater motivation and knowledge," namely the fact that journalists and researchers are content with the story that Halos offer and are not motivated to probe more deeply.

51 President Bush's 2001 poll ratings were cited by Walczak, Lee, Richard S. Dunham, and Mike McNamee, "Selling the Ownership Society," *Business Week,* September 6–13, 2004, based on data from Pew Research Center for the People & the Press. The same effect has been described by Robb Willer, "The Effects of Government-Issued Terror Warnings on Presidential Approval Ratings," *Current Research in Social Psychology* 10, no. 1 (2004).

51 "Poll: Bush Ratings Hit New Low," CBS News Poll, October 6, 2005.

53 The Staw study is reported in Staw, Barry M., "Attribution of 'Causes' of Performance: A General Alternative Interpretation of Cross-Sectional Research on Organizations," *Organizational Behavior and Human Performance* 13 (1975): 414–32. Staw conducted other studies on the theme of organizational performance, including Staw, Barry M., Pamela I. McKechnie, and Sheila M. Puffer, "The Justification of Organizational Performance," *Administrative Science Quarterly* 28 (1983): 592–600.

55 The Downey study is reported in Downey, H. Kirk, Thomas Chacko, and James C. McElroy, "Attributions of the 'Causes' of Performance: A Constructive, Quasi-Longitudinal Replication of the Staw (1975) Study," *Organizational Behavior and Human Performance* 24 (1979): 287–99.

56 The quotes from John Opel come from Perry, Nancy J., "America's Most Admired Corporations," *Fortune,* January 9, 1984.

57   "button-down culture," "rigid bureaucracy," and "complacent
       executives" were quoted from Kirkus Reviews. Carroll, Paul, *Big
       Blues: The Unmaking of IBM*, New York: Crown, 1993.

57   *The Economist*, "Tough at the Top: A Survey of Corporate Lead-
       ership," October 25, 2003. The full list was: "A sound ethical
       compass; The ability to make unpleasant decisions; Clarity and
       focus; Ambition; Effective communication skills; The ability to
       judge people; A knack for developing people; Emotional self-
       confidence; Adaptability; Charm."

58   "its $40 billion market [capitalization] has collapsed to $4 bil-
       lion." George, Bill, *Authentic Leadership: Rediscovering the Secrets to
       Creating Lasting Value*, San Francisco: Jossey-Bass, 2003, p. 168.

59   "with all his might to keep from being broken up." George,
       2003, p. 117.

59   "significant damage to its business and its reputation." Yoffie,
       David B., and Mary Kwak, "Playing by the Rules: How Intel
       Avoids Antitrust Litigation," *Harvard Business Review*, June
       2001, pp. 119–22.

60   "and a tarnished image. Just ask Bill Gates." Yoffie and Kwak,
       2001, p. 120.

60   Descriptions of Microsoft as "combative and rude" and using
       bullying and other "unfair tactics to compete in markets where
       its technology was inferior." Markoff, John, "Papers Shed New
       Light on Microsoft Tactics," *International Herald Tribune*, March
       25, 2004, p. 11.

60   The case study was called "Bill Gates and the Management of
       Microsoft," Philip M. Rosenzweig, Harvard Business School
       Case Study 392-019, 1992.

60   Some of James Meindl's most important works in this stream
       include Meindl, James R., Sanford B. Ehrlich, and Janet M.
       Dukerich, "The Romance of Leadership," *Administrative Science
       Quarterly* 30 (1985): 78–102; Meindl, James R., and Sanford B.
       Ehrlich, "The Romance of Leadership and the Evaluation of Or-
       ganizational Performance," *Academy of Management Journal* 30,
       no. 1 (1987): 91–109; and Salancik, Gerald R., and James R.
       Meindl, "Corporate Attributions as Strategic Illusions of Man-
       agement Control," *Administrative Science Quarterly* 29 (1984):
       238–54.

60   From the opinion of Justice Potter Stewart in *Jacobellis v. Ohio*,
       378 U.S. 184 (1964). The full paragraph reads as follows: "Under
       the First and Fourteenth Amendments criminal laws in this area
       are constitutionally limited to hard-core pornography. I shall
       not today attempt further to define the kinds of material I un-
       derstand to be embraced within that shorthand description; and

perhaps I could never succeed in intelligibly doing so. But I know it when I see it, and the motion picture involved in this case is not that."

61   *Fortune*'s annual survey was first called *America's Most Admired Companies*; today the poll is the *World's Most Admired Companies.*

62   "just what we would expect given the salient and tangible nature of financial results." Brown, Brad, and Susan Perry, "Removing the Financial Performance Halo from Fortune's *Most Admired Companies*," *Academy of Management Journal* 37, no. 5 (1994): 1347–59.

62   The two studies that showed that a company's financial performance explained between 42 percent to 53 percent of the variance of the overall rating are Fombrun, Charles, and Mark Shanley, "What Is in a Name?: Reputation Building and Corporate Strategy," *Academy of Management Journal* 33: pp. 233–58; and McGuire, Jean B., Thomas Schneeweis, and Ben Branch, "Perceptions of Firm Quality: A Cause or Result of Firm Performance," *Journal of Management* 16, no. 1 (1990): 167–80.

62   Hjelt, Paola, "The World's Most Admired Companies," *Fortune,* March 8, 2004, pp. 30–37.

63   Carvajal, Doreen, "Champion in Hearts of Employees," *International Herald Tribune,* August 11, 2004, p. 11. If the portfolio had changed every year to include the current list of companies, the return would have been 15.21 percent—assuming we ignore transaction costs.

63   The ways that concepts such as "respect" were measured were found at the *Great Place to Work* website, www.greatplace-towork.com.

63   Cisco's rankings as a *Great Place to Work* were listed on the website.

Chapter Five

67   Narver, John C., and Stanley F. Slater, "The Effect of Market Orientation on Business Performance," *Journal of Marketing,* October 1990, pp. 20–35. I have, in this passage, used the terms "customer orientation" and "market orientation" interchangeably.

69   "manage the crisis as effectively as we did." Aguilar, Francis, and Arvind Bambri, "Johnson & Johnson, Philosophy and Culture (A)," Harvard Business School Case Study 384–053, 1983.

69   In 2004, Johnson & Johnson's shared values seemed to be as strong as ever. See London, Simon, "J&J Stands Proudly by Its Leader's Words," *Financial Times,* August 31, 2004, p. 10.

69 "a set of relatively consistent values and methods of doing business." Kotter, John, and James Heskett, *Corporate Culture and Performance*, New York: Free Press, 1992, p. 16.

69 "just what we'd expect given the Halo Effect." Kotter and Heskett, 1992, pp. 20–21. In their letter accompanying the survey, they advised respondents: "Please rate the firms listed on the accompanying sheet on a scale of one to five, assigning one to a firm that you believe has a strong culture. Try to disassociate your rankings from the way in which these firms have performed in recent years." This last caution recognized the potential for attributions based on performance, but whether it would be sufficient to defuse the tendency for Halos, given what we have seen in other settings, is questionable and was not tested by the authors.

70 "while low-performing companies averaged just 3.7." Kotter and Heskett, 1992, p. 37.

71 "can have a huge payoff." Amazon.com website review, July 2004.

72 "usually outperform companies that don't." There are, of course, arguments to the contrary, notably Clayton Christensen's work on disruptive technologies, which suggests companies can fail if they stay *too* focused on today's customers and neglect the needs of potential future customers. See Christensen, Clayton M., *The Innovator's Dilemma: When New Technologies Cause Great Firms to Fail*, Boston: Harvard Business School Press, 1997.

74 "A correlation, by itself, explains nothing." Locke, Edwin A., "The Nature and Causes of Job Satisfaction," in M. D. Dunnette (ed.), *Handbook of Industrial and Organizational Psychology*, Chicago: Rand McNally, 1976, pp. 1297–1349. Steven Levitt and Stephen Dubner, on p.10 of their best seller, *Freakonomics: A Rogue Economist Explores the Hidden Side of Everything*, New York: Penguin, 2005, made much the same point: "Just because two things are correlated does not mean that one causes the other. A correlation simply means that a relationship exists between two factors—let's call them X and Y—but it tells you nothing about the direction of that relationship. It's possible that X causes Y; it's also possible that Y causes X; and it may be that X and Y are both being caused by some other factor, Z."

74 The Bain & Company statement "Our clients outperform the market 4 to 1" was found January 2006 at www.bain.com/bainweb/About/what_we_do.asp. That each point represented a quarter-by-quarter comparison of a portfolio of Bain's clients in that quarter with the market was explained by e-mail in January 2006 by Bain's head of press relations, Cheryl Krauss.

75   A longitudinal design may help overcome simple errors of correlation and causality but cannot definitively prove causality. If we trace our thinking back to David Hume and other philosophers of science, we have to admit that causality can never be proven in a definitive fashion; all we have are observations and experience. I am grateful to Michael Raynor for this point.

75   Showing that financial performance, measured by return on assets and earnings per share, did a better job of predicting employee satisfaction than the reverse, is from Schneider, Benjamin, Paul J. Hanges, D. Brent Smith, and Amy Nicole Salvaggio, "Which Comes First: Employee Attitudes or Organizational, Financial, and Market Performance?," *Journal of Applied Psychology* 88, no. 5 (October 2003): 836–51.

76   Jaworski, Bernard J., and Ajay K. Kohli, "Market Orientation: Antecedents and Consequences," *Journal of Marketing* 57 (July–August 1993): 53–70.

77   "in their efforts to attain higher business performance." Jaworski and Kohli, 1993, p. 64.

77   "have greater funds to invest in socially responsible pursuits." See, for example, pp. 52–54 of Paine, Lynn Sharp, *Value Shift: Why Companies Must Merge Social and Financial Imperatives to Achieve Superior Performance,* New York: McGraw-Hill, 2003.

78   "have both immediate and continuing financial impacts." Ruf, Bernadette M., Krishamurty Muralidhar, Robert M. Brown, Jay J. Janney, and Karen Paul, "An Empirical Investigation of the Relationship Between Change in Corporate Social Performance and Financial Performance: a Stakeholder Theory Perspective," *Journal of Business Ethics* 32 (2001): 143–56. Another study about CSR that used KDL data and found a positive relationship was Shawn L. Berman, Andrew C. Wicks, Suresh Kotha, and Thomas M. Jones, "Does Stakeholder Orientation Matter?: The Relationship Between Stakeholder Management Models and Firm Financial Performance," *Academy of Management Journal* 42, no. 5, October 1999.

78   *The Economist* suggested that many CSR initiatives were little more than examples of "good management." "The Good Company: A Review of Corporate Social Responsibility," *The Economist,* January 22, 2005.

78   "to avoid problems of correlation and causality." They note, for example, the problem of "managerial assessment of HRM effectiveness"—a recognition that the Halo Effect may color ratings.

79   "on three widely followed measures of firm performance." Huselid, Mark A., Susan E. Jackson, and Randall S. Schuler, "Technical and Strategic Human Resource Management Effec-

tiveness as Determinants of Firm Performance," *Academy of Management Journal* 40, no. 1 (1997): 184.

79   "are a potential source of competitive advantage." Huselid, Jackson, and Schuler, 1997, p. 186.

79   Wasserman, Noam, Nitin Nohria, and Bharat Anand, "When Does Leadership Matter?: The Contingent Opportunities View of CEO Leadership," Harvard Business School working paper, 2001.

79   "the choice of a chief executive is crucial." Quoted in Joyce, William F., Nitin Nohria, and Bruce Roberson, *What Really Works: The 4+2 Formula for Sustained Business Success*, New York: HarperBusiness, 2003, p. 200.

80   "or simply a reflection of firms that are better managers across all functions." Huselid, Mark A., and Brian E. Becker, "Methodological Issues in Cross-Sectional and Panel Estimates of the Human Resource-Firm Performance Link," *Industrial Relations* 35, no. 3 (July 1996): 403.

81   Pinker's observation is from p. 38 of Pinker, Stephen, *How the Mind Works*, London: Penguin Books, 1997.

82   This last category, which they called "segment-specific effects," captures the company's practices, the effectiveness or the organization, and the skills of its managers. McGahan, Anita, and Michael E. Porter, "How Much Does Industry Matter, Really?," *Strategic Management Journal* 18 (1997): 15–30. The exact phrase was: "This last category, segment-specific effects, encompasses all business-segment differences, including diversity in market share, differentiation, heterogeneity in fixed assets, differences in organizational practices, differences in organizational effectiveness, heterogeneity in activity configurations, anomalies in accounting practices, and differences in managerial competence."

Chapter Six

83   Twain, Mark (Samuel L. Clemens), *The Annotated Huckleberry Finn: The Adventures of Huckleberry Finn*, New York: W. W. Norton & Co., 2001, p. 203.

84   "which are the backbone of this book." Peters, Thomas J., and Robert H. Waterman Jr., *In Search of Excellence: Lessons from America's Best-Run Companies*, New York: Warner Books, 1982, p. 24.

84   "Which is completely wrong." Peters, Tom, "Tom Peters' True Confessions," *Fast Company*, December 2001, p. 81.

84   "no theory that I was out to prove." Peters, 2001, p. 81.

85   "were the eight principles of *Search*." Peters, 2001, p. 84.

87   "you can't get any of these without virtually everyone's commit-
        ment." Peters and Waterman, 1982, p. 17.

87   "we had to come up with some quantitative measures of per-
        formance" and "we faked the data." Peters, 2001, p. 84.

88   "conduct scores of workshops for thousands of managers." Pe-
        ters and Waterman, 1982, p. 25.

88   "suffered significant earnings declines that stem from serious
        business problems, management problems, or both" and "that
        fell by the wayside overstressed some attributes and ignored
        others" from "Who's Excellent Now?," *Business Week,* November
        5, 1984.

93   "You can always worry about proving the facts later." Peters,
        2001, p. 86.

94   "underlying timeless, *fundamental principles* and patterns that
        might apply across eras." Collins, James C., and Jerry I. Porras,
        Built to Last: Successful Habits of Visionary Companies, New York:
        HarperBusiness, 1994, p. 17 of the 1997 paperback edition.

95   "to make petri dishes of corporations, but we can't; we have to
        take what history gives us and make the best of it." Collins and
        Porras, 1994, pp. 20–21.

95   Vast quantities of data are mentioned in Collins and Porras,
        1994, p. 19.

96   "as Collins and Porras themselves recognized." Collins and Por-
        ras, pp. 245–46.

96   "The *In Search of Excellence* for the 1990s has arrived. It is *Built to
        Last*." Collins and Porras, inside quote on the second page of
        the 1997 paperback edition.

96   "a master blueprint for building organizations that will prosper
        long into the future." *Built to Last,* back cover of the 1997 paper-
        back edition.

96   "You can build a visionary company." Collins and Porras, p.
        xxiv.

96   "a revolution in our understanding of what makes companies
        successful over the long haul." Collins and Porras, inside quote
        on second page of the 1997 paperback edition.

97   "Let the evidence speak for itself." Collins and Porras, p. 21.

98   Gary Hamel and Liisa Välikangas compared the eighteen vi-
        sionary companies to the Dow Jones Industrial Average rather
        than the S&P 500 but got similar results. In "The Quest for
        Resilience," *Harvard Business Review,* September 2003, pp.
        52–63, they write: "Over the last ten years, just six of these
        companies managed to outperform the Dow Jones Industrial
        Average."

102   "their longevity, their ability to last." Foster, Richard N., and
        Sarah Kaplan, *Creative Destruction: Why Companies That Are Built
        to Last Underperform the Market—And How to Successfully Transform
        Them,* New York: Random House, p. 8.

103   "In the long run, the markets always win." Foster and Kaplan,
        pp. 8–9.

104   "in fact, on the hypothesis that there is a perennial lull."
        Schumpeter, Joseph A., *Capitalism, Socialism, and Democracy,*
        New York: Harper, 1975 (orig. pub. 1942), pp. 82–85.

104   Ghemawat, Pankaj, *Commitment: The Dynamics of Strategy,* New
        York: Free Press, 1991.

104   "the erosive forces of imitation, competition, and expropria-
        tion." Waring, Geoffrey F., "Industry Differences in the Persis-
        tence of Firm-Specific Returns," *American Economic Review,*
        December 1996, pp. 1253–65.

104   McGahan, Anita M., "Competition, Strategy, and Business Per-
        formance," *California Management Review* 41, no. 3 (Spring
        1999).

105   Most people don't intuitively grasp the phenomenon of regres-
        sion toward the mean. Amos Tversky and Daniel Kahneman, psy-
        chologists who pioneered much research into human judgment
        under uncertainty, explained: "We suggest that the phenomenon
        of regression remains elusive because it is incompatible with the
        belief that the predicted outcome should be maximally represen-
        tative of the input, and hence that the value of the outcome vari-
        able should be as extreme as the value of the input variable."
        "Judgment Under Uncertainty: Heuristics and Biases," *Science* 185
        (1974): 1124–31.

105   The studies by Ghemawat and McGahan are just two of the
        many that have shown the same general tendency. Robert Wig-
        gins at the University of Memphis and Timothy Ruefli at the
        University of Texas at Austin reviewed many such studies and
        concluded not only that profits erode, but that the rate of ero-
        sion is becoming faster and faster—owing to increasing competi-
        tive pressures, sometimes called hypercompetition. They quote
        Schumpeter: "Practically every enterprise [is] threatened and
        put on the defensive as soon as it comes into existence." Wig-
        gins, Robert R., and Timothy W. Ruefli, "Schumpeter's Ghost:
        Is Hypercompetition Making the Best of Times Shorter?,"
        Strategic Management Review 26 (2005): 887–911.

Chapter Seven

106   Bing, Stanley, "Quantum Business," *Fortune*, October 4, 2004, p. 104.

107   Several direct quotes come from Joyce, William F., Nitin Nohria, and Bruce Roberson, *What Really Works: The 4+2 Formula for Sustained Business Success*, New York: Harper Business, 2003: "but none greater than this: What really works?" is from p. 3; "the ones that do indeed really matter" is from p. 5; "conducted with scientific rigor and verified by measured fact" is from p. 6; and "the link between 4+2 practices and business success was astonishing" is from p. 15.

112   Kirby, Julia. "Toward a Theory of High Performance," *Harvard Business Review*, July–August 2005, pp. 30–39. Kirby discusses several of the studies discussed in this book—including Peters and Waterman, Collins and Porras, Kotter and Heskett, Zook and Allen, Joyce, Nohria, and Roberson, and Foster and Kaplan. The article makes a number of good points but does not address two fundamental problems: the reliance on data from sources that are likely to be shaped by the Halo Effect and the relative nature of company performance.

113   All of these bullet points come from Alex. Brown, except for the mention of "sophisticated client/server technology that improved merchandise management, bringing savings of $240 million," which is from Santosus, Megan, "A Seasoned Performer," *CIO*, January 15, 1995.

114   "to post still higher financial returns than Kmart." Buchanan, R. F., "Kmart Corporation—Company Report," October 9, 1990, Alex. Brown & Sons, The Investor Group, Boston, p. 4.

115   "but Wal-Mart had done the same two years earlier." Foley, Sharon, but "Wal-Mart Stores, Inc.," Harvard Business School Case Study 9-794-024, rev. 1996, p. 6.

115   For background on General Motors and its falling market share, see Welch, David, and Dan Beucke, "Why GM's Plan Won't Work," *Business Week*, May 9, 2005.

116   The cover declared: "The groundbreaking five-year study of the secrets of the world's best companies." "improving upon specific practices virtually guarantees a company's superior performance." is from Joyce, Nohria, and Roberson, 2003, p. 12.

117   "death march of financial analysis" and the description of fifteen years of stock market returns near the general average, "punctuated by a transition point," and "in the most unlikely of situations" are all from Collins, 2001, p. 6.

118   "from financial ratios to management turnover." Collins, 2001,
       p. 9.

118   On pp. 211–12 of *Good to Great,* Collins addresses questions
       about statistical significance, given that there were only eleven
       companies in the study. He writes that his team consulted a
       statistician at the University of Colorado, who observed that the
       problem of statistical significance applies only when sampling
       of data is involved, but that Collins instead made a purposeful
       selection to arrive at these eleven companies. That's correct, but
       not necessarily a point in favor of this research design. Selecting
       companies on the basis of outcomes would not be problematic
       if there were independence between independent and depend-
       ent variables, but that is not the case, as much of the data come
       from sources that are commonly distorted by the Halo Effect.
       Next, on p. 212, Collins quotes a professor of applied mathe-
       matics at the University of Colorado, who concluded that there
       was "virtually no chance that we simply found eleven random
       events that just happened to show the good-to-great patterns we
       were looking for. We can conclude with confidence that the
       traits we found are strongly associated with transformations
       from good-to-great." *Associated with,* yes, but not in the causal
       way that Collins so strongly implies when he claims to have ex-
       plained why some companies make the leap from good to great
       while others do not. Did the observed traits *lead to* good-to-great
       transformations, or do companies that underwent these transi-
       tions tend to be described as having these traits? The fundamen-
       tal argument of this book is that the latter explanation is the
       more likely one, given the likelihood of Halos in his data set.

119   Interview questions are from Collins, 2001, pp. 240–41.

119   Self-reporting can be valuable when used in conjunction with
       other data and when conducted in such a way as to minimize
       biases of retrospection. See, for example, the discussion of
       Robert K. Yin in *Case Study Research: Design and Methods,* New-
       bury Park, CA: Sage Publications, 1984. Collins and his team
       do not show evidence of recognizing the limitations of their
       methods, which relied on retrospective interviews, journal arti-
       cles, and other such accounts, nor do they show any effort to
       compensate for the problems inherent in those data.

119   "and rebuilding it again." Collins, 2001, p. 10. Collins recalled
       that he would "make a presentation to the team on that specific
       company, drawing potential conclusions and asking questions.
       Then we would debate, disagree, pound the table, raise our
       voices, pause and reflect, debate some more, pause and think,

discuss, resolve, question, and debate yet again about 'what it all means.'" As we know from Barry Staw's research, these sorts of discussions are likely to be suffused with the Halo Effect.

120   "extract order from the mess—to go from chaos to concept." Collins, 2001, p. 11.

120   I've borrowed an image from James Joyce's *Ulysses,* who also describes a heavenly hockey stick: "And they beheld Him even Him, ben Bloom Elijah, amid clouds of angels ascend to the glory of the brightness, at an angle of forty-five degrees over Donohoe's in Little Green street like a shot off a shovel." Joyce, James, *Ulysses, The Corrected Version,* New York: Random House, 1986, p. 283.

121   "largely a matter of conscious choice." Collins, 2001, p. 11.

121   A close look at the eleven *Great* companies shows that in the fifteen years prior to the inflection point, they actually *declined* slightly relative to the market. The message? *Don't worry if you're not doing well right now. Your company, too, can go from merely good to truly great.*

121   Berlin, Isaiah, *The Hedgehog and the Fox: An Essay on Tolstoy's View of History,* Chicago: Elephant Paperback, 1993.

122   Tetlock, Philip E., *Expert Political Judgment: How Good Is It? How Can We Know?,* Princeton, N.J.: Princeton University Press, 2005.

125   "universal answers that can be applied by any organization." Collins, 2001, p. 5.

125   "certain immutable laws of organized human performance (the physics) will endure." Collins, 2001, p. 15.

125   "emitted by atoms to eight or ten decimal places." Emanuel Derman, *My Life as a Quant: Reflections on Physics and Finance,* New York: John Wiley, 2004, p. 15. At the level of subatomic particles, some of this precision breaks down, and physicists cannot describe phenomena with the same reassuring accuracy, but Collins does not invoke the image of physics to suggest uncertainty; quite the contrary, his reference to physics is meant to suggest precision and predictability.

Chapter Eight

129   "to become the focus of attention or celebrity." Booker, Christopher, *The Seven Basic Plots: Why We Tell Stories,* London: Continuum Books, 2004, p. 585. "miraculous transformation in their fortunes" is from p. 52.

129   Anders, George, "Homespun Strategist Offers Career Advice,"

Wall Street Journal Online, January 13, 2004, www.careerjournal. com/myc/climbing/20040113-anders.html.

133   Bertrand, Marianne, and Antoinette Schoar, "Managing with Style: The Effect of Managers on Firm Policies," *Quarterly Journal of Economics* 118, no. 4 (November 2003): 1169–1208. This journal, it bears mentioning, is among the more scholarly economics journals, hardly light reading for practicing managers. The authors refer to other papers that have sought to measure the impact of managerial characteristics on firm performance and correctly point out that "these papers do not control for firm fixed effects and therefore cannot separate manager effects from firm effects." Those papers include the working paper by Wasserman, Nohria, and Anand (2001), which was mentioned as an effort to study the impact of leadership on firm performance in chapter 5.

133   Bloom, Nick, Stephen Dorgan, John Dowdy, John Van Reenen, and Tom Rippin, "Management Practices Across Firms and Nations," Centre for Economic Performance, London School of Economics, June 2005, p. 3. Interpretation of the 10 percent explanation of total firm performance comes from correspondence by e-mail with Nick Bloom, July 2005: "On the variance of TFP [total firm performance] explained this is based on the R-squared numbers from the regressions adjusted for measurement error. For the countries it is just based on saying that the U.K.-U.S. TFP gap is about 20% to 40% and the management gap would be associated with about a 3% to 5% TFP gap, so this accounts for about 15% of the variation. Of course on these we know nothing about causation." Commenting more broadly on studies of firm performance, Nick Bloom wrote: "TFP is really a measure of our ignorance and we are now a bit less ignorant about one component—management—and so find unexplained TFP falls."

135   "simultaneously goes ahead to make such inference." March, James G., and Robert I. Sutton, "Organizational Performance as a Dependent Variable," *Organization Science* 8, no. 6 (November–December 1997): 698. Reference to the "schizophrenic tour de force" in which "the demands of the roles of the consultant and teacher are disassociated from the demands of the role of the researcher" is on p. 703.

136   "Barns' Storming," *The Economist,* March 12, 2005, p. 57. Extraordinary fees like these suggest something else, a sort of conspicuous consumption as described by the economist Thorstein Veblen. Since it is hard to gauge accurately the value of such speeches, the high fee serves as a signal of high market value.

140   "poor powers to add or detract" is a phrase borrowed from
       Abraham Lincoln's Gettysburg Address: "The brave men, living
       and dead, who struggled here, have consecrated it far above our
       poor powers to add or detract."

141   Articles cited in this section include Ekman, Ivar, "Lego Braces
       for Big Changes," *International Herald Tribune*, July 23, 2005, p.
       9; Austen, Ian, "Lego Plays Hardball with Right to Bricks," *Inter-
       national Herald Tribune*, February 3, 2005, p. 11; and the Lego
       press release of October 21, 2004, *www.Lego.com*. The declining
       prospects for toy companies were described by Erika Kinetz in
       "Putting Away Childish Things," *International Herald Tribune*,
       April 2–3, 2005, pp. 16–17. "By most standards the toy industry
       is coming apart at the seams. Kids just are not buying toys as
       they used to, and the industry is scrambling to adjust. Sales in
       Western Europe, Japan, and the United States—the three largest
       toy markets by sales—have been stagnant for several years." Part
       of the problem is the growth of electronic toys and mobile
       phones; further squeezing toy companies is the consolidation
       of retail channels. The imperative, according to the reporter, was
       to broaden their audience, expand their appeal, and venture
       into "consumer electronics, media, education, fashion, and
       even home décor hybrids." Just about anything, it seems, other
       than sticking to a dying core.

Chapter Nine

144   "performing different activities from those of rivals or perfor-
       ming similar activities in different ways." Porter, Michael E.,
       "What Is Strategy?," *Harvard Business Review*, November–De-
       cember 1996, pp. 62.

145   "well understood by employees, customers, partners, and in-
       vestors." Joyce, Nohria, and Roberson, 2003, p. 16.

145   "and then figured out where to drive it." Collins, *Good to Great*.
       Collins's argument is circular, since it suggests we can identify
       "right" and "wrong" people irrespective of the company's strat-
       egy. In fact, certain people and their skills may be more or less
       appropriate given what the company is trying to do—the activi-
       ties it performs, the markets in which it competes, and the
       sources of differentiation it pursues. As an example, consider
       Harrah's Entertainment, which was mentioned in chapter 1.
       When Gary Loveman took the company in a different direc-
       tion—a strategic choice of emphasizing an information-based ap-
       proach to customer data management—some of the people who

had been considered among the best performers were no longer needed. Loveman even replaced a senior marketing manager who had just been named Employee of the Year. Was that person suddenly "wrong"? Not in an absolute sense, but relative to the strategic direction, evidently so.

145 For purposes of this discussion, I use the terms "risk" and "uncertainty" interchangeably, although strictly speaking there is an important difference between the two. Risk is generally meant to involve known probabilities, while under conditions of uncertainty, probabilities are not known. Playing roulette is therefore a game of risk—we know the odds, and we know the payoffs, and we can place our bets accordingly. Predicting the damage caused by a massive earthquake involves uncertainty—we don't know the timing or magnitude and cannot forecast with precision the damage. By that definition, most of what I refer to here comes under the heading of uncertainty.

146 "when you're looking in the mirror." Guralnick, Peter, *Last Train to Memphis: The Rise of Elvis Presley,* New York: Little, Brown, 1994, p. 227 of the paperback edition.

147 Christensen, Clayton M., *The Innovator's Dilemma: When New Technologies Cause Great Firms to Fail,* Boston: Harvard Business School Press, 1997.

147 Robert R. Wiggins and Timothy Ruefli have shown that industries differ in the persistence of performance, with high-tech industries showing faster erosion of high performance than more stable industries. They also showed that all industries seem to have shortening periods of persistence, meaning that *the Delusion of Lasting Success* is becoming even more pronounced. See Wiggins, Robert R., and Timothy W. Ruefli, "Schumpeter's Ghost: Is Hypercompetition Making the Best of Times Shorter?," *Strategic Management Review* 26 (2005): 887–911.

149 To see the importance of knowing the profile of the overall population, imagine that 90 percent of all companies had a single core and the other 10 percent had more than one. In that case, if 78 percent of successful companies had a single core, we would find that companies with more than one core tended to have a greater likelihood of success on a proportionate basis, $22/10 = 220$ percent versus $78/90 = 87$ percent. Zook's study isn't the only one to make this sort of mistake. Neil Harper and Patrick Viguerie of McKinsey & Co. explored much the same topic in a 2002 article (Harper, Neil W. C., and S. Patrick Viguerie, "Are You *Too* Focused?," *McKinsey Quarterly,* "Special Edition: Risk and Resilience," 2000, pp. 28–37). Their study of more than 4000 major American companies from 1990 to 2000

found that focused companies outperformed the average of their industry peers by 8 percent, but moderately diversified companies outperformed the average by 13 percent. The conclusion: Moderate diversification is at least as good as—and probably better than—greater focus. But just like the Bain study, the McKinsey study is unable to tell us whether moderate diversification *leads to* high performance or whether companies that perform well refrain from further diversification. Unless we can look at the data over time and compare the results of different decisions undertaken by companies facing similar circumstances, we can't say.

149   It should be possible to conduct such a study by gathering data over time (a longitudinal design) using an appropriate methodology such as event-history analysis, of course with the proviso that our data are not corrupted by Halos.

150   See March, James G., and Zur Shapira, "Managerial Perspectives on Risk and Risk-Taking," *Management Science* 33 (1987). They write: "In historical perspective, we have no difficulty distinguishing those who have been brilliant risk-takers from those who have been foolish gamblers, however obscure the difference may have been at the time they were making their decisions. Post hoc reconstruction permits history to be told in such a way that 'chance,' either in the sense of genuinely probabilistic phenomena or in the sense of unexplained variation, is minimized as an explanation."

151   "are the stuff of execution." Bossidy, Larry, and Ram Charan, with Charles Burck, *Execution: The Discipline of Getting Things Done,* New York: Random House Business Books, 2002, p. 9.

151   The origins of sociotechnical systems goes back to Eric Trist, A. K. Rice, Eric J. Miller, and their colleagues of the Tavistock School during the 1950s and 1960s.

152   "idiosyncratic contingency." Becker, Brian E., Mark A. Huselid, Peter S. Pickus, and Michael F. Spratt, "HR as a Source of Shareholder Value: Research and Recommendations," *Human Resource Management* 36, no. 1 (1997): 41.

152   Peter Cappelli and Anne Crocker-Hefter of the Wharton School doubted whether there exists any single set of "best" practices. Rather, they observed, "there are examples in virtually every industry of highly successful firms that have very distinct management practices." Their examples ranged from companies (Sears and Nordstrom, or Boston Consulting Group and McKinsey & Co) to business schools (Harvard and Wharton) to football teams (the San Francisco 49ers and the Oakland Raiders), each of which had very different management

practices from those of its pair, but all of which were successful in their field. They note: "Even practices that appear to have been demonstrated to be 'best' in some firms never seem to sweep over the business community as a whole." Cappelli, Peter, and Anne Crocker-Hefter, "Distinctive Human Resources Are Firms' Core Competences," *Organizational Dynamics* 24 (1996): 7–21.

152   Murphy, James D., *Flawless Execution: Use the Techniques and Systems of America's Fighter Pilots to Perform at Your Peak and Win the Battles of the Business World,* Los Angeles: Regan Books, 2005.

153   Edmondson, Gail, "What He'll Do with Renault," *Business Week,* April 25, 2005, p. 19.

154   The description of execution of Allied-Signal is from Tichy, Noel, and Ram Charan, "The CEO as Coach: An Interview with AlliedSignal's Lawrence A. Bossidy," *Harvard Business Review,* March–April 1995, p. 72.

154   The description of execution at Dell is from Bossidy, Larry, and Ram Charan, with Charles Burck, *Execution: The Discipline of Getting Things Done,* New York: Random House Business Books, 2002, pp. 16–18.

155   "What we failed to do is execute the strategy." See www.informationweek.com/showArticle.jhtml?articleID=29100212.

155   For stories about the replacement of Carly Fiorina, see Morrison, Scott, "HP Sacks Chief Executive Fiorina but Stresses Strategy Will Not be Changed," *Financial Times,* February 10, 2005, p. 1; and Morrison, Scott, "HP Turns to NCR for Its New Chief," *Financial Times,* March 30, 2005, p. 1.

155   A review of the strategic issues facing Hewlett-Packard were well summarized by *Business Week* in "Carly's Challenge," by Ben Elgin, December 13, 2004, pp. 48–56. A devastating critique, which addressed the full gamut of problems, from strategy to execution, was provided by Carol J. Loomis, "Why Carly's Big Bet Is Failing," *Fortune,* January 24, 2005. See also "Exit Carly," *The Economist,* February 12, 2005, p. 63.

155   Lee, Louise, and Peter Burrows, "Dell's Edge Is Getting Duller," *Business Week,* November 14, 2005, p. 43. According to the authors, some of the strategic issues facing Dell concerned the relative importance placed upon consumer versus corporate markets, as well as its approach to China.

156   "it's a paradox. Now deal with it." Peters, 2001, p. 90.

Chapter 10

157   Mention of Ballmer reading Collins's *Good to Great* is from Greene, Jay, "Troubling Exits at Microsoft," *Business Week*, September 26, 2005, p. 55.

158   Wiggins and Ruefli, 2005, write that "sustained competitive advantage has become less a matter of finding and maintaining a single competitive advantage and more a case of finding a series of competitive advantages over time and concatenating them into a sustained competitive advantage."

158   "as enduring as it appears at a distance." Lester, Tom, "Learning How to Fail in Business," *Financial Times*, September 29, 2003.

158   Strategy professor Jay Barney writes: "Firms that enjoy above normal returns may do so because of unique insights and abilities they controlled when the strategies generating high current returns were chosen. On the other hand, these firms might also have been lucky." Barney, Jay B., "Strategic Factor Markets: Expectations, Luck, and Business Strategy," *Management Science* 32, no. 10 (October 1986): 1231–1241.

160   "What has guided my career in both business and government." Rubin and Weisberg, p. 7.

160   "Success came by evaluating" Rubin and Weisberg, p. 7.

160   "Flux and uncertainty made risk arbitrage quite nerve-racking." Rubin and Weisberg, p. 46.

160   The Becton-Dickinson and Univis transaction is explained in Rubin and Weisberg, pp. 42–46.

161   "under considerable pressure—and the law of averages." Rubin and Weisberg, p. 46.

162   "that is likely to lead to the best results." Rubin and Weisberg, p. xii.

164   "This device became a big hit." Grove, Andrew S., *Only the Paranoid Survive: How to Exploit the Crisis Points That Challenge Every Company*, New York: Doubleday, 1996, p. 83.

165   "still keep an eye on it because its speed and course may change." Grove, 1996, p. 102.

165   "won't articulate the shape of the [future]?" Grove, 1996, pp. 152–53.

166   "fear of being wrong and fear of losing all can be powerful motivators." Grove, 1996, p. 117.

167   Quotes from Jeffrey Garten's article are from "Andy Grove Made the Elephant Dance," *Business Week*, April 11, 2005, p. 11.

167   Quotes from Tedlow's article are from "The Education of Andy Grove," *Fortune*, December 12, 2005, pp. 33–41.

168   "has been the most sure-footed of Silicon Valley companies."

Markoff, John, "The Disco Ball of Failed Hopes and Other Tales from Inside Intel," *New York Times*, November 29, 2004. *Business Week* also profiled Intel as one of the great business innovators; see Edwards, Cliff, "Supercharging Silicon Valley," *Business Week*, October 4, 2004, p. 8.

168   "has been shaken over the past year." Nuttall, Chris, "Intel Inside Out: The Chip Industry Leader Adapts to Changing Consumer Demands," *Financial Times*, February 9, 2005, p. 15.

168   "one of the best manifestations incorporating Intel values of risk-taking, discipline, and results orientation I have ever seen here." Edwards, Cliff, "Inside Intel," *Business Week*, January 9, 2006, pp. 43–53.

170   Comments delivered at IMD's *Orchestrating Winning Performance*, Lausanne Switzerland, June 26, 2005.

Bibliography

Books

Aronson, Eliot. *The Social Animal,* 5th ed., New York: W. H. Freeman & Co., 1988.

Barham, Kevin, and Claudia Heimer. *ABB: The Dancing Giant.* London: FT Pitman Publishing, 1998.

Berlin, Isaiah. *The Hedgehog and the Fox: An Essay on Tolstoy's View of History.* Chicago: Elephant Paperback, 1993.

Booker, Christopher. *The Seven Basic Plots: Why We Tell Stories.* London: Continuum Books, 2004.

Bossidy, Larry, and Ram Charan, with Charles Burck. *Execution: The Discipline of Getting Things Done.* New York: Random House Business Books, 2002.

Burgelman, Robert A. *Strategy Is Destiny: How Strategy-Making Shapes a Company's Future.* New York: Free Press, 2002.

Carlin, George. *When Will Jesus Bring the Pork Chops?* New York: Hyperion, 2004.

Carroll, Paul. *Big Blues: The Unmaking of IBM.* New York: Crown Publishers, 1993.

Christensen, Clayton M. *The Innovator's Dilemma: When New Technologies Cause Great Firms to Fail.* Boston: Harvard Business School Press, 1997.

——, and Michael E. Raynor. *The Innovator's Solution: Creating and Sustaining Successful Growth.* Boston: Harvard Business School Press, 2003.

Collins, James C., and Jerry I. Porras. *Built to Last: Successful Habits of Visionary Companies.* New York: HarperBusiness, 1994.

Collins, Jim. *Good to Great: Why Some Companies Make the Leap . . . and Others Don't.* New York: Random House Business Books, 2001.

Derman, Emanual. *My Life as a Quant: Reflections on Physics and Finance.* New York: John Wiley, 2004.

Feynman, Richard P. *The Pleasure of Finding Things Out: The Best Short Works of Richard P. Feynman.* London: Penguin Books, 1999.

Foster, Richard N., and Sarah Kaplan. *Creative Destruction: Why Companies That Are Built to Last Underperform the Market—And How to Successfully Transform Them.* New York: Currency, Random House, 2001.

George, Bill. *Authentic Leadership: Rediscovering the Secrets to Creating Lasting Value.* San Francisco: Jossey-Bass, 2003.

Ghemawat, Pankaj. *Commitment: The Dynamics of Strategy.* New York: Free Press, 1991.

Gould, Stephen Jay. *Full House: The Spread of Excellence from Plato to Darwin.* New York: Three Rivers Press, 1996.

Grove, Andrew S. *Only the Paranoid Survive: How to Exploit the Crisis Points That Challenge Every Company.* New York: Doubleday, 1996.

Guralnick, Peter. *Last Train to Memphis: The Rise of Elvis Presley.* New York: Little, Brown, 1994.

Hitchens, Christopher. *Letters to a Young Contrarian.* New York: Basic Books, 2001.

Joyce, James. *Ulysses, the Corrected Version.* New York: Random House, 1986.

Joyce, William F., Nitin Nohria, and Bruce Roberson. *What Really Works: The 4+2 Formula for Sustained Business Success.* New York: HarperBusiness, 2003.

Kotter, John, and James Heskett. *Corporate Culture and Performance.* New York: Free Press, 1992.

Levitt, Steven D., and Stephen J. Dubner. *Freakonomics: A Rogue Economist Explores the Hidden Side of Everything.* New York: Penguin, 2005.

Marcus, Alfred A. *Big Winners and Big Losers: The Four Secrets of Long-Term Business Success and Failure.* Upper Saddle River, N.J.: Pearson Education Inc., 2006.

Micklethwait, John, and Adrian Wooldridge. *The Witch Doctors: What the Management Gurus Are Saying, Why It Matters, and How to Make Sense of It.* London: Heinemann, 1996.

Murphy, James D. *Flawless Execution: Use the Techniques and Systems of America's Fighter Pilots to Perform at Your Peak and Win the Battles of the Business World.* Regan Books, 2005.

O'Reilly, Charles III, and Jeffrey Pfeffer. *Hidden Value: How Great Compa-*

nies Achieve Extraordinary Results with Ordinary People. Boston: Harvard Business School Press, 2000.

Paine, Lynn Sharp. *Value Shift: Why Companies Must Merge Social and Financial Imperatives to Achieve Superior Performance.* New York: McGraw-Hill, 2003.

Peters, Thomas J., and Robert H. Waterman Jr. *In Search of Excellence: Lessons from America's Best-Run Companies.* New York: Warner Books, 1982.

Peters, Tom. *Liberation Management: Necessary Disorganization for the Nanosecond Nineties.* London: Pan Books, 1992.

Pinker, Stephen. *How the Mind Works.* London: Penguin Books, 1997.

Rubin, Robert E., and Jacob Weisberg. *In an Uncertain World: Tough Choices from Wall Street to Washington.* New York: Random House, 2003.

Schumpeter, Joseph. *Capitalism, Socialism, and Democracy.* New York: Harper, 1942.

Shaw, George Bernard. *Pygmalion.* London: Penguin Books, 1916.

Simon, Herbert A. *Models of My Life.* New York: Basic Books, 1991.

Taleb, Nassim Nicholas. *Fooled by Randomness: The Hidden Role of Chance in Life and in the Markets.* New York: Texere, 2004.

Tetlock, Philip E. *Expert Political Judgment: How Good Is It? How Can We Know?* Princeton, N.J.: Princeton University Press, 2005.

Twain, Mark (Samuel L. Clemens). *The Annotated Huckleberry Finn: The Adventures of Huckleberry Finn.* New York: W. W. Norton & Co., 2001.

Waters, John K. *John Chambers and the Cisco Way: Navigating Through Volatility.* John Wiley & Sons, 2002.

Yin, Robert K. *Case Study Research: Design and Methods.* Newbury Park, CA: Sage Publications, 1984.

Zook, Chris, with James Allen. *Profit from the Core: Growth Strategy in an Era of Turbulence.* Boston: Harvard Business School Press, 2001.

Articles

"Global Most Admired: The World's Most Admired Companies," *Fortune,* October 2, 2000.

"Who's Excellent Now?," *Business Week,* November 5, 1984, pp. 46–48.

"Fortune 500 Largest U.S. Corporations," *Fortune,* April 18, 2005.

"Poll: Bush Ratings Hit New Low," CBS News Poll, October 6, 2005.

"The Good Company: A Review of Corporate Social Responsibility," *The Economist,* January 22, 2005.

"Tough at the Top: A Survey of Corporate Leadership," *The Economist,* October 25, 2003.

"Barns' Storming," *The Economist,* March 12, 2005, p. 57.

ABB Annual Reports, ABB Corporate Communications Ltd., Dept. CC-BI, P.O. Box 8829, CH-8050, Zurich, Switzerland.

Aguilar, Francis, and Arvind Bambri. "Johnson & Johnson, Philosophy and Culture (A)," Harvard Business School Case Study 384-053, 1983.

Anders, George. "Homespun Strategist Offers Career Advice," *Wall Street Journal Online,* January 13, 2004.

Austen, Ian. "Lego Plays Hardball with Right to Bricks," *International Herald Tribune,* February 3, 2005, p. 11.

Barham, Kevin, and Claudia Heimer. "Creating the Globally Connected Corporation," *Financial Times Mastering Management,* June 1997, pp. 12–14.

Barney, Jay B. "Strategic Factor Markets: Expectations, Luck, and Business Strategy," *Management Science* 32, no. 10 (1986): 1231–41.

Bartlett, Christopher A. "ABB's Relays Business: Building and Managing a Global Matrix," Harvard Business School Case Study 9-394-016, 1993.

Becker, Brian E., Mark A. Huselid, Peter S. Pickus, and Michael F. Spratt. "HR as a Source of Shareholder Value: Research and Recommendations," *Human Resource Management* 36, no. 1, (1997): 47.

Bennis, Warren, and James O'Toole. "How Business Schools Lost Their Way," *Harvard Business Review,* May 2005.

Berman, Shawn L., Andrew C. Wicks, Suresh Kotha, and Thomas M. Jones. "Does Stakeholder Orientation Matter?: The Relationship Between Stakeholder Management Models and Firm Financial Performance," *Academy of Management Journal* 42, no. 5 (October 1999).

Bertrand, Marianne, and Antoinette Schoar. "Managing with Style: The Effect of Managers on Firm Policies," *Quarterly Journal of Economics* 118, no. 4 (November 2003): 1169–1208.

Bilefsky, Dan, and Anita Raghavan. "How ABB Tumbled Back Down to Earth," *Wall Street Journal Europe,* January 23, 2003.

Bilefsky, Dan, Goran Mijuk, and Brandon Mitchener. "In a Surprise Move, ABB Replaces CEO–Appointment of Successor to Centerman Raises Questions on Management," *Wall Street Journal Europe,* September 6, 2002.

Bing, Stanley. "Quantum Business," *Fortune,* October 4, 2004 p. 104.

Bloom, Nick, Stephen Dorgan, John Dowdy, John Van Reenen, and Tom Rippin. "Management Practices Across Firms and Nations," Centre for Economic Performance, London School of Economics, June 2005, p. 3.

Brown, Brad, and Susan Perry. "Removing the Financial Performance Halo from Fortune's Most Admired Companies," *Academy of Management Journal* 37, no. 5 (1994): 1347–59.

Buchanan, R. F. "Kmart Corporation–Company Report," Boston: Alex. Brown & Sons, Investext Group, October 9, 1990, p. 4.

Burrows, Peter. "Cisco's Comeback," *Business Week*, November 24, 2003, pp. 42–48.

Byrne, John A., and Ben Elgin. "Cisco Behind the Hype." *Business Week*, January 21, 2002.

Cappelli, Peter, and Anne Crocker-Hefter. "Distinctive Human Resources Are Firms' Core Competences," *Organizational Dynamics* 24 (1996): 7–21.

Carvajal, Doreen. "Champion in Hearts of Employees," *International Herald Tribune*, August 11, 2004, p. 11.

Christensen, Clayton M., and Michael E. Raynor. "Why Hard-Nosed Executives Should Care About Management Theory," *Harvard Business Review*, September 2003, pp. 67–74.

Clark, Nicola. "Fraying Brand Image at Britain's WH Smith," *International Herald Tribune*, April 26, 2004, p. 9.

Coggan, Philip. "World's Most Respected Companies," *Financial Times, Special Report*, November 18, 2005.

Cooper, William H. "Ubiquitous Halo," *Psychological Bulletin* 90, no. 2 (1981): 218–44.

De Jonquieres, Guy. "Europe's Most Respected Companies," *Financial Times*, September 18, 1996, p. 1 of survey.

Doonar, Joanna. "Brand MOT: Lego," *Brand Strategy*, February 10, 2004.

Downey, H. Kirk, Thomas Chacko, and James C. McElroy. "Attributions of the 'Causes' of Performance: A Constructive, Quasi-longitudinal Replication of the Staw (1975) Study," *Organizational Behavior and Human Performance* 24 (1979): 287–99.

Edmondson, Gail. "What He'll Do with Renault," *Business Week*, April 25, 2005, p. 19.

Edwards, Cliff. "Supercharging Silicon Valley," *Business Week*, October 4, 2004, p. 8.

———. "Inside Intel," *Business Week*, January 9, 2006, pp. 43–53.

Ekman, Ivar. "Lego Braces for Big Changes," *International Herald Tribune*, July 23, 2005, p. 9.

Elgin, Ben. "Carly's Challenge," *Business Week*, December 13, 2004, pp. 48–56.

Fleming, Charles. "New Chairman of ABB Aims to Tighten Business Focus," *Wall Street Journal Europe*, November 23, 2001.

Flower, Joe. "The Cisco Mantra," *Wired* 5.03 (March 1997).

Foley, Sharon. "Wal-Mart Stores, Inc.," Harvard Business School Case Study 9-794-024, rev 1996.

Fombrun, Charles, and Mark Shanley. "What Is in a Name?: Reputation Building and Corporate Strategy," *Academy of Management Journal* 33, no. 2 (1990): 233–58.

Garten, Jeffrey S. "Andy Grove Made the Elephant Dance," *Business Week*, April 11, 2005, p. 11.

Goldblatt, Henry. "Cisco's Secrets," *Fortune*, November 8, 1999.

Gomes, Lee. "Cisco Tops $100 Billion in Market Capital—Passing Milestone in 12 Years May Be Speed Record," *Wall Street Journal*, July 20, 1998.

Greene, Jay. "Troubling Exits at Microsoft," *Business Week*, September 26, 2005, pp. 53–60.

Hamel, Gary, and Liisa Välikangas. "The Quest for Resilience," *Harvard Business Review*, September 2003, p. 52.

Hammonds, Keith H. "Michael Porter's Big Ideas," *Fast Company*, March 2001, pp. 150–55.

Harper, Neil W. C., and S. Patrick Viguerie. "Are You *Too* Focused?," *McKinsey Quarterly*, 2002 Special Edition: Risk and Resilience, pp. 28–37.

Hjelt, Paola. "The World's Most Admired Companies," *Fortune*, March 8, 2004, pp. 30–37.

——. "The World's Most Admired Companies," *Fortune*, March 14, 2005, pp. 41–45.

Huselid, Mark A., Susan E. Jackson, and Randall S. Schuler. "Technical and Strategic Human Resource Management Effectiveness as Determinants of Firm Performance," *Academy of Management Journal* 40, no. 1 (1997): 171–88.

Huselid, Mark A., and Brian E. Becker. "Methodological Issues in Cross-Sectional and Panel Estimates of the Human Resource-Firm Performance Link," *Industrial Relations* 35, no. 3 (July 1996): 400–22.

Jaworski, Bernard J., and Ajay K. Kohli. "Market Orientation: Antecedents and Consequences," *Journal of Marketing* 57 (July–August 1993): 53–70.

Karlgaard, Rich. "Interview with Percy Barnevik," *Forbes*, December 5, 1994, pp. 65–68.

Kennedy, Carol. "ABB: Model Merger for the New Europe," *Long Range Planning* 25, no. 5 (October 1992).

——. "ABB's Sun Rises in the East," *Director*, September 1996, pp. 40–44.

Kets de Vries, Manfred. "Leaders Who Make a Difference," *European Journal of Management* 14, no. 5 (1996): 486–93.

——. "Making a Giant Dance," *Across the Board* 31, no. 9 (October 1994): 27–32.

Kinetz, Erika. "Putting Away Childish Things," *International Herald Tribune*, April 2–3, 2005, pp. 16–17.

Kirby, Julia. "Toward a Theory of High Performance," *Harvard Business Review*, July–August 2005, pp. 30–39.

Kupfer, Andrew. "The Real King of the Internet," *Fortune*, September 1998.

Lester, Tom. "Learning How to Fail in Business," *Financial Times*, September 29, 2003.

Locke, Edwin A. "The Nature and Causes of Job Satisfaction," in M. D. Dunnette (ed.), *Handbook of Industrial and Organizational Psychology*. Chicago: Rand McNally, 1976, pp. 1297–1349.

London, Simon. "J&J Stands Proudly by Its Leader's Words," *Financial Times*, August 31, 2004, p. 10.

Loomis, Carol J. "Why Carly's Big Bet Is Failing," *Fortune*, January 24, 2005.

Loveman, Gary. "Diamonds in the Data Mine," *Harvard Business Review*, May 2003, pp. 109–113.

MacCarthy, Clare. "Deputy Chief Sacked as Lego Tries to Rebuild," *Financial Times*, January 9, 2004, p. 25.

Manette, Nicole. "Cisco Fractures Its Own Fairy Tale," *Fortune*, May 14, 2001.

March, James G., and Robert I. Sutton. "Organizational Performance as a Dependent Variable," *Organization Science* 8, no. 6 (November–December 1997): 698–706.

March, James G., and Zur Shapira. "Managerial Perspectives on Risk and Risk-Taking," *Management Science* 33, (1987).

Markoff, John. "Papers Shed New Light on Microsoft Tactics," *International Herald Tribune*, March 25, 2004, p. 11.

——. "The Disco Ball of Failed Hopes and Other Tales from Inside Intel," *New York Times*, November 29, 2004.

McClenahen, John S. "Percy Barnevik and the ABBs of Competition," *Industry Week*, June 6, 1994, pp. 20–24.

McGahan, Anita M. "Competition, Strategy, and Business Performance," *California Management Review* 41, no. 3 (Spring 1999): 74–101.

——, and Michael E. Porter. "How Much Does Industry Matter, Really?," *Strategic Management Journal* 18, (1997): 15–30.

McGuire, Jean B., Thomas Schneeweis, and Ben Branch. "Perceptions of Firm Quality: A Cause or Result of Firm Performance?," *Journal of Management* 16, no. 1 (1990): 167–180.

Meindl, James R., Sanford B. Ehrlich, and Janet M. Dukerich. "The Romance of Leadership," *Administrative Science Quarterly* 30 (1985): 78–102.

Meindl, James R., and Sanford B. Ehrlich. "The Romance of Leadership and the Evaluation of Organizational Performance," *Academy of Management Journal* 30, no. 1 (1987): 91–109.

Mijuk, Goran. "Pensions Case Against Ex-CEOs of ABB Is Ended," *Wall Street Journal Europe*, October 6, 2005.

Moore, Angela. "Mattel Earns Rise, but Barbie Sales Snag," Reuters, July 19, 2004.

Morosini, Piero. "ABB in the New Millenium: New Leadership, New Strategy, New Organization," IMD Case Study, 3-0829, 2000.

Morrison, Scott. "HP Sacks Chief Executive Fiorina but Stresses Strategy Will Not Be Changed," *Financial Times,* February 10, 2005, p. 1.

——. "HP Turns to NCR for Its New Chief," *Financial Times,* March 30, 2005, p. 1.

Narver, John C., and Stanley F. Slater. "The Effect of Market Orientation on Business Performance," *Journal of Marketing,* October 1990, pp. 20–35.

Nuttall, Chris. "Intel Inside Out: The Chip Industry Leader Adapts to Changing Consumer Demands," *Financial Times,* February 9, 2005, p. 15.

Orwell, George. "Notes on Nationalism," *England, Your England and Other Essays.* London: Secker & Warburg, 1945.

Perry, Nancy J. "America's Most Admired Corporations," *Fortune,* January 9, 1984.

Peters, Tom. "Tom Peters' True Confessions," *Fast Company,* December 2001, p. 90.

Platt, John R. "Strong Inference," *Science* 146, no. 3642, (October 16, 1964).

Porter, Michael E. "What Is Strategy?," *Harvard Business Review,* November–December 1996.

Quick, Rebecca. "Tiny Dogs and a Dream: Beating Cisco," *Wall Street Journal,* June 4, 1998.

Rapoport, Carla, and Kevin Moran. "A Tough Swede Invades the U.S.," *Fortune,* June 29, 1992, pp. 76–79.

Reinhardt, Andy. "Can Nokia Get the Wow Back?," *Business Week,* May 31, 2004, pp. 18–21.

——, and Peter Burrows. "Crunch Time for the High Tech Whiz," *Business Week,* April 28, 1997, p. 80.

Rosenzweig, Philip M. "What Do We Think Happened at ABB?: Pitfalls in Research About Firm Performance," *International Journal of Management and Decision Making* 5, no. 4 (2004): 267–81.

——. "Bill Gates and the Management of Microsoft," Harvard Business School Case Study, 1991.

Ruf, Bernadette M., Krishamurty Muralidhar, Robert M. Brown, Jay J. Janney, and Karen Paul. "An Empirical Investigation of the Relationship Between Change in Corporate Social Performance and Financial Performance: A Stakeholder Theory Perspective," *Journal of Business Ethics* 32, no. 2 (2001): 143–56.

Salancik, Gerald R., and James R. Meindl. "Corporate Attributions as Strategic Illusions of Management Control," *Administrative Science Quarterly* 29 (1984): 238–54.

Santosus, Megan. "A Seasoned Performer," *CIO,* January 15, 1995.

Schares, Gail E. "Percy Barnevik's Global Crusade," *Business Week,* December 6, 1993, pp. 56–59.

Schlender, Brent. "Computing's Next Superpower," *Fortune*, May 12, 1997, pp. 64–71.

Schneider, Benjamin, Paul J. Hanges, D. Brent Smith, and Amy Nicole Salvaggio. "Which Comes First: Employee Attitudes or Organizational, Financial, and Market Performance?," *Journal of Applied Psychology* 88, no. 5 (October 2003): 836–51.

Serwer, Andy. "There's Something About Cisco," *Fortune*, May 15, 2000.

Simonian, Haig. "Optimistic ABB Turns the Corner," *Financial Times*, July 30, 2004.

Staw, Barry M. "Attribution of 'Causes' of Performance: A General Alternative Interpretation of Cross-Sectional Research on Organizations," *Organizational Behavior and Human Performance* 13 (1975): 414–32.

——, Pamela I. McKechnie, and Sheila M. Puffer. "The Justification of Organizational Performance," *Administrative Science Quarterly* 28 (1983): 592–600.

Taylor, William. "The Logic of Global Business: An Interview with Percy Barnevik," *Harvard Business Review*, March–April 1991, pp. 91–105.

Tempest, Nicole, and Christian G. Kasper. "Cisco Systems, Inc.: Acquisition Integration for Manufacturing (A)," Harvard Business School Case Study 9-600-015, 1999.

Thorndike, Edward L. "A Constant Error in Psychological Ratings," *Journal of Applied Psychology* 4 (1920): 469–77.

Thurm, Scott. "Cisco Profit Before Charges Rises 33% as Revenue Growth Keeps Accelerating," *Wall Street Journal*, February 3, 1999.

——. "Joining the Fold: Under Cisco's Systems, Mergers Usually Work," *Wall Street Journal*, March 1, 2000.

——. "Superstar's Pace: Cisco Keeps Growing but Exactly How Fast Is Becoming an Issue—As Debate over Its Stock Mounts, the Outcome Could Have Big Ripples," *Wall Street Journal*, November 3, 2000.

Tichy, Noel, and Ram Charan. "The CEO as Coach: An Interview with AlliedSignal's Lawrence A. Bossidy," *Harvard Business Review*, March–April 1995.

Tomlinson, Richard, and Paola Hjelt. "Dethroning Percy Barnevik," *Fortune*, April 1, 2002, pp. 38–41.

Tversky, Amos, and Daniel Kahneman. "Judgment Under Uncertainty: Heuristics and Biases," *Science* 185 (1974): 1124–31.

Walczak, Lee, Richard S. Dunham, and Mike McNamee. "Selling the Ownership Society," *Business Week*, September 6–13, 2004.

Waring, Geoffrey F. "Industry Differences in the Persistence of Firm-Specific Returns," *American Economic Review*, December 1996, pp. 1253–65.

Wasserman, Noam, Nitin Nohria, and Bharat Anand. "When Does Leadership Matter?: The Contingent Opportunities View of CEO Leadership," Harvard Business School working paper, 2001.

Weber, Joseph, Peter Burrows, and Michael Arndt. "Management Lessons from the Bust," *Business Week,* August 20, 2001.

Welch, David, and Dan Beucke. "Why GM's Plan Won't Work," *Business Week,* May 9, 2005.

Wiggins, Robert R., and Timothy W. Ruefli. "Schumpeter's Ghost: Is Hypercompetition Making the Best of Times Shorter?," *Strategic Management Review* 26 (2005): 887–911.

Willer, Robb. "The Effects of Government-Issued Terror Warnings on Presidential Approval Ratings," *Current Research in Social Psychology* 10, no. 1 (2004).

Woodruff, David. "ABB Unveils New Board, Overhaul–Structural Plan Aims to Shift Focus from Products to Corporate Customers," *Wall Street Journal Europe,* January 12, 2001.

——. "Shares of ABB Slide 8.5% in Zurich on Disappointing Report of Results–New Chairman Vows to Boost Earnings, Revenue at Industrial Conglomerate," *Wall Street Journal Europe,* February 14, 2001.

——, and Almar Latour. "Barnevik Gets Harsh Verdict in Court of Public Opinion–Former ABB Chief Is Disgraced in Pension Row," *Wall Street Journal Europe,* February 18, 2002.

Yoffie, David B., and Mary Kwak. "Playing by the Rules: How Intel Avoids Antitrust Litigation," *Harvard Business Review,* June 2001, pp. 119–22.

Acknowledgments

My first thanks go to Gordon Adler, my good friend and colleague at IMD, who heard me talk about some of the themes in this book over the last several years and encouraged me to write them down. My wife, Laura Rosenzweig, and my father, Mark Rosenzweig, read drafts of early chapters and offered comments and encouragement. Other colleagues read various chapters and responded with enthusiasm: Thank you to Dan Denison, Peter Killing, and John Walsh. My deepest gratitude goes to those who read the entire manuscript in considerable detail (sometimes more than once) and offered many valuable comments, large and small: Bill Fischer, Tomi Laamanen, Anita McGahan, Michael Raynor, Mark Rosenzweig, and Tom Vollmann. I appreciate the time they spent, and the care they took, to challenge my assumptions, to point out my mistakes, to sharpen my thinking, and to offer ideas for improvement. The book is immeasurably better for their contributions.

IMD, the International Institute for Management Development in Lausanne, Switzerland, where I've been a faculty member since 1996, is one of the world's leading centers for management research and education. IMD is above all a practical institute, with a curiosity about business ideas and their application to real world situations. That spirit has been a fertile ground for the thinking that led to this book. I am very grateful to IMD's leaders during this last decade, Peter Lorange and Jim

Ellert. I also wish to thank my faculty colleagues for their friendship and support, and for allowing me to contribute to the institute while balancing family life abroad. Not many organizations would take such a flexible and constructive stance—IMD has done so, for which I and my family are thankful.

Marine Frey has assisted me for the past two years, tracking down articles and library books, preparing bound versions of drafts, and managing correspondence. She combines several qualities long associated with Switzerland—efficiency, reliability, and discretion—with others that I appreciate in anyone, regardless of passport—good cheer, irreverence, and a sly sense of humor. John Evans, director of IMD's Information Centre, and his entire staff helped enormously in gathering articles. In particular, John played a key role in working with Standard & Poor's to collect the Compustat data shown in the appendix and described in chapters 6 and 7.

Daniel Bial, my literary agent, believed in this project from the outset and has been a superb partner throughout the entire process, from initial contact through completion. Fred Hills at Free Press provided many ideas that have been pivotal in shaping the manuscript. I have greatly appreciated their counsel and support. Without Dan and Fred, I would probably still be muttering to myself about storytelling that masquerades as science. Thanks also to the many people at Free Press who helped to edit, design, and produce the book, including Marty Beiser, Phil Metcalf, Davina Mock, and Eric Fuentecilla.

Before closing, I would like to offer a word of appreciation to some of the teachers who most influenced me at important times in my life: from Berkeley High School, Donald Schrump and Gordon "Buddy" Jackson (1945–1971); from UC Santa Barbara, Roy Savoian and William Ebenstein (1910–1976); and from the University of Pennsylvania, John Kimberly, Kenwyn Smith, and Edward Bowman (1925–1998). My sincere thanks to them all for their guidance and for the examples they set.

Finally, special thanks to my lovely wife, Laura, who recognized the fun I've had with this project and never complained about waking up to the sound of the keyboard in the next room going tap-tap-tap.

Index

About the Author

Phil Rosenzweig is a professor at IMD, the International Institute for Management Development, in Lausanne, Switzerland, where he works with leading multinational companies on questions of strategy and organization.

A native of Northern California, Phil studied economics at UC Santa Barbara and business administration at UCLA. After six years at Hewlett-Packard, he moved to Philadelphia and earned a Ph.D. at the Wharton School, University of Pennsylvania, in 1990. He was on the faculty of Harvard Business School for six years before joining IMD in 1996. Phil and his wife, Laura, have two children, Tom and Caroline.